A SEXUAL LEXICON

Lawrence Paros

An Owl Book
HENRY HOLT AND COMPANY
New York

Copyright © 1984 by Lawrence Paros
All rights reserved, including the right to reproduce
this book or portions thereof in any form.
Published by Henry Holt and Company, Inc.,
115 West 18th Street, New York, New York 10011.
Published in Canada by Fitzhenry & Whiteside Limited,
195 Allstate Parkway, Markham, Ontario L3R 4T8.

Library of Congress Cataloging-in-Publication Data
Paros, Lawrence.
The erotic tongue: a sexual lexicon / Lawrence Paros.
           p.   cm.
          "An Owl book."
Reprint. Originally published: Seattle: Madrona, 1984.
          ISBN 0-8050-0796-2 (pbk.)
1. Sex—Terminology.   2. Sex—Terminology—Anecdotes, facetiae,
    satire, etc.   3. English language—Slang.   I. Title.
HQ23.P37   1988   87-36970
306.7'014—dc19   CIP

First published by Madrona Publishers, Inc., in 1984.
First Owl Book Edition—1988

Printed in the United States of America
        1   3   5   7   9   10   8   6   4   2

ISBN 0-8050-0796-2

To Beth and Jennifer,
words of love and respect

A Word from the Author

To prevent any charge of immorality being brought against this work, the editor begs leave to observe, that when an indelicate or immodest word has obtruded itself for explanation, he has endeavoured to get rid of it in the most decent manner possible; and none have been admitted but such, as either could not be left out, without rendering the work incomplete, or in some measure, compensate by their wit, for the trespass committed on decorum. Indeed respecting this matter, he can with great truth make that same defence that Falstaff ludicrously urges in behalf of one engaged in rebellion, viz, that he did not seek them, but like rebellion in the case instanced, they lay in his way, and he found them.

— Jon Badcock, writing as Jon Bee,
Dictionary, 1823

The Contents

Acknowledgments

The Erotic Tongue expresses its appreciation to its sources, especially the late Eric Partridge, the wordmaster who provided an indispensable series of guides to the language. Those works include *A Dictionary of Slang and Unconventional English; Origins, A Short Etymological Dictionary of Modern English; Shakespeare's Bawdy; Slang, To-day and Yesterday; Words, Words, Words!;* and *A Dictionary of Catch Phrases.*

It was the estimable Partridge who first introduced me to Dr. John S. Farmer and W. E. Henley and their seven-volume *Slang and its Analogues* (1890–1914); Captain Bee (John Badcock) and his *Dictionary of the Turf etc.* (1823); as well as the irascible Francis Grose and his *Classical Dictionary of the Vulgar Tongue* (1785), all of which I have drawn upon quite heavily.

Other major works consulted include: Thomas Brewer, *Dictionary of Phrase and Fable;* Henry N. Cary, *The Slang of Venery;* John Ciardi, *A Browser's Dictionary;* Stuart Berg Flexner, *I Hear America Talking* and *Listening to America;* H. L. Mencken, *The American Language;* J. L. Dillard, *American Talk, Where Our Words Come From* and *Lexicon of Black English;* Hugh Rawson, *A Dictionary of Euphemism and Other Doubletalk;* Richard A. Spears, *Slang and Euphemism;* Lester V. Berrey and Melvin Van den Bark, *The American Thesaurus of Slang;* Harold Wentworth and S. B. Flexner, *Dictionary of American Slang;* Robert Wilson, *Forbidden Words;* and of course, *The Oxford English Dictionary.*

Special thanks to Dr. Reinhold Aman for his personal support and encouragement and to his precious *Maledicta, The International Journal of Verbal Aggression* – a treasurehouse of profanity. And of course the boys on the street corner and in locker rooms everywhere – without whom it never would have been possible.

ACKNOWLEDGEMENTS

To Andy Hoffman for his insights and editorial assistance; to the good people who read the manuscript in its more primitive phases: Barney Brawer, Steve and Nancy Berger, and Angela Smith; Elliott Negin for the support which I needed, and the artwork I never used; Lois Smith, Shereen Heath, and Memory Myers for the patience and skill with which they translated reams of notes into legible copy; Linda Paros who covered my asterisk each step of the way; Sara and Dan Levant, a.k.a. Madrona Publishers, who literally took my words for *IT* and put their money where my mouth was. And J.M.P., phantom sponsor of the arts.

the
EROTIC
tongue

ONE

Words for the Wise

Banish the use of those four-letter words
Whose meanings are never obscure.
The Angles and Saxons, those bawdy old birds,
Were vulgar, obscene and impure.
But cherish the use of the weak-kneed phrase
That never quite says what you mean;
Far better to stick with your hypocrite ways
Than be vulgar or coarse or obscene.

> — Anon., "Ode to Those Four-Letter
> Words," 20thC.

Nature her custom holds, let shame say what it will.

> — Shakespeare, *Hamlet*

Another *sex* book? Spare us! With the recent spate of publications, journals, magazines and how-to-do-it manuals, we now have more knowledge than we know what to do with, spelling out in agonizing detail the technique and the joy of it all, and made so simple, even a child can do it — with parental discretion, of course.

However, there still remains one last step on the road to total sexual enlightenment: writing and talking about it properly. This is no simple task, for *sex* is easier done than said.

Research has recently revealed an entire body of sexual language waiting to be mastered. We call it *The Erotic Tongue*.

Most people are only slightly familiar with *The Erotic Tongue*, primarily through a small group of words which polite society considers taboo. These are words which have often evoked a hysterical response; they are symbols of a deeper, darker side of ourselves that we'd rather not acknowledge.

The Moral Majority considers these words obscene. Feminists point out their aggressive character and the contempt they show toward women. Children love these words, finding them useful for dramatic effect, for capturing the attention of the adult world and making it more responsive to their presence. Mom and Dad are less than pleased on hearing their children use them, having picked up on Freud's connection between use of dirty words and toilet training and, as some point out, are as quick to wash out their children's mouths as to give them enemas. Ordinary adults also find occasion to deploy these words as a declaration of independence, an editorial statement against the forces of restraint and convention. Or, as one commentator described their use – an oral *fart* of sorts.

But there is much more to the lexicon than the four-letter words and their friends. We also have technical and scientific words for *sex,* as well as words that are refined and even border on the poetic.

Euphemisms (from the Greek "to sound well") make up a good part of *The Erotic Tongue.* They are neat little rhetorical devices by which we cloak otherwise naked thoughts.

We take a taboo word and rephrase it with sufficient taste and delicacy as to make it acceptable. There are many ways to euphemize a word: We can render it somewhat abstract; make up words that are longer and more complex, the bigger being the better; we can understate; use indirection; or simply substitute a foreign word. This explains those frantic folks screaming, *"Merde!"* as they run madly to the *facilities* in order to effect a simple act of *defecation.*

Euphemisms, however, are not without their problems. They can be escapist, uninspiring, and unimaginative. Another difficulty is that once they have attained a certain popularity, they become so closely identified with the words they are meant to replace that they themselves come to be considered obscene. A euphemism's life is not an easy one. As Ernest Weekly pointed out in 1930 in his *Romance of Words,* the euphemism is by inevitable association doomed from its very birth.

Given the shifting supply of "good" words and the increasing demand for them, it's apparent that what is needed is a comprehensive venereal vocabulary, and we have it in *The Erotic Tongue.* Here are slang, rich and colorful; euphemisms, flowery, arcane, and remote; and quaint words rescued from Standard English, worthy of recycling. All are suggestive of the romanticism, cynicism, violence, and humor with which the actors, the parts, and the act itself have been viewed throughout history. It also includes words of the four-letter variety.

The Erotic Tongue does not eschew the use of "dirty words." After all, they are an integral and vital part of the lexicon, but their use does call for judicious application and proper mix so that readers and listeners might sample the great variety of expressions available without the senses becoming dulled by saturation.

Master *The Erotic Tongue* and you too will find yourself able to talk dirty and command respect. Expand and sophisticate your venereal vocabulary. Obscenity, by itself, is the last refuge of the vulgarian and the crutch of the inarticulate *motherf**ker.*

July 3, 1978

BULLETIN

WASHINGTON (UPI) – The Supreme Court Monday upheld, 5–4, a ban against airing seven "filthy" words when children might be listening. The broadcast industry called it "a harsh blow to freedom of expression of every person in this country."

Justice John Paul Stevens' opinion rested on the unique characteristics of broadcasting: Society's right to protect children from "inappropriate speech" and the right of unwilling adults not to be assaulted with offensive speech.

Justices Potter Stewart, William Brennan, Byron White and Thurgood Marshall dissented on the ground that Congress intended to prohibit obscene speech – not words deemed merely "indecent."

The words involved were *c**ks**ker, c**t, f**k, motherf**ker, p*ss, s**t,* and *t*t.*

5

When people read the story of the Supreme Court decision in their newspapers, they found something missing—the words. Most editors apparently were terrified of putting them into print.

The *Portland* (Maine) *Press Herald* hit upon a somewhat ingenious compromise, offering to mail a list of the seven "dirty" words to anyone who requested them and enclosed a self-addressed envelope. After a story about the *Press Herald's* offer was carried by the Associated Press, about sixty requests were received at the paper, mostly from out-of-state residents from as far away as British Columbia and West Germany. The correspondents included such notables as the author of *The Erotic Tongue*. *Rolling Stone,* on September 7, 1978, tried to put things in perspective:

> Maybe words really are as dangerous as sticks and stones, more dangerous than ideas, in fact, because the Supreme Court will fight like a *motherf**ker* to protect our ideas; they just want to ban some of the ideas our words are made of.

In more genteel quarters these words are frequently described as four-letter words, a term that, according to Eric Partridge, originated in 1928 with the publication of *Lady Chatterley's Lover,* as well as with a parallel phrase, *the four-letter man,* a term of derision that came into use about the same time—a roundabout way of calling someone a *s**t*. As a rule, four-letter words can contain more or less than four letters (one referred to in the Supreme Court decision contains twelve), but they invariably deal with the taboo topics of either *sex* or the toilet. *The Erotic Tongue* does not give a *s**t* about the latter.

The Big F

I was walking along this *f**king* fine morning, *f**king* sun *f**king* shining away, little country *f**king* lane, and I meets up with this *f**king* girl, *f**king* lovely she was, so we gets into *f**king* conversation, and I takes her over a *f**king* gate into a *f**king* field, and we has *sexual intercourse.*

> — An Australian "rigamarole" quoted by
> Wayland Young in *Eros Denied,* mid-
> 20thC.

In the beginning there was *the act.* It was damn good fun but also somewhat scary. It struck fear and generated awe in those who first experienced it. They surrounded it with mystery and circumscribed its use. When they later found a way to express themselves, they transferred the dread and awe into the word. The word closest to *the act* reminds us most dramatically of our discomfort. It is the *Big F,* more commonly known as the *f**k.*

My Word!

Whence came the *f**k?* Nobody really knows. Some think it derives from the acronym for *For Unlawful Carnal Knowledge.* Others argue that the word comes from the sound of the act itself: in and out, in and out, in and out—"ph-ck," "ph-ck," "ph-ck"—sounds which only a trained ear could distinguish.

There is no consensus among serious students of the language. They used to believe that the word originated with the

French *foutre,* or the Latin *futuere,* a theory now pretty much discounted.

If etymologists appear somewhat aroused by the topic, it's only because there are those who find *f**k*'s origins in the German *ficken,* to "strike, beat, knock, or bang," a theory that converges nicely with the fact that men today *hit on* a woman (*make sexual advances*). Over the years, synonyms have included *thump, smack, batter, stuff, punch, ram, jolt, cramp, poke,* and *wallop*—leaving little doubt as to how men conceived *the act. Ficken's* roots are the Indo-European *peik,* meaning "enmity," "evil," "maliciousness," the *p* becoming an *f* when it moved into the Germanic. It later made us "fickle," descriptive of one who shifts affections, initially in an evil, later a benign fashion, as well as "fey," which is Old English *faege,* for "fated to die," which John Ciardi suggests may be at the base of the sixteenth-century slang *to die*—to have an *orgasm.*

Ficken makes a strong case, but most now favor the Latin root *pug,* "to prick," giving us the Roman *pugil,* "boxer" or "puncture," and the link between sex and violence. The leading candidate, however, appears to be *firk.* The word was used widely and frequently from the eleventh through the seventeenth centuries, and was defined as "a sharp blow, or a thrust." It also meant "to stir up, cheat, move about briskly, to be frisky or jiggish."

On yet another side, a small minority go with derivation from the Greek word *phuteo* for "sowing, planting, or begetting."

Any way you look at it, the *f**k* appears to be a many-sided thing—the beginning of life, inconstancy, and random violence.

Love at First Cite

Late to arrive, the word didn't appear in print until 1503. It quickly made the rounds of several sixteenth-century Scottish poems and then, with the exception of the writings of John Wilmot, Earl of Rochester (usually referred to as Rochester), the great seventeenth-century lech, went underground, not to attain legitimacy until the *Lady Chatterley* case in 1951.

Its inclusion in dictionaries can only be described as uneven. There are references to it in a number of early volumes, but you can search through most popular dictionaries of the nineteenth and twentieth centuries and nary a *f**k* will you find. It is absent from H.L. Mencken's masterful work on the American language. For years you couldn't find it in Webster's *New International Dictionary* or in the *Oxford English Dictionary*—the OED—the most comprehensive work on the language, one that prides itself on being "conceived in a scientific spirit." Makes one wonder, doesn't it, how they could care so deeply about words and at the same time not really give a *f**k*.

The dictionary-makers finally did come around, but not till 1965. By then, "nice" people had forgotten completely how to *f**k*, and the word had become our principal four-letter outcast. Mere mention of it caused flesh to creep and cheeks to flush. Few people spoke of it openly. Only the kids were telling it like it *f**kin'* is. And for them it was only *beautif**kingful,* far *f**kin'* out, and outta *f**kin'* sight.

A Word of Caution

Because it was unwelcome both at home and at school, many of the kids took the *Big F* to the streets. There they created the mean *motherf**ker,* a legendary figure who attained prominence in the sixties, as in *"up against the wall, motherf**ker!"*

It wasn't long before the ranks swelled to include the jive *motherf**ker,* the dirty *motherf**ker,* and the exotic *muh-f**kah.* This is to say nothing of your basic, no-frills *mother* (also *mutha*).

Generally considered the worst forms of verbal abuse, these expressions can also become terms of respect, as when one street-corner man wishes to pay homage to another's toughness. They should, however, only be used with great care, or you too could end up calling for your mamma.

Fighting Words

It was on the battlefield where the *f**k* found itself most at home and was accorded the greatest respect. Young men who had been taught to eschew the *Big F* in word and deed because of its obscene nature were suddenly confronted with an even greater obscenity—war. Knowing no other way to describe the *screwed-up* nature of things, they reached down into the depths of their souls and resurrected the forbidden *f**k*. Compelled to express the depth of their physical and mental misery, they truly felt *f**ked and far from home.*

The experience repeated itself in World War II with appropriate comments about the military. The original military *f**k-up* occurred in the British army around 1939 as an *MFU*, evolving into the great all-purpose *SNAFU* (Situation Normal, All *F**ked* Up) shortly thereafter. *SNAFU* eventually made it into polite society, albeit in a slightly "fouled-up" form, but those in the know, still regard it as *SUSFU* (Situation Unchanged, Still *F**ked* Up).

A Many-splendored Thing

Most people are familiar only with *f**k's* violent side, and few appreciate the word's complex character. The *f**k* is nature's all-purpose word, able to express every mood and capture the tenor of every occasion. The one thing it isn't, is simple, as with this *f**kin'* business.

Given the proper inflection, the word can express an entire range of sentiments:

Confusion:	What the *f**k?*
Despair and dismay:	*F**ked* again, or Truly *f**ked.*
Liberation:	What the *f**k!*
Helplessness:	*F**ked* by the fickle finger of fate.
Concern:	Doesn't anyone give a *f**k?*
Surprise, dismissal, or rejection, with the help of various objects:	Oneself—*F**k* me! Inanimate object—*F**k* it! Helpless creature—*F**k* a duck!
Futility:	What the *f**k?* or Who gives a *f**k* anyway?
Absence of meaningful action:	*F**king* around, or *f**king* off.

What better way to end this disquisition than by simply getting the *f**k* out of here?

Take My Word for IT

This is the way we say *it* in our time
When carnal and unmarried love is meant:
I mean we do not *make the double back,*
Or *die:* We *sleep together.* We *conjugate.*

> —Winfield Townley Scott, Sonnet XV,
> *c.* 1940

When we summarily dismissed the *f**k* from our working vocabulary, we added more than 1,500 expressions to take its place. Eric Partridge, the noted wordsmith, remarked as to how the large number of phrases "bear witness to the fertility of the English language and to the enthusiastic English participation in the universal fascination of *the creative act.*" Other critics saw the dismissal as a form of cowardice and hypocrisy.

Many of the substitute terms are vivid and expressive, oft-times ingenious. But none has proved more popular and inoffensive than *doing IT.* For years everyone was *doing IT, doing IT, doing IT,* and everyone knew exactly what *IT* meant. Occasionally there was a screw-up, and somebody mistakenly took out the garbage, but for the most part, *IT* came off as intended.

In 1934 the censors declared *doing IT* "too suggestive" and banned *IT, doing,* and *doing IT* from the airwaves. This low blow deprived Rudy Vallee of the right to sing his greatest stage and radio hits, including "Let's Do It," "Do It Again," and "You Do Something to Me." Today, America is again *doing IT,* with gusto. Of all the expressions we have for *the act,* the inarticulate favor *doing IT* over all the others. Joan Rivers assured women everywhere that there's really nothing to *IT,* "Just close your eyes, lie back, and pretend you're having an operation."

IT couldn't be any easier.

Do IT *Yourself*

Doctors *do IT* with patience
Lawyers *do IT* briefly
Accountants *do IT* figuratively
Publishers *do IT* periodically

_____*do IT*_____
_____*do IT*_____
_____*do IT*_____

Dante *did IT* divinely
Marx *did IT* in a revolting fashion
Michaelangelo *did IT* on the ceiling
Moses *did IT* on the rush
Sinatra *did IT* my way

_____ *did IT* _____
_____ *did IT* _____
_____ *did IT* _____

Making Do

Though a lady repel your advance, she'll be kind
Just as long as you intimate what's on your mind.
You may tell her you're *hungry,* you *need to be swung,*
You may mention the *ashes that need to be hauled,*
Put the lid on her sauce pan, but don't be too bold;
For the moment you're forthright, get ready to duck—
For the girl isn't born yet who'll stand for "Let's *f**k!*"

—"Ode to Those Four-Letter Words"

In "polite society" they have their own ways of *doing IT,* albeit in a drab and somewhat colorless fashion.

None is more popular than *making love.* Couples have been *making love* in the sense of paying court or wooing one another since 1580. They've been *making love* as we *do IT* only since around 1950. That meaning wasn't even formally recognized in our dictionaries until 1976.

Another recent favorite is *having sex,* which has been used since the late twenties or thirties.

Sex comes from the Latin *secare,* "to cut or divide," and we first used the word to designate the two major categories of humanity we have come to know and love as male and female. According to Greek mythology, we began life as a perfect four-armed and -legged he/she unit. Unfortunately, we were so taken with ourselves as works of art that our manner offended the mighty Zeus. He cut us down to size, severing us into two separate entities.

We later used the word *sex* not only for dividing the sexes, but to refer to qualities of being male or female. Over time we assigned specific attributes to each category. These distinctions were dutifully recorded in the esteemed OED, making it all very official. The male was described as "the better" and "the sterner" sex; the female, as "the fairer," "the gentler," "the softer," and "the devout" sex. Women were also called "the second" sex. For a period of time between the sixteenth and seventeenth centuries, when people spoke of "the sex," they had women in mind.

We obviously had a problem, and we called on the word itself to bridge the gap between the sexes. In the twentieth century we began to use *sex* to describe the means of forging a new togetherness, a way of helping us get our act together. Today, when we use the word *sex,* it generally refers to that unifying process.

Being with a woman often said it all, underscoring the closeness or coziness in the act. And there's no one closer than our *relations* (19thC.). Men and women are also said *to be familiar with* (15thC.) or *on familiar terms with* one another. Before the fifteenth century some even considered them *overfamiliar.*

But such *familiarity* breeds *intimacy* nowadays. That began around 1884, with people *being intimate with each other.* Today, there is talk of people *being intimate* or *on intimate terms.* The nice part about it is you can also have intimates without necessarily *f**king* them.

You Should Know Better

I've only *slept with* the men I've been married to.
How many women can make that claim?
 —Elizabeth Taylor

You can't get any more *intimate* than by *spending the night with someone* or *sleeping with someone.* We've been *sleeping with each other* that way since the ninth century, and celebrated it as such in poetry from Chaucer to Whitman. *Sleeping with some-*

body, however, is not without its critics. Alan Sherman in *Rape of the Ape* noted, "Since time began nobody has been able to *copulate* while asleep. Even if it were possible it would be impolite."

It was especially easy to be *intimate* in the Old Testament. All the more important people already *knew* each other there. *Knowing* a person was synonymous with *f**king* that person, and the word was applied to both sexes. Men *knew* women, and women *knew* men. Later, we only had *knowledge of a woman* (c. 1425), where to *know* her was to *love* her. *Knowing* a man, however, came to count for very little, and self-knowledge, not at all.

A little knowledge continued to be a very dangerous thing. We eventually gained *carnal knowledge* (c. 1686), from the Latin *carnus*, "meat," which made it possible for us to know each other in the flesh, advanced students ostensibly being able to distinguish between eye of the round and chuck.

In God We Trust

They didn't *know* everything, however. The all-time Biblical favorite remained *to go in unto,* a phrase that appears liberally throughout the Old Testament. There are dozens of references to it as when, for example, Onan *went in unto his brother's wife.* The expression is a real bell-ringer. It makes *the act* sound as romantic as pulling your car into your neighbor's garage.

You might not guess it from the Old Testament, but for the Jews, the *f**k* has always been a matter of *doing the agreeable* (19thC.) — no guilt, no pain, no anxiety. Though they took seriously the injunction to "multiply and be fruitful," they never sought to disguise or suppress the pleasure.

Good sex was considered a *mitzvah,* an exemplary deed. The most pious reserved Friday night for *doing IT* with their wives, choosing the most holy day, the Sabbath, to perform this most sacred and blessed act.

The Christian attitude toward sex originated with the Church leaders and authorities, who did much to shape and influence future attitudes on the topic.

Each came at it differently. St. Augustine believed it a problem that began in Eden when we first unleashed our *con-*

cupiscence (from the Latin for "to desire eagerly"), a strong and unnatural appetite previously subject to the dictates of will, and he was most troubled by the lack of control that accompanied *the act.* Pope Gregory I was angered more by *the act* itself and that which impelled it than by the *voluptus carne,* the "pleasure of the flesh" which accompanied it and obscured its true purpose—*procreation.* For St. Thomas Aquinas, *sex* primarily offended his sense of orderliness, being contrary to the dictates of reason.

Before you could say "hellfire, brimstone, and damnation," people began feeling guilt. Soon they found themselves *doing the naughty* (19thC.), feeling naughtiness in the pleasure prior to, during, and subsequent to *the act.* The medieval Church worked hard to eliminate guilt by simply cutting down on the number of occasions on which one might feel pleasure. It recommended abstinence on Thursdays in memory of the capture of Jesus; on Fridays in memory of his death; on Saturdays in honor of the Virgin Mary; on Sundays in memory of the Resurrection; and on Mondays in commemoration of the departed souls. *The act* was also forbidden forty days before Easter, Pentecost, and Christmas, and never on special feast days or during Lent. Thus was born the appointment book.

Those who made it, dressed for the occasion. They donned the medieval *chemise cagoule,* a plain shift that totally covered the female save for a suitably placed hole through which the *penis* could perform its work, effectively generating new sinners for the Church to save.

Cleaning Up Your Act

Love has pitched her mansion in the place of
excrement.

—W.B. Yeats

Inter faeces et urinem nascimur.
We are born between feces and urine.

—St. Augustine

It was easy for the Church to convince people that *sex* was a dirty business. Reinforced by the proximity of the sexual parts to, and their close association with, the process of elimination of waste, it was only a matter of time before sex came to be identified with the elimination process, a way of transferring from one individual to another such waste matter as may have accumulated in one's body.

Church authorities loved the image. It was perfect: Man eliminated into woman, and her *vagina* was the repository for his filth. They could even sanction the role the *prostitute* played as a common sewer to help carry away men's garbage. Chaucer's Parson wrote of whores "that must be likened to a common *gong* [a toilet] where men purged their ordure."

The theme was soon picked up in the language. Especially popular during the 1930s was the practice of *getting one's ashes hauled.* A not unnatural thing, for when fires are raging, ashes are the natural residue. Someone has to remove them. After all, neatness counts, even in sex. It's another bond between sexual release and body hygiene.

You'll find variations of this in contemporary blues songs, with reference to how *"my garbage can is overflowing"* and won't you please *"empty my trash."* We speak of sex as *easing oneself* (20thC.), and *doing one's business* (20thC.). Some even refer to *IT* as *number three* (20thC.), an apparent also-ran behind numbers one and two, *p∗ssing* and *s∗∗tting* respectively.

Hundreds of years after Chaucer's Parson, a boy in Sylvia Plath's *The Bell Jar* described his first sexual experience with a *whore* as being "as boring as going to the toilet." Phillip Wylie in *Opus 21* recounts how books of advice for young men attaining the age of desire sought to dissuade them from seeking the company of *prostitutes.* They employed not the toilet but the bathtub to make their point, asking indignantly, "Would you walk into a cheap hotel, find that the stranger before you had left the tub filled with dirty bath water, and immerse yourself in it?"

Sex is great, but it's really difficult to keep it clean.

Latin Lovers

As dirty as *IT* is, men of the cloth always prefer talking about *IT* to *doing IT.* They are especially good at catching others in *the act*—but always in Latin. They never catch you *f**king,* only *copulating, fornicating, having conjugal relations* or engaged in *coitus.* When not so occupied, you can find them sitting in judgment as to whether a marriage has indeed been *consummated.*

Copulation, or *coupling,* comes from the Latin *copulatus,* "being linked or tied together"—a form of *sexual union. Conjugal* means "to join with," from *jugam,* "the yoke" (as many have experienced it). *Fornicate* (before 1300) originates with the *fornices,* the dark archways under the Roman colosseums where *ladies of loose morals* used to ply their trade. When many of the brothels of Rome went underground, they then became identified as *fornices.* We later turned the goings-on into *fornication,* transforming the regular customers into *fornicators.*

When in *coitus* or practicing *coition* couples simply *"went together"* (from the Latin *co* and *ire*). *Consummation* is sometimes the highest form (*summa*) of togetherness (*con*), thus saying it all as far as the Church was concerned.

You're an Animal!

The entire exercise, however, was not without value. Thanks to Christianity we uncovered our bestial nature. There we were, *bulling* (18thC.), *hogging* (19thC.), and *tomming* (19thC.). The animals themselves had better things to do. Sheep *tupped* (c. 1549), horses *covered* (c. 1535), birds *trod* (before 1250), foxes were *at clicket* (17th–18thC.), and dogs were *in line.* Deer and cats were forever *rutting.* It all sounded so good that before you knew it, we had appropriated these same expressions for ourselves.

There was no denying the quality of the *service.* The best literary *service* can be found in *Othello* where Iago warns Brabantio that Othello and Desdemona are *getting it on* together.

> . . . Even now, now, very now,
> an old black ram is *tupping*
> your white ewe. . . .
>
> You'll have your daughter *cover'd*
> with a Barbary horse. . . .

Your daughter and the Moor are now
making the beast with two backs.

Standing Tall in the Saddle

Quoth she, "What is this so still and warm?"
" 'Tis Ball, my nag, he will do you no harm."
"But what is this hangs under his chin?"
" 'Tis his bag he puts his provender in."
Quoth he, "What is this?"
Quoth she, " 'Tis a well where Ball, your nag,
   can drink his fill."
"But what if my nag should chance to fall in?"
"Catch hold of the grass that grows on the slip
   brim."
"But what if the grass should chance to fail?"
"Shove him in by the head, pull him out by
   the tail."

> — Thomas D'Urfey, "The Trooper," in
> *Songs of Wit and Mirth or Pills to
> Purge Melancholy,* 1719

My father was no jockey, but he sure taught me
   how to ride;
He said first in the middle, then you swing from
   side to side.

> — Quoted in Le Roi Jones, *Blues People,*
> *c.* 1963

Surely, it was no surprise, then, to find ourselves *horsing around* (19thC.), or *playing at stallions and mares* (c. 1850). The man generally *mounted* (c. 1592) or *did a mount* and *rode the mare* (c. 1850). And the woman, well . . .

Ride as *f**k* was first recorded before 1250 and was Standard English for *the act* until around 1780. Man first *rode* and later woman was said to *get* or *have a ride* (19thC.). In *Antony and Cleopatra,* the Egyptian queen, thinking of her love who is far away at war, remarks, "O happy horse to bear the weight of Antony."

It's all good clean fun, but if you were with your neighbor's wife, you were open to the charge of *riding in another man's saddle,* the *saddle* long having stood for the female *pudendum.*

Autoeroticism

When my baby go to bed,
It shines like a morning star.
When I crawl in the middle,
It rides me like a Cadillac car.

> — Georgia Bill, "Scary Day Blues," early 20thC.

The days of *lascivious carriage* are over. We now have a *classy chassis* (c. 1940) with good car maintenance and an entire sub-vocabulary to describe it, including the *valve job* (19th-20thC., from the *vulva*), a *body job,* and a *lubrication.* What better place to *get your oil changed* than at your local *service station?* The basic parts include the *piston* (rod) and *connecting rod* (both 20thC.), and the *coupling pin* (19th-20thC.).

Good maintenance means everything. It is said that the American man caresses and pampers his car like a favorite mistress — or is it the other way around? e.e. cummings couldn't have agreed more.

> . . . (having thoroughly oiled the universal
> joint tested my gas felt of
> her radiator made sure her springs were o.
> k.) i went right to it flooded-the-carburetor
>   cranked her
> up, slipped the
> clutch . . .

> — *She Being Brand,* 1926

Making History

IT's detractors could take nothing away from *IT*'s proud history. From time immemorial, *IT* was *what mother did before me* and *what Eve did with Adam.* The commonfolk have been at it for centuries: *quiffing* (18th-20thC.), *tiffing* (late 18th-early

19thC.), *niggling* (c. 1565-1820), *snizzling* (c. 1923), *foining* (late 16th-17thC.), *nubbing* (18th-early 19thC.), and *nugging* (late 11th-mid-17thC.).

When not so engaged you could find them *jiggling* (c. 1845), *bouncing* (late 19thC.), *shaking* (verb, 16thC.; noun, c. 1860), and *humping* (c. 1760-1850). Taking great pains to be anatomically correct, they've been *belly-bumping, tummy-tickling, rump-splitting* (all 19thC.), *joining faces,* and *rubbing bacons.*

Back in 1398, they loved to *swive.* But the oldest expression we have in English for the *tickle-tail function* (17th-20thC.) is to *sard* (c. 950) as in the old Nottingham saying, "Go teach your granddam to *sard!*" – a rank insult of the times and possibly the first recorded example of the "dozens," a remark somewhat equivalent to our own, "Your mother swims out to meet troopships!"

Doing unto Others

Originally, *IT* was just a *job* (16thC.) – good work if you could get it. Over time, it came to be viewed as an act of charity, doing for those unable to do for themselves, as *to do a woman's job for her* (c. 1850). When woman's work was synonymous with the kitchen, one could get her *a handle for the broom* (18thC.), *give her cannister a rattle* (Robert Burns), *do some ladies' tailoring* (c. 1815), or *mend her kettle* (18thC.).

Doing a woman's job is not without problems. It requires skill, dexterity, and determination. Many a fellow has started a *job* he later couldn't finish.

For many it's been a real *grind* (late 16thC.), from the movement involved, giving us his *grinding tool,* her *grindstone,* and the *grinding house* (all 19thC.), and bumps and *grinds.* One actively disposed to *the act* was said to be *on the grind* (19th-20thC.). You'll find numerous references to *grinding* in books and songs from bawdy Restoration ballads to twentieth-century blues. Three centuries ago it was said,

Digbie's lady takes it ill,
that her lord *grind* not at her mill.

– *Ladies' Parliament,* 1647

Things improved over time, and by the 1930s Bessie Smith was singing,

> The woman has a *grinder*,
> The best one [she] could find.
> The man *grinds* her coffee,
> 'Cause he has a brand new *grind*.

Write On!

IT soon evolved from a real *grind* into the highest form of communication. Once it entailed *conversation* (from the Latin *conversari*, "to keep company with") and *correspondence* (both 19thC.). Before the era of the ball-point pen, when a boss did *IT* with his secretary or the clerical help, he simply *dipped his pen in the office ink* (20thC.). On occasion, he didn't have the resources to finish his message. His "ink was run, his pen was done" (*c.* 1650). Alas, there was also *no lead in his pencil*.

Giving Them the Business

Words are cheap in a world based on money and politics, making it inevitable that we would have both sexual *commerce* and *business* in the nineteenth century. *Intercourse* originally referred to the normal flow of communications and commercial transactions between localities. But in 1798 we also discovered *sexual intercourse*. It proved so popular that *intercourse* developed a *traffic* (19thC.) of its own.

Since then most *traffic* has not been sexual, though an interesting intersection of the two meanings occurred during the sixties when, for promotional purposes, Ralph Ginzburg had his magazine *Eros* postmarked from Intercourse, Pennsylvania—thereby putting the *Big F*'s stamp on the U.S. mails.

The Body Politic

The Democrats are *doing IT* to their secretaries
and the Republicans are *doing IT* to the country.

—Joan Mondale

21

Politically, most know congress as a serious assembly or gathering of persons, but it's also been described as *amorous* and *sexual* (16th-19thC.). Few would argue with the definition, including James Boswell, who wrote in his journal, "I picked up a fresh, agreeable young girl called Alice Gibbs and we had a very agreeable *congress.*"

Others also have found *congress* agreeable and amorous. The more famous congressional *liaisons* have included Elizabeth Ray with Representative Wayne Hays, and Fanny Foxe with Wilbur Mills. It appears that the highest position to which every office-holder aspires is that same *congress.* It is synonymous with the treatment given the American people by that body, as well as their extracurricular activities.

Do you know where your senator is tonight?

Pretty Please

Fanny: There are words which sound better and are often used before company, instead of *"swiving"* and *"f**king,"* which is too gross and downright bawdery, fit only to be used among dissolute persons. To avoid scandal, men modestly say, *"I kissed her, made much of her, received a favor from her,"* or the like.

> — *The School of Venus, or The Ladies*
> *Delight Reduced into Rules of Practice,*
> 1744

Well, it is sort of a favor. Isn't it? I mean when a girl lets you kiss her and, you know, go on from there — feel her up and you know, the rest of it — go all the way, and the rest of it. I mean, isn't it a favor? What's in it for her? I mean if she's not getting paid or anything?

> — Jules Feiffer, *Carnal Knowledge,*
> 1971

When *The New York Times* and other august publications report such goings-on, they often describe them as *sexual favors* or plain *favors. Favors* traditionally are *granted* or *bestowed, lavished upon,* or *yielded.* William Safire, the columnist and wordsmith, defines such *favors* as the hats, bonbons, noise-makers and other souvenirs one brings back from an orgy.

Favors can be granted by both sexes. For a time, it was men who *did* or *worked their kind,* did the *act* or *deed of kind* (c. 1230), or *did a kindness* (18th-20thC.), but for the most part, it's been women who've extended every courtesy, thus making *courtesans* out of many of them. Often they've given everything save the *last favor.* Moll Flanders proudly reported, "Though he took these freedoms with me, it did not go to that which they call the *last favor.*" Makes you wonder, doesn't it, that *sex* might indeed be a favor of sorts.

Favors are generally helpful, but *connections* also help. Boswell reported trying to track down a certain "Signor Gonorrhea," finally narrowing his search to one of his many *paramours.* Confronting her with his condition, he then argued with her, pointing out, "Madam, I have had no *connections* with any woman but you these two months." As Boswell's experience reminds us, it's sometimes as important to miss *connections* as to make them.

Nice of You to Drop In

These two did often *do the two-backed beast* together . . .
in so far that at last she became *great with child.*

— Rabelais, translated by Sir Thomas
Urquhart, 1653

If all this still seems too serious, perhaps you should simply treat it as fun. Shakespeare made the *beast with two backs* and *went groping for trout in the peculiar river,* one aspect of the sport that somehow eluded both Sir Isaac Walton and our English teacher. For a bit of even more offbeat recreation a man could try *burying* or *dipping his wick* (c. 1850). A contemporary parallel is *dunking the love muscle* (20thC.), a great phrase that makes *the act* sound as if it were something akin to bobbing for apples.

Games People Play

There hath a question been of late
Among the youthful sort;

What pastime is the pleasantest
And what the sweetest sport?
And it hath been adjudged
As well by great and small
That of all the pastimes none is like to
Uptails all.

> —Thomas D'Urfey, "Uptails All," in
> *Songs of Wit and Mirth,* 1719

Sexual athletes, front and center! It's time for the *first game ever played,* the *sport of Venus* (19thC.).

It's the sport of the masses, the *national indoor sport* (20thC.), the *old ball game* (20thC.), the *game of inches* where every young man *pitches woo* (1920s) and dreams of making a *hit* (mid-20thC.).

It features something for everyone. For the young moderns there's *jogging, pole-vaulting* (both 18th-19thC.), *broad-jumping,* a *bit of bouncy-bouncy* and a little *one-on-one* (all 20thC.), while historical buffs can play at *pushpin* (17th-18thC.), *take a turn on the aphrodisiacal tennis court,* or opt for *a spot of Cupid's archery* (both 19thC.).

You don't need a cast of thousands, either, only *a little o' the one with t'other* (18th-20thC.). And it's so simple anyone can *do IT,* merely a little *in-and-in* (17th-early 19thC.), or some *in-and-out* (17thC.).

Tennis, Anyone?

Tennis? Not when you can play at
    Two-handed Put (18th-early 19thC.)
    Pully-Hauly (late 18thC.)
    Pickle-Me-Tickle-Me (mid-17th-18thC.)
    Cuddle-My-Cuddle (D'Urfey)
or have
    A Rootle
    A Poopnoddy
    A Squeeze and a Squirt (all 19th C.)

It's a game in which there is always a winner, *where you can lose the match and still pocket the stakes* (18thC.). By mid-twentieth century it definitely was not a matter of winning or losing – or even how you played the game – but simply a matter of *scoring.*

Take a Card, Any Card

If you're not up for sports, perhaps you'd settle for a quiet game of cards – maybe a somewhat unusual game called *Irish Whist* (19thC.). The woman *plays the jack against the ace,* and the *jack takes the ace.*

Jack has long been synonymous with the *he-thing* and the *ace* (particularly the *ace of spades*) for more than three centuries has been identified with the female counterpart, from the shape and color of pubic hair. When *jack* takes the *ace* the game is over – nothing else remains to be played.

All That Jazz

Cards aren't your bag, either? We could always *make beautiful music together,* starting with a little *fiddling about* (17thC., "to caress familiarly"), going on to some *strumming* (*c.* 1780) and some *tromboning* (late 1880s). The classic blend of *sex* and music is *jazz,* a popular expression from the thirties and forties for *doing IT* – like the music, emotional, rhythmic, and improvisational. David Dalby, an authority on the African element in American English, finds the word's roots in *jas* and *jasy,* the core of which is "to speed up, excite, exaggerate, or act in an unrestrained way." The first jazz in this country was performed by Black musicians in *bawdy houses,* firmly establishing the link between the music and *sex.* Streetwalkers later approached prospective customers with the line, "Hey, big boy, what about some *jazz* tonight?"

Jam and *jam sessions* have also been used in that same way. A lovelorn column in a British newspaper featured the following advice: "Quicker than a penguin sliding down an icicle, that's how quickly a necking session can turn into a *jam session.* And you're the one in a *jam.*"

25

Invitation to the Dance

Sukey that danced with the cushion,
An hour from the room has been gone;
And Barnaby knew by her blushing
That some other dance had been done.

— D'Urfey, "The Winchester Wedding,"
in *Songs of Wit and Mirth,* 1719

Oscar Wilde called dance "a vertical expression of a horizontal urge." And a Gene Kelly you don't have to be to do the *mattress jig* (18th-19thC.), the *reel o'Stumpie* (Scot., 18th-20thC.), the *blanket hornpipe* (*c.* 1810), or the *four-legged frolic* (*c.* 1850).

The more experienced do the routine *box step* (20thC.) or the *matrimonial polka* (*c.* 1850). You can dance them best to some *sheet music* (19th-20thC.), or to the *tune of the shaking of the sheets together*—an old English country melody.

We have dance steps and sexual positions. Wayland Young in *Eros Denied* commented that both dancing and *f**king* are not a series of positions but, rather, a flow of movement. He considered the fact that we refer to sexual positions in this context as the result of blocked imaginations.

Those who believe that *f**k* comes from an acronym for *F*or *U*nlawful *C*arnal *K*nowledge maintain that it was used as a form of covert shorthand for recording cases of rape and sodomy. Some trace it to the Puritan Massachusetts Bay Colony; others to medieval times. Neither claim can be substantiated. As for reference works, *f**k* first appeared in 1598 in Florio's English-Italian Dictionary, *A Worlde of Wordes,* but it wasn't until 1671 in a dictionary edited by one Steven Skinner that the word received an entry of its own in correct alphabetical order. What then followed was a series of erratic placements. Nathaniel Bailey (*c.* 1725) identified it as "a term used of a goat." John Ash (1775) called it "a low, vulgar word . . . to have to do with a woman." Francis Grose's *Classical Dictionary of the Vulgar Tongue,* published in 1785, featured a "f__k duck," the man who had care of the poultry aboard a ship of war. The word surfaced briefly in John Farmer and W.E. Henley's multivolume *Slang and Its Analogues,* a nineteenth-century survey of the common tongue, but disappeared from the single-volume abridgement.

Freed at last by the U.S. Supreme Court decision on *Lady Chatterley's Lover* in 1951, the word soon gained new life. James Jones included some 258 *f**k*s in his original manuscript of *From Here to Eternity,* published that same year, though his editor later edited them down to a mere 50. Overnight the word became the darling of contemporary novelists, leaving us all wondering what it was that people did prior to D.H. Lawrence. We had rediscovered the *f**k* with a vengeance.

The *Big F*'s formal coming out includes: *The Penguin Dictionary,* 1965; *The American Heritage Dictionary,* 1969; and at last the *OED* in its 1972 supplement.

† † †

*F**k* has been formally banned from the House of Commons of Her Britannic Majesty's Parliament in Westminster, London. The decision fell upon the

Speaker of the House, one George Thomas. According to the *Manchester Guardian,*

> As long as I am Speaker I shall consider that an unparliamentary expression. None of us would use it in our own homes, and I hope that this House can maintain a better example to the country.

† † †

World War II begat a host of lesser imitations of *SNAFU,* the best of which include *COMMFU* (a Complete Monumental Military *F**k-up*), *FUBAR* (*F**ked Up* Beyond Recognition), *FUBB* (*F**ked Up* Beyond Belief), *FUMTU* (*F**ked Up* More Than Usual), *GFU* (General *F**k-up*), and *IMFU* (Immense Military *F**k-up*). Complicating matters even further were Joint Anglo-American *F**k-ups* (*JAAFU*) and Joint Anglo-Chinese *F**k-ups* (*JACFU*). With luck, things were *SAMFU* (Self-Adjusting Military *F**k-ups*), but often they could only be described as *TARFU* (Things Are Really *F**ked Up*) or *TAFUBAR* (Things Are *F**ked Up* Beyond All Recognition).

† † †

Yo mama and other such terms of abuse sprang from, and are part of, an exercise popular in the Black community called the dozens (mother-rhyming), a game played on street corners by Black youth as a form of recreation or, as Rap Brown described it, a popular form of recreation much "like White folks play Scrabble." It's a verbal duel, the purpose of which is to destroy your opponent with words. Dozens originated in an African tradition where there is a great reliance on oral expression, one in which people express references to one another's mothers, often imputing incestuous relations as part of the verbal give and take.

> I *f**ked* your mama
> Till she went blind.

Her breath smells bad,
But she sure can *grind*.

I *f**ked* your mama
For a solid hour.
Baby came out
Screaming Black Power.

Elephant and the Baboon
Learning to *screw*
Baby came out looking
Like Spiro Agnew.

> — H. Rap Brown, "Street Talk," in
> *Rappin' and Stylin' Out,* Thomas
> Kochman, ed., 1972

† † †

The Irish have always been on the butt end of sexual language. They and the Dutch were to the eighteenth and nineteenth centuries what the Polish are to the twentieth.

An Irish Wedding:	Emptying a *s**t-house*
Irish Confetti:	Semen
Irish Root:	Penis
Irish Toothache:	Priapism (i.e., to get one's Irish up)
Irish Dip:	Sexual intercourse
Irish Clubhouse:	Brothel
Irish Fortune:	A woman's *private parts*

† † †

Wentworth and Flexner's *Dictionary of American Slang* records this anecdote from Stephen Longstreet's 1951 book *The Pedlocks.* "Have you heard the story of the old Irish woman who was asked if she'd ever been bedridden? 'Hundreds of times,' she answered, 'and once in a sled.' "

THREE

Sticks and Stones

Hey-diddle-diddle,
Mine's in the middle.
Where's yours?

— Anon., *c*. 1950s

If *sex* be an act, we all have parts to play with. Most of us know them as the *carnal parts* (early 18thC.), the *natural parts* (mid-16thC.), the *naturals* (17thC.), the *parts below* (17thC.), the *underparts* (mid-19thC.), the *privy parts* (*c*. 1565), the *private parts* (*c*. 1885), the *privates* (20thC.), and the ever-favorite *genitals* or *genitalia*, from the Latin *gignere*, "to beget." In literate circles they're our *pudenda* (*c*. 1634), from the Latin *pudere*, "to shame" — giving us "that of which we are ashamed," which tells a lot about our feelings toward them.

Few speak well of these parts, many not at all. Even the great H.L. Mencken was struck dumb in their presence. He omitted any mention of them by name in his classification of the body parts — reasoning that there was no place for such items in a book meant to be read before the domestic hearth.

However, the days of domestic hearths are over, replaced by the age of sexual enlightenment. The times call for candor. We've found out everything about *the act;* it's now time we learned our parts.

I'll tell you a little story,
    Just a story I have heard;
And you'll swear it's all a fable
    But it's gospel, every word.

When the Lord made father Adam,
  They say He laughed and sang;
And sewed him up the belly
  With a little piece of *whang*.

But when the Lord was finished
  He found He'd measured wrong;
For when the *whang* was knotted
  'Twas several inches long.

Said He, " 'Tis but eight inches
  So I guess I'll let it hang."
So He left on Adam's belly
  That little piece of *whang*.

But when the Lord made mother Eve
  I imagine He did snort,
When He found the *whang* He sewed her with
  Was several inches short.

" 'Twill leave an awful gap," said He,
  "But I should give a damn,
She can fight it out with Adam
  For that little piece of *whang*."

So ever since that day
  When human life began,
There's been a constant struggle
  'Twixt the woman and the man.

> —Anon., "Whang," 20thC.

Stand Up and Be Counted

Much luck to you *members*
Just try to never let me down
And keep to your place.

> —Thom Gunn, *Das Liebesleben,*
> mid-20thC.

Welcome to the club! Ours is exclusive. Women are simply not admitted. *Members* (c. 1290) in good standing include the *sex-*

31

ual member, the *carnal member,* the *virile member* (18thC.), the *male member,* the *privy member* (c. 1297), the *dearest member* (Robert Burns), and even the *unruly member.*

"I don't know how to put it sir, but you simply don't measure up."

We have more than 600 ways of referring to our *members.* Heading up the rolls is the right honorable *pr**k,* derived from the Old English *prica* for "dot or point." Its distinguished lineage goes back to 1592 and an OED citation: "The passing boye lifte up his *pr**k.*" Three years later Shakespeare lifted it for *Romeo and Juliet,* causing Mercutio to pun, "The bawdy hand of the dial is now upon the *pr**k* of noon."

*Pr**k* was standard English until 1700, after which it became a vulgarism, evidence of its popularity. Most recently, we have used it to describe a particularly offensive, irascible, or unscrupulous male personality. He's a rogue, a scoundrel, and a knave—one who under no circumstances can be trusted. *Pr**k* has also been used to register an exclamation. The Spanish cry out, *"Carajo!"* The English-speaking world opts for "Gad!" "Gatso!" and "Gadzooks!" all corruptions of *carazo* from the Italian *cazzo, pr**k.* Regardless of its common usage, the *pr**k* continues to be an outcast in polite society. As George Carlin noted, "You can prick your finger, but you cannot finger your *pr**k.*"

Tails of Old

That strives to stand that cannot go,
 That feeds the mouth that cannot bite.
It is a friar with a bald head
 A staff to beat a cuckold dead.
It is a gun that shoots point blank;
 It hits betwixt a maiden's flank.
A shift of cupid's cut,
'Twill serve to rove, to prick, to butt;
'Twas ne'er a maid but by her will
Will keep it in her quiver still.

—Anon., *A Riddle,* 18th-19thC.

Of all our *members,* it's the *penis* that has won widest acceptance. It made its first recorded appearance in 1684 in a medical dictionary and over the years established itself as the most respected *member* in the field. It alone has gained public exposure and access to places a *pr**k* could never go.

In truth, *penis* has an ignoble pedigree. Though it's a good Latin word, Ovid, the Roman poet and *pornographer* had no use for it. Literally, *penis* means "tail" (Standard English for the part, mid-14th–mid-18thC.) – and a definite put-down. Freud, however, tells us that women feel otherwise, that they elevate it to new heights when experiencing *penis envy,* an urge repressed at an early age to possess male power and exercise the male prerogative. A more succinct update in *Psychology Today* defines *penis envy* as "the desire to be red, wrinkled, and four inches long."

Simply Fascinating

Man has always been of two minds in dealing with his *pr**k.* It's been both an object of great pride and of great shame. Back in ancient times, it was treated with reverence and worshipped as the source of fecundity and perceived to be the power behind motherhood, fertility, food and the seasonal cycles. In Egypt and Greece symbolic representations of it, huge *phalluses* (late 18th-20thC. from the Greek for *pr**k*), were carried about in solemn religious processions. In Rome, images of *pr**ks* could be found everywhere. There were *pr**ks* at the doors of shops, *pr**ks* at the city gates, and *pr**ks* attached to the chariots of famous generals. Even drinking glasses and goblets were cast in their shape.

Believing that the *phallus* possessed magic powers and was especially effective in warding off the evil eye, the Romans also cast good-luck charms in the shape of male organs, which they wore about the neck. Supposedly, the evil eye became so taken with the sight of the *pr**k* that its attention was diverted from the intended victim. These charms were called *fascina* or "little bundles" from which we get the word "fascinating."

Things change over time, but no one knows why the *pr**k* remained a *penis* but ceased being fascinating.

For the Birds

Before the barn-door crowing
The c∗∗k by hens attended
His eyes around him throwing,
Stands for a while suspended.
Then one he singles from the crew,
And cheers the happy hen
With How do you do and How do you do
And How do you do again.

—John Gay, song from *The Beggar's Opera*, 1728

A more modern contender for the top spot, and definitely trying harder, is the c∗∗k (16th-20thC.). Many even consider it the most popular expression that we have for the *male organ*. The c∗∗k is part of a larger Greco-Roman tradition of putting wings on images of the *phallus*. The same instinct also gave us the *bird* in nineteenth-century England. In Italian the word *uccello* has the same meaning. The colloquial German features *Vogelin*, which literally means *"to bird"* and figuratively "to f∗∗k." In the United States our fine-feathered friends include the *canary* (20thC.), found along the eastern seaboard, and the southern-based *pecker* (20thC.), noted for its repeated and rhythmic thrusts.

C∗∗k's rise to the top has not been easy. Early in the nineteenth century a wave of anti-c∗∗k sentiment swept the land. It was part of a general purge of language deemed offensive — transforming legs into limbs and bulls into he-cows. C∗∗k suddenly disappeared, not only from private conversations but from the family farm. Poultry farmers referred to their holdings as "boy birds" and "gentlemen fowl." In war, men pulled back the roosters of their guns. And throughout, folks had nothing to sustain them but a little rooster-eyed optimism. He's staged a comeback, however. Today, the average male is c∗∗kier than ever, though there are those detractors who would describe his appearance and character as more like a turkey.

"Esther, have you ever seen a man?" . . .
"No," I said. "Only statues." . . .

I stared at Buddy while he unzipped his chino pants. . . .

He just stood there in front of me and I kept staring at him. The only thing I could think of was turkey neck and turkey gizzards, and I felt very depressed.

— Sylvia Plath, *The Bell Jar*, 1971

Little Things Mean a Lot

*C**k* and *pr**k* are especially vivid and evocative words, but most people consider them obscene and socially unacceptable. Talking about them often occasions a violent reaction.

In response to our personal discomfort and out of deference to the sensitivity of others, we often substitute a less emotionally laden term. *Penis* is a case in point. Latin lends class and respectability, and as a dead language, it threatens very few.

But the *penis* just wouldn't do. In its own lackluster fashion it failed to capture the true glory of a man's *organ*. As safe as the *penis* was, it was also incredibly dull — dull — dull.

Women compounded matters by rendering it somewhat nondescript as *it*, his *whatchamacallit*, and his *thing*. *Things* couldn't have been any worse, all *things* being equal.

Man tilled his fertile imagination, finding new ways to do his *pr**k* justice, extolling its virtues and singing its praises. He promoted it heavily as his *manhood* (20thC.), though admittedly choosing a rather strange place in which to carry it. He reminded females that it was the *delight of women* (20thC.), somewhat of an exaggeration, though it has been a source of amusement for them as a *toy* or *plaything* (both 20thC.). On a more exotic plane, he encouraged woman to admire his *animated ivory* (18thC., John Cleland) and gaze longingly upon his *pego* (from the Greek for "fountain," early 18thC.).

And what better way to keep her body in tune than with a *whistle*, a *flute*, or an *organ*? The *flute* (18thC.) traditionally has stood for *pr**k* going all the way back to ancient Rome, and much *marriage musick* (18thC., for children bawling) has been produced on the *family organ* (18thC.). We had but to see the man *in full orchestra* (late 19th-20thC., *penis* and *testicles*).

Man was determined to find the right metaphor, that none

35

but himself should sell his *organ* short.

Judge: did he introduce his *organ*?
She: It was more like a *flute,* Your Honor.

Funny, You Don't Look Jewish

Mayor Koch of New York City, responding to a request that he pose with a tiger: "No, the mayor is not
a coward, and the mayor is also not a *schmuck.*"

And it was man himself, along with his ambivalence toward
his own *organ,* that contributed most to its decline and fall. Consider his *schmuck* and his *putz,* two of our more popular terms
for the *pr**k.* They're two rather nice words that come to us
from the Yiddish via the German. Their value is further en-
hanced by their meaning as "ornaments, jewelry, or finery," the
putz further conveying the sense of being in full dress.

"What jewels!" you say. Not so. Though these words once
had a positive connotation, man chose to use them in the opposite sense. He employed *schmuck* and *putz* not to praise his
fellow men, but to humiliate and insult them, linking prototypes
of the *penis* to male personalities in a particularly negative way,
and coming up with two separate types.

Your typical *schmuck* is a benign *pr**k,* gentle, inoffensive,
and full of fun. In a playful moment, he will slip out of your
BVDs and warmly rub against your thigh. He is the bed-wetter
and the premature ejaculator. He gropes, muddles, and flip-
flops about—and does an awful lot of plain dumb things.
Though he's insecure and indecisive, most *schmucks* are incredibly lovable. As the man said, "I never met a *schmuck* I didn't
like."

The *putz* is his antithesis. He's a nasty and immoral fellow
who cares little for others. Ever combat-ready, he is constantly
striking out against the world. A real *mother-f**ker,* and there
isn't a jockstrap that can contain him. *Putz* is the mindless
Neanderthal, the embodiment of violence and immorality.
When you call someone a *putz,* you're telling him that he's a real
*pr**k.* The difference between a *schmuck* and a *putz?* It's as fun-

damental as the difference between Gerald Ford and Richard Nixon.

> Better to be a king for an evening than a *schmuck* for a lifetime.
>
> — *The King of Comedy,* 1983

Meat and Potatoes

There was no confusion when it came to food. It was both natural and inevitable that eating be a featured activity of *The Erotic Tongue,* with food itself playing the most important parts.

Man's bill of fare deals primarily with fine *meat,* either *beef* or *pork* (20thC., also used as a verb, as *to pork her*), as is your wont. But his *sweetmeat* (19thC.) is often in such demand that there are times when you may have to settle for something less, perhaps a *weenie* (16thC.) or *sausage* (19thC.). Worse yet, you might have to make do with an old *hambone* (the topic of many an old blues song), some *marrowbone* (19thC.), or even just some plain *gristle* (c. 1850).

The main dish? *Meat and two vegetables* — the full spread. You can select from *une asperge* (Fr., "asparagus stalk"), or the unique *potato finger.* But we'd consider it especially crude if you suggested to the young lady that she take a *carrot!* Equally offensive is the French *Et ta soeur, aime-t-elle les radis?* ("And your sister, does she like radishes?" i.e., does she have a go at it?)

Fresh Fruit

> From the tattered banana tree after waiting
>   months . . .
> Unexpectedly, from the highest shoot, a huge
> Thing detached itself, leaving the sheath
> Curving, purpling, thrusting out an emergent
> Flower, that lifted . . .
>
> — Charles G. Bell, "Banana," early 20thC.

There's no better way to bring dinner to a close than with something special. Perhaps some fruit? Cheeky lads making advances to town girls (*c.* 1905-1920) used to encourage them to "have a banana!" The phrase originated with an old British music-hall ditty, "I had a banana with Lady Diana," reportedly updated with the 1981 royal nuptials as "I had some fruit with the royal brute."

Bo Derek, America's sex symbol for the '80s, issued a similar invitation in her recent version of *Tarzan.* There we find her in the water face to face with the ape man. In one of the more memorable scenes in the history of contemporary cinema, she looks languidly into his eyes and coyly remarks, "I'm a virgin. You must be one too," while slowly — oh, so slowly — peeling a banana. Though this was a screen first, men have been *getting their bananas peeled* (*c.* 1930-36) long before Bo.

The Moslems also had the right idea, believing the forbidden fruit in the Garden of Eden to be not an apple, but a banana. But what's a banana against the Bard's *poperine pear:*

> O Romeo, that she were, O, that she were
> An open *arse* [*etcetera* in some editions],
> Thou a *poperine pear*!
>
> —Shakespeare, *Romeo and Juliet*

That's "pop 'er in" — and possibly the single worst pun on *pr**k* in the history of Western literature.

May we also suggest the *sugar stick* or the *(ladies')* lollipop (both 19thC.)? For those looking for something less explicit, we have some *pudding,* or *pudden,* from the *pudenda.* Would you for an *apple turnover* (mid-20thC.)?

The Greeks and Romans favored *phallus*-shaped cakes, and the Egyptians enjoyed bread and pastries in the shape of both male and female *sex organs.* You could order them individually or joined in *union.* Hardly a thing of the past, since you can still find such exotic fare in specialized bakeries in our more cosmopolitan cities.

A fitting ending to a meal, which men described as the *dear morsel* and a *yum-yum* (both 19thC.).

Names Can Never Harm Me

He: Honey, would you like to see Oliver Twist?
She: Why not, I've seen it do everything else.

Food is elemental, but people are number one. The ancients often gave the *phallus* image human features—face, hands, feet, all of which served to further emphasize its importance. It was also as a person, linguistically, that the *penis* evolved most fully and truly came into its own. A noted nineteenth-century shop-keeper used to greet his more dandified customers with the greeting, "And how is your *small person* today?" This is hardly unusual, for in *The Erotic Tongue,* our parts play very real people indeed.

And what a gallery of greats we have, with dignitaries drawn from the Bible, Mythology, the Classics, and the Imagination. *The master of ceremonies* can make the initial introductions beginning with *Julius Caesar* (*c.* 1840) and the Cyclops, *Polyphemus* (19thC.). There's somebody for everybody.

Those traveling in literary circles might prefer *Dr. Johnson* (18th-19thC.). According to Eric Partridge, "There was no one that *Dr. Johnson* was not prepared to stand up to." Yet there's always someone to take up the challenge. In the film *Putney Swope* (1969), Putney's girlfriend tells him, "I'm going to bend your *Johnson!*" A somewhat disquieting and uncomfortable notion calling for some flexibility on the Doctor's part.

On a first-name basis, *Peter, Dick,* and *John* stand out. *Peter* began as *St. Peter,* who held the keys to heaven, but after he had used them regularly for a few hundred years, and clearly was no longer a saint, he was reduced to just plain *Peter,* a long-time favorite name for the *pr**k.* But *Peter* is nowhere near as popular as he once was, having hit his stride among America's teen-agers in the 1940s and '50s. In the Ozarks, however, he's still the word for the *family organ.* Vance Randolph, the noted folklore specialist, tells the story of the novice minister who both embarrassed and flabbergasted his congregation by innocently inquiring as to how many *Peters* there were out there. It was a real gaffe. In that part of the country, one never refers to *Peter* in mixed company. A son is never named *Peter.* And nothing, but nothing, ever *peters* out.

John, the commonest name in the English language, has often given his name to the commonest *organ,* as has *Johnnie,* a favorite of "cultured" nineteenth-century females. We are told that women have also been hot for a man's *Jones* (20thC., U.S.), *John's* family name. But our featured performer is *John Thomas* (*c.* 1840), an old pet name for a flunky or a servant, an important figure in world literature who was also the hero of *Lady Chatterley's Lover* and without whom there would not have been a story.

> "John Thomas! John Thomas! . . ."
> "Ay," said the man, stretching his body almost painfully.
> "He's got his root in my soul has that gentleman! An' sometimes I don't know what ter do wi' him. Ay, he's got a will of his own, an' it's hard to suit him. Yet, I wouldn't have him killed."
> "No wonder men have always been afraid of him!" she said. "He's rather terrible."

Jack (19thC.), a nickname for *John,* has also stood for the *penis* and its *erection,* as has *Jock* (before 1790), from which we got the jockstrap by which today's male supports his *hanging Johnny.* Nothing—well almost nothing—could contain a *roaring jack.* A *jack-in-the-box* (19thC.) was your pop-up surprise, the *box* being the likeliest place in which a man might place it.

Though *John* apparently has fallen out of favor, it's *Dick* (since 1860) who continues to hang in there.

This is one *Dick* that is not derived from Richard. He originates with *dirk,* a short dagger used by sneak thieves in Old England. And its name derives from *Derrick,* the notorious hangman at Tyburn Prison whose improved gallows design was the prototype of the modern crane, and who was evidently a real *pr∗∗k,* at that.

There's little left to say except that there's no need to be uncomfortable with the naming process. Some of our best friends are *genitals* (20thC.). As Leonardo da Vinci, who himself lived without *sex,* reminded us:

> . . . this creature has often a life and intelligence separate from this man, and it would appear that the man is in the wrong in being ashamed to give it a name or to exhibit it, seeking, rather, constantly to cover and conceal what he ought to adorn and display with ceremony.

Best Foot Forward

How's your middle leg?
Come here till I straighten it out.

—James Joyce, whore in *Ulysses,* 1922

The personification of the *pr**k* represented its high point. But even then, men felt only partially confident. Few came to its defense. Except for Walt Whitman, who raised his *thumb of love,* others refused to even lift their *little fingers* (19thC.) on its behalf.

Finally, someone put his foot down — what psychologists call "displacement downward." None were more adamant than the authors of the Old Testament. If you can believe St. Jerome and his Vulgate translation of the Bible, all references the authors of the Bible made to the foot are nothing more than veiled allusions to the *penis.*

It's all very possible: in the Ancient East, *foot* and *leg* were familiar euphemisms for a man's *thing.* When a man *spilled water at a woman's feet,* he *ejaculated.* When he *washed his feet,* he actually bathed his *penis* in a woman's *vagina.* The man who suffered with diseased feet in reality had come down with *venereal disease.*

This usage promises to kick off a whole new thing linguistically. There's no end of possibility what with getting a leg up on someone, shaking a leg, and putting your foot in it. That, of course, is only if the shoe fits. . . .

Stick to It

. . . At winter's frost, or heat in June
The *fiddle* here is out of tune
Fiddles alone are not to blame.
The *sticks* must often take the shame;
Too often feeble, short or limber chosen.
And often fail for lack of resin.

—"The Question," *New Crazy Tales,*
1783

More than food, more than a plaything, more than a celebration of personhood or a small part thereof, the *pr**k* is also a highly useful instrument, even in its most primitive form—the *stick*.

Whatever your *shtick*, we've got it: *night sticks, holy poles*, and the *sceptres of authority* (all 19thC.). Satisfaction guaranteed. Thy *rod* and thy *staff* they comfort me. They should more than meet your needs as well.

Tools of the Trade

So wild and wooly and full of fleas
Whose *tool* hung down below his knees.

> —Rudyard Kipling, *The Bastard King of England*

I ne'er knew a woman to find fault with
a long *toole* before.

> —Beaumont and Fletcher, *Faithful Friends*, 1613

Sticks were also man's first *tools*, a popular term for the *pr**k* from the middle of the sixteenth century until the eighteenth. Though we speak only rarely of it today, the *tool* remains an ever useful and versatile *instrument* (19thC.). It's the *baby-maker* (late 19thC.), or the *means of generation* (1791). In another vein, it's the *P-maker* or the *waterworks* (both mid-19thC.)—all very functional and no-nonense.

The *tool's* utility has increased even further with advances in technology. Since the industrial revolution it has expanded to include all sorts of machines: the *grinding tool*, the *pile-driver*, as well as everyone's favorite, the *fornicating engine*, popularly known as the little engine that could.

The Dream Machine

She can do more with a *swipe*
than a monkey can do with a banana.

> —Iceberg Slim, *Pimp: The Story of My Life*, 1967

As *love's engine* (19thC.), the *organ* proved a smash hit. Starting as a *gentle tittler, jigger,* and a *wriggling pole* (19thC.), it made its greatest impact as a *poker, rammer,* and *gooser.* Best known for the force with which it hit, it produced the *dong* (mid-20thC., Aust. and N.Z., "to strike" or "punch"), the *swipe* (20thC., U.S. Black, "to deal a rather severe blow"), and the *whang* (19th-20thC., "to strike a heavy and resounding blow"), the final stroke.

Cutting Loose

The *penis* mightier than the sword.

— Mark Twain

But tools of peace easily become tools of war. It began with the sword, the *gladius* of ancient Rome whose effectiveness went unchallenged. Centuries later, the sword was but one weapon in Adam's arsenal. You could find everything there you might possibly need to carry love's battles to a successful conclusion: the *lance of love, love's battering ram, love's sensitive truncheons,* the *shafts of delight* (18thC.), and *love's dribbling dart.* There were also *pikes, sabers, spears,* and *clubs,* all described with *love, pleasure,* and *delight,* and all in the name of *Venus* or *Cupid.* We would *break a lance* with someone (19th-20thC.), meaning to enjoy a woman. Soon we would have the *artillerie de Cupide* or *de Venus* (19thC.) for the arts and accompaniments of *venery.*

In *The Erotic Tongue* we turn sex and war on their heads. Benign parts become instruments of war. In politics, implements of battle often become organs of peace. What next? A *missile of Venus* launched from love's pad—a double-duty weapon, allowing us to exit with both a bang and a whimper?

Great Guns!

Is that a gun in your pocket, or are you just glad to see me?

— Mae West

Here, Pistol, I charge you with a cup of sack.
Do you discharge upon mine hostess.

— Shakespeare, *Henry IV,* Part 2

Times change as do our weapons. Today, most go off with a *bang.* Men join the army, and it's there that they learn the important difference between a rifle and a gun. The man who fails to master that distinction is required to stand guard with one hand on his *penis,* the other on his rifle, while loudly repeating this quatrain for all to hear:

This is my rifle
This is my gun;
This is for shooting
This is for fun.

Men also learned to keep their *weapons* in good working order through periodic checkups, a.k.a. the *dangle-parade* (W.W.II). This includes *short-arm inspection,* medical inspection of the *penis* while at rest, and *long-arm inspection,* while at "attention" (both W.W.II).

Even with all this care, men still carelessly discharged their *weapons.* Many times, it was the woman who *drew their fireworks,* causing the woman to receive a *shot up the straight* (19thC.) or *a shot betwixt wind and water* (late 19thC.), often leaving M'lady, you guessed it, in a *banged-up* state.

At other times, in the case of an overly active trigger finger, a man *went off at half-cock* – a sober reminder that though power grows out of the end of a gun, good *sex* is more than a one-shot proposition.

That's About the Size of It

"Is this your *yard?*" quoth she,
"Is this your tailor's measure?
It is too short for me;
It is not standard measure."

– Ballad, 18thC.

"Generally speaking," Fanny Hill reminded us, "it is in love as it is in war, where the longest weapon carries it." So encouraged, man has gone to great lengths in describing his *rod* (19th-20thC.). One of the more durable expressions we've ever known is the *yard.* It was originally a *stick,* but for almost two hundred years, from 1590 to 1780, *yard* was our most common literary term for the *pr**k*.

Most found the *yard* quite acceptable. As Eric Partridge notes, it never suffered the unfavorable social reputation of *c**k, pr**k,* or *tool* and was always deemed an appropriate way of *getting* or *taking a woman's measure* (late 18th-mid-19thC.).

> To the goal of her pleasure she drove very hard
> But was tripp'd up ere half-way she ran,
> And tho' everyone fancied her life was a *yard,*
> Yet it proved to be less than a span.
>
> — Gravestone of one Sally Salisbury,
> 18thC.

By 1850 it had become obsolete. Yet the *yard* lives on in every man's fantasy, though the details of the fantasy clash. We have the old adage, "Short and thick does the trick" (18thC.), as well as Robert Burns's "Nine inch will please a lady," while contemporary folk hyperbole immortalizes the *man with a nine-inch pr**k and a twelve-inch tongue who can breathe through his ears.* In our world, however, it's the *three-inch fool* (*The Taming of the Shrew*) who clearly is the rule.

You're a Hard Man!

> Now with your hand
> provoke my *foe* to rise.
>
> — Ovid

> Now pierced is her virgin-zone
> Soon she feels the
> *foe* within it.
>
> — Rochester, *The Lucky Minute,* 1670

The size of our *members,* despite all the discussion, varies most with the conditions. Ordinarily, it's nothing but a good-natured *flap-doodle* (late 17thC.), *dingle-dangle* (c. 1895), or *twiddle-diddler.*

However, when hard times hit, the *bald-headed hermit* emerges as *Old Slimy,* a *mutinous rogue* sure to strike fear into the hearts of maidens everywhere. As the *belly ruffian* and the *terror of virgins,* he is clearly her *foe.*

When the *old man's got his Sunday clothes on* (19thC.), he's at his finest and his biggest. But it may be for naught; he's often dressed up with no place to go.

Rising to the Occasion

A standing *pr**k* has
no conscience.

— English proverb, 18thC.

When the *pr**k* stands up
The brain goes to sleep.

— Yiddish proverb

Some have interpreted this puffing up as arrogance, and others as an illness of sorts — an *Irish toothache* (19thC.), the *horn-colic* (mid-18th-mid-19thC.), a *swelling,* or perhaps even a *hidden tumor.* But it's really nothing serious, only your everyday *erection* (1594) or *priapism* (1598), after Priapus, the Greek and Roman god of potency and virility, son of Aphrodite and Bacchus, who was always depicted as *tumescent* (1859). The commonfolk knew it best as a *stand-on* (19thC.), a *stiff-and-stout* (mid-17th-20thC.), a *hard-on* or *hard-'un* (adjective *c.* 1860, noun *c.* 1890), and, in times of want, a *hard-up* (late 19thC.).

Ofttimes it's unintentional, a social gaffe of sorts: a *boner* (19thC.) or simply a *horn* (mid-18thC.) for which no one in particular gives a toot.

Lucky Stiffs

Q: What is the difference between dark and hard?
A: It stays dark all night.

Some may knock it, but for most men, the *pr**k's* been a source of real *pride.* In the seventeenth century, they had both a *proud inclination of the flesh* and *grew proud below the navel.*

Early risers made it a *pride-of-the-morning* or a *morning pride* (both late 19th-20thC.). Among the Maoris, a chieftain felt especially proud when he woke up with an erection prior to a battle. It was considered an extremely good omen.

It's all for the best he didn't know he was *p∗ss-proud* (late 18th-20thC.) — it was nothing more than a matter of urine retention. After all, pride goeth before a fall.

What Goes Up?

Time to say good-bye? Say it with flowers. May we suggest the *flowery shrub*, the *sensitive plant* (c. 1779), *love's nectar-laden stalk*, the *man root*.

Few things stand as proud as the *arbor vitae* (c. 1732) in full flower. As Richard Brinsley Sheridan described it in *The Geranium,*

> How straight upon its stalk it stands. . . .
> The tree of life, this tree that tempted Eve,
> the crimson apples hang so fair.
> Alas! What woman could forebear? The tree by
> which we live.

But the fall is never far behind, and all fade after the heat. Rochester noted, "Now languid lies in this unhappy hour. Shrunk up and sapless like a withered flower."

A posy can turn a farewell into an until-we-meet-again. But with this wretched horticultural specimen added to our roster, our membership drive sadly concludes.

Wild Oaths

However, there are still some lesser items to discuss. In the nineteenth century they knew them as *witnesses to one's virility,* and with good reason. *Testicles* (c. 1425) derives from the Latin *testis,* "witness," and *testiculus,* "the little witness" — related directly to "testify" and "testament," because at one time it was customary for men to pledge faith or swear testimony by holding or touching one another's *genitals.* The event is recorded several times — where else — in the Old Testament.

You'll find reference to such testimony in I Chronicles 29:24, where the chiefs and captains of Israel take hold of Solomon's *genitals* as a gesture of loyal submission. In Genesis 24:9 the servant was slightly off target when he placed his hand under Abraham's *thigh*.

You might consider the entire subject detestable. In which case, according to John Ciardi, you'd be swearing against it or hating the subject from the bottom of your *balls*.

Hang It All!

The blowen was nutts upon
the kiddey because he is well-hung.

The girl is pleased with the youth
because his genitals are large.

> —Anon., *The Lexicon Balantronicum,*
> 1811

Over the years, the little fellows have borne witness anony-mously—in the shadow of their more famous counterpart—known only as *thingmajigs* (c. 1880), *dojiggers, tarriwags* (17thC.), *talliwags* (late 18thC.), *whirlygigs* (late 17th-early 18thC.), and *twiddle-diddles* (c. 1786).

At their best, they've simply hung in their well as *bobblers, swingers, pounders* (Dryden), and *danglers*. One who was *well hung* (19th-20thC.) was said to be *hung like a bull* or *like a stallion* (18th-20thC.), or even *hung like a rabbit* (20thC.)! Those with lesser assets were *hung like chickens,* a demeaning remark giving one no reason at all to crow.

A Real Gem!

"Your ladyship sets too high a price on my weakness."
"Sir, I can distinguish gems from pebbles."
"Are you so skilled in *stones*?"

> —Ben Jonson, *Silent Woman,* 1609

Hit 'em high
Hit 'em low
Hit 'em where
The *cherries* grow

> —Anon., football cheer, 20thC.

Clearly, people set great value by them, but you'll never find them in Tiffany's—*the family jewels* (20thC.), that is. John Cleland described them as his *inestimable bulse of ladies' jewels,* but they've also been everything from inexpensive *baubles* (19thC., *bobbles?*) and *trinkets* to precious *rocks* and *stones. Stones* is one of our more venerable words for the items, dating back to the twelfth century, but around the middle of the nineteenth century *stones* came to be considered vulgar and was deemed appropriate only in reference to the *testicles* of a horse.

Noah Webster left no stone unturned when he published his expurgated version of the Bible in 1833 and transformed all references to them as *stones* into *peculiar members* (*peculiar,* as belonging to one person only). In Deuteronomy 23:1, they became classified as top *secrets,* with the warning that "he that is wounded or mutilated in his *secrets* shall not enter into the congregation of the Lord."

More recently, *stones* are back in our good graces, while it's our *rocks* that we've been *getting off* (20thC., U.S.).

Rounding out our collection are *pebbles, marbles, agates,* and *goolies* (late 19thC., from "gully," a game of marbles). Naturally, we have *cherries, berries, nutmegs* (17thC.), *marrons* (French for "chestnuts"), *love apples* (19thC.), and *little acorns* . . . from which grows the mighty oak. *Glans* is Latin for "acorn," which coincides nicely with the *glands, sex glands,* and *interstitial glands,* all favorite euphemisms from the 1920s and '30s.

The most interesting designation of all is the *nuts* (18th-20thC.), often described as "tight" and "hard," though they are really soft and vulnerable. This leaves us all in a quandary when it comes to *getting one's nuts cracked,* a painful but pleasurable practice from the 1920s. Mencken reminds us that during the early '20s *nuts* "had connotations that made [the word] seem somewhat raw," leading nice people to replace them with *nerts,* thereby *breaking everyone's nuts* in the process.

The Way the B*lls Bounce

"*B*lls!*" said the Queen.
"If I had two, I could be King."

— Anon., 20thC.

It takes *b∗lls* to play soccer.

—Bumper sticker, 1982

We're most nuts about our *b∗lls* (10thC.), the term by which we know them best. *B∗lls* have demonstrated exceptional versatility and service to the language. If you're looking for courage, look no further. It takes *b∗lls* to acquit yourself like a man, often *b∗lls the size of watermelons.* Even Hemingway's heroes required real *cajones* (Spanish for *"b∗lls"*), in order to show grace under pressure.

Truly *b∗llsy* but also somewhat *bollixed* or *balled-up* were the Skopts, a religious sect at the time of Catherine II and Alexander I, which initiated new members into the cult by searing their *b∗lls* with a hot iron. The sect died out—but the rites entered the language as our "baptism of fire."

B∗lls have also served us well as an important interjection, part of our long-standing tradition of using the better half of the body to register emotion. They express surprise and exasperation ("Nuts!") as well as incredulity and disappointment ("Nonsense!").

"Baloney!" you say? As Partridge reminds us, that word comes not from sausage but from the gypsy *pelone*—for *b∗lls.*

Functionally speaking, it would be difficult to imagine the sports world without balls. Absolutely critical to most of our games, they are governed by definite rules as to their use. It's proper for men to play ball but not to play with their *b∗lls.* And when a ball bounces up and hits the catcher *you-know-where*, it is said to "ring his bell."

Everyone has detractors, and there are those disrespectful of the *b∗lls'* ties to the male ego. We call such women *castrators* or *b∗ll-busters* (20thC.). But *b∗lls* finally achieved their deserved recognition as part of the vocabulary of the counterculture of the sixties when they became a full-fledged verb. You could now tell everyone how "I love to *b∗ll* my old lady!" While the 1981 World Series was being played, the Rendezvous Cinema, at 54th Street off Seventh Avenue in Manhattan, a block and a half away from series headquarters, premiered a flick called *Ball Game . . .* rated X.

How really important are they? *B∗lls* are the ultimate motivator. Former Nixon aide and born-again Christian Charles Colson kept a reminder posted on a wall, "If you've got them by the *b*lls*, their hearts and minds will follow."

The Whole Bag of Tricks

Pego like an upstart Hector . . .
Would fair have ruled as Lord Protector
Inflam'd by one so like a goddess
I scarce could keep him in my *codpiece*.
—Ned Ward, *London Spy*, 1709

*B*lls* usually come handsomely packaged in an appropriate container, often a bag. For this reason, the word "bag" itself hasn't had an easy time of it. It was banned from use in Kansas during the 1920s because it reminded people of the *scrotum* (*c.* 1597), and in Appalachia it was replaced by "sack" and "poke" for the same reason.

The sixteenth-century word for it was *culls*, either an abbreviated version of *testicles* or a variation of *culeus*, Latin for "bag." In Old English, the bag came disguised as a *cod* (*c.* 1398), encouraging countless scabrous puns.

Shakespeare had us *"changing the cod's head for the salmon's tail."* And Mark Twain grew it to monumental proportions as the subject of a long-suppressed poem, "The Mammoth Cod."

Man once carried his *fancy work* and all his precious *gear and tackle* in a sex glove called a *brayette* by the French (from Latin *braca*, which is linked to the Aryan *bhrag*, "a covering for the loin and thighs") and a *codpiece* by the English.

Originally intended to protect him during combat, it became a popular objet d'art during the fifteenth to seventeenth centuries. The glove was embroidered and colorfully decorated, often including fancy work, a pocket in which he also placed his handkerchief, loose change, and a piece or two of fruit, thereby rounding out his assets. It was an outstanding addition to his wardrobe, inspiring admiration, speculation, and discussion as to what the bulge divulged. Borachio in *Much Ado About Nothing* mentions an imagined Hercules "where his *codpiece* is as massie as his club."

51

Today, we hear only of the notorious *bucket of b*lls* (mid-20thC.), leaving everyone wondering when, if ever, man will finally learn to contain himself properly.

A Last Verbal Bouquet

The orchid comes to us from the Latin *orchis,* from the Greek word for *testicles,* based on the similarity in shape between the roots of the plant and a man's *b*lls.* No one probably would have noticed this if John Ruskin, the nineteenth-century writer and art critic, had not personally championed a cause to change the name, so angry was he that such a vile word should be used to describe so delicate and beautiful a flower.

His efforts, however, did not succeed. But it was a good try. Thus we had, *"Orchids* to you, John!" as an early twentieth-century curse, a later variation of which was, *"Testicles* to you!"

Consensus has it that the *c**k* derives from the rooster, from its shape as well as its proud and active nature, originating with the Latin *coccus,* from "cococococco," the cock's cry. But there are those who disagree. John Ciardi, for one, disputes this derivation, basing his case on *kak,* Indo-European for the male *genitalia.* He argues that the *pr**k* influenced the word we have for the rooster, rather than the other way around.

Which really came first, the chicken or the . . .?

Though the *c**k* appears jaunty and confident, he's anything but cocksure. He may think of himself as a strictly all-male bird, but a close look at his history shows quite the contrary. Not only does this most masculine of birds have a feminine side to him, but, according to J.L. Dillard, the lexicographer of Black English, he once denoted exclusively the female organ in the Black community of the Southern United States and the Caribbean. This usage originated in nineteenth-century England where women ofttimes used *c**k* as a verb in a passive sense, as "to want *c**king*" or "to get *c**ked.*" From there, it was a natural transition to refer to the female *pudendum* as a *c**t.*

† † †

If it's sheer size you fancy, you can't beat the Yiddish *schlang* (also *schlange* and *schlong*) from the German *schlange* for "snake." In 1967 Phillip Roth's Portnoy reminisced about his father's:

> "His *schlang* brings to mind the firehoses along the corridors at school. *Schlang:* the word somehow captures exactly the brutishness, the meatishness that I admire so, the sheer mindless, weighty and unselfconscious dangle of that living piece of hose through which he passes water as thick and strong as rope. . . ."

† † †

What else is in a name? Biblical buffs might settle on *Old Adam, Abraham, Nebuchadnezzar* (c. 1860-1915),

Conqueror of the Holy City, or *Nimrod* (19thC.), the mighty hunter.

For followers of fiction we've got *Sir Martin Wagstaff, Master John Goodfellow* (Urquhart), and *Captain Standish,* stout, "who made his dame cry out" (Joseph Ebsworth). On a more formal basis there's the *Rector of the Females* (Rochester), the *Captain of My Body* and *His Majesty in Purple Cap* (19thC.).

Among the commonfolk, you could always reach for *Timothy Tool* (*c.* 1845), slip in *Daintie Davis* (19thC.), or *Little Davy* (Scot. 19thC.), and, as an act of charity, show *Old Blind Bob* the way—all quicker than you can say *Jack Robinson* (both 19thC.)

† † †

Don't have a leg to stand on? Try the *best leg of three.* But forget about *the hind leg,* an old Ozark expression for the *a∗s.* We've also had the *privy limb* since the thirteenth century and the *joint,* a contemporary Black term that goes back to the nineteenth-century fowl and our inability to say "leg" in polite society.

We have *joy sticks* (20thC.), *dip sticks* (19thC.), *cream sticks* (*c.* 1920), and *trap sticks* (late 19thC.). We have *fiddlesticks* (*c.* 1800) to go with the *fiddle* as the female *pudendum.* We have *sticks* for a hundred purposes and *sticks* for every occasion. For leaders, the *sceptre of authority* (18thC.); for authorities, the *night stick* (19thC.); for the celebratory, the *Maypole* (*c.* 1758), which truly was a symbol of *phallus* worship around which celebrants would dance; for the religious, the *holy pole* (19thC.) and the *pilgrim's staff* (18thC.). Those among us inclined toward magic might prefer the *wand of love* (19thC.)—a phrase that conveys the true wonder of the apparatus.

For something truly special, there's *Aaron's rod,* the basis of not one but two miracles performed in the pages of the Old Testament. In Numbers 17:8, Aaron places it before the ark, and Jehovah causes it to bloom and bear ripe almonds. In Exodus 7:9-12, when he casts it to the ground, God transforms it into a serpent. The feat is also performed by Pharaoh's sorcerers, but, as a spectacular bit of showmanship, Aaron's rod-serpent swallows up all the others. It was the perfect symbol for the *penis* – the fount of all creative activity and the unassailable power that envelops and engulfs all about it.

† † †

The *engine*, or *machine of love*, is often described by the work it does; *bum-tickler* (18th-19thC.), *quim-wedge* (19thC.), *rump-splitter* (c. 1560-1800), *beard-splitter* (c. 1849), *bush-whacker* (18thC.), *plug-tail* (mid-18th–mid-19thC.), *kidney wiper, liver turner, womb brush,* and *tickle-tail.*

† † †

The oldest English word for the *testicles* that we have on record is the *beallucas* (before 10thC.). We later had the *ballokes* (c. 1382) or *ballocks* and the verb *to ballock* (19th-20thC.), from which we got our "Ballocky Bill the Sailor" – a *b∗llsy* old salt if there ever was one. Time and his yearning for acceptability would mellow him into the children's favorite, Barnacle Bill, with hardly a hint of his salacious character.

FOUR

The Gender Gap

The portions of a woman that appeal to man's depravity
    Are constructed with considerable care,
And what at first appears to be a simple little cavity
    Is in fact a most elaborate affair.

Physicians of distinction have examined these phenomena
    In numerous experimental dames;
They have tabulated carefully the feminine abdomina,
    And given them some fascinating names.

There's the *vulva*, the *vagina*, and the jolly *perineum*,
    And the *hymen*, in the case of many brides,
And lots of other little things you'd like, if you could see 'em,
    The *clitoris*, and other things besides.

So isn't it a pity, when we common people chatter
    Of these mysteries to which I have referred,
That we use for such a delicate and complicated matter
    Such a very short and ordinary word.

                  —Anon., cited by Peter Freyer, "It" in
                      Mrs. Grundy, 1963

    No one particularly likes going into the *hole* (16thC.), but this isn't your ordinary run-of-the-mill cavity. It's *your better 'ole* (16th-19thC.), and ever since Eden the center of man's attention. His preoccupation with it has led him to embellish it: as the *sweet-scented hole* (c. 1690, Rabelais), the *touch-hole* (17th-20thC.), the *aperture of bliss* (16th-20thC.), and *your hole-of-holes* (16thC.). He has also named it the *gap* (19th-20thC.), *crack* (16th-

20thC.), *slot* (20thC.), *cranny* (20thC.), and *nook*, from which we get our favorite, *nooky* (or *nookie*, early 20thC.), though some argue that *nooky* derives instead from to *nug* (17th-19thC.), or to *nock* (late 16th-18thC.), two of our more venerable expressions for the *Big F.*

Over time, your basic *hole* assumed new dimensions as the *crevice* (19th-20thC.), the *bottomless pit* (18th-early 19thC.), the *Great Divide* (c. 1925), and the *Grand Canyon* (20thC.). It got religion with the *holy-of-holies* and the *temple of low men* (as opposed to the temple of *hymen*), puns calculated to bring us all to our knees.

Starting from Scratch

O gracious *hymen*!
Cure this dire mishap
Sew up this mighty
Rent or fill this *gap.*

— Robertson of Struan, *Poems,* 1746

Nobody really knows where the *hole* came from, though Captain Grose, the roguish eighteenth-century lexicographer, had his own ideas about it. His version opens with an angel who had been employed in forming women, forgetting to cut off their *parts of generation*. Enter Lucifer who took it upon himself to set matters right.

Taking a somewhat direct approach to the problem, he placed himself in a sawpit with a scythe fixed to a stick in his hand and directed the women to straddle the pit. He then gave each the *mark of the beast* (c. 1715). The pit being too deep for the length of his instrument, tall women received only a moderate scratch, but little women, because their legs were so short and more within his reach, received a somewhat larger cut. The long and the short of it? They both went home with an *everlasting wound* (17thC.), known in some quarters as the *divine scar* (18thC.).

The Devil, henceforth, was to be known as *Old Nick* or *Ole Scratch*; and the *c**t*, as *slit* (17th-20thC.), *nick*, and *gash* (both 16th-20thC.).

As men saw it, women were left forever with an aching

57

void. Soon men began employing these terms not only for the organ but for the sex act itself, and, unable to distinguish one from the other, for women collectively. This may have been the meanest cut of all.

Gimme a C!

It's a *cavern of joy* you are thinking of now
A warm, tender *field* just awaiting the plow.
It's a quivering *pigeon* caressing your hand
Or that sweet little *p∗ssy* that makes a man stand
Or perhaps it's a *flower*, a *grotto*, a *well*,
The *hope of the world*, or a *velvety hell.*
But friend, heed this warning, beware the affront
Of aping a Saxon: don't call it a *c∗∗t.*

—"Ode to Those Four-Letter Words"

M'lady's *privates* consist of a number of parts. Those which are featured most prominently are the *vulva* (c. 1548, Latin for "wrapper"), and the *vagina* (c. 1682, Latin for "sheath"). However, the whole world knows them better collectively as the *c∗∗t.*

C∗∗t is a grand old word, not underground, not slang. You'll find variations of it in Old and Middle English, Middle Low and Low German, Old Norse, and Dutch.

For years, it was believed that *c∗∗t* derived from *cunnus,* the Latin word for the female *genitals,* but no one could explain how the *t* got into *c∗∗t.* It was left for Eric Partridge to discover the word as related to the Old English *cwithe,* womb, finding the root of the matter in *cwe,* (or *cu*), which signifies "quintessential physical femininity"—a root that appears in a host of words from "cradle" and "cow" to "queen" and "cunning."

The word has been taboo in writing and in speech since the fifteenth century. Between 1700 and 1959 it was considered obscene, and it was a legal offense to print it in full. John Fletcher, in *The Spanish Curate* (17th C.), reminded us that to write *sunt* (Latin for "they are") with a *c* is "abominable"—creating a *fie-for-shame* (c. 1820) or a *hey-nonny-no* (c. 1690-1750). Shakespeare spelled it out clandestinely, and sneaked it by the bluenoses in *Twelfth Night* when Malvolio exults, "By my love, this is my lady's hand!, these be her very *C*'s, her *U*'s, 'n' her *T*'s, and thus makes she her great *P*'s."

Lexicographers, however, generally avoided any reference to *c**t* in their dictionaries, leaving a long-standing gap. Francis Grose's *Dictionary of the Vulgar Tongue* met it halfway and awarded it four stars, ****, in his second edition in 1788, noting that the word came from the Greek *kovvos* ("bead or trinket") and the Latin *cunnus,* and then, to add insult to injury, referred to it as "a nasty name for a nasty thing." Now really! For years, she was denied access to the OED. Only Partridge argued the injustice of her exclusion: "OED gave *pr**k,* why this further insult to women?" It wasn't until 1976 that it finally was given an entry of its own.

But even in its formal absence it has occupied a very special place in the English language. Not just "a bawdy *monosyllable* such as boys write upon walls" (Farmer and Henley) but the *venerable monosyllable* (pre-1788-pre-1915).

As Grose reminds us, there are thousands of monosyllables in the English language, but there is only one that is the *definite article* (18thC.).

Amo, amas,
I loved a lass
And she was tall and slender;
Amas, amat,
I laid her flat
And tickled her *feminine gender.*

— Henry N. Cary, *The Slang of Venery,*
1916

You Don't Say

However positive and reinforcing it could be, *c**t* has been a pejorative for women all the way back to Roman times and the *cunnus.* According to Partridge the word was used frequently by soldiers during World War I in such expressions as "You silly (or great) *c**t.*" More recently, Dustin Hoffman called it to our attention while promoting his movie *Tootsie,* in which he plays a man playing a woman. Displaying his newly raised consciousness on matters sexual, he notes, "If a man is obsessed with getting things right, he's called difficult. If I were a woman, I'd be called a *c**t.*"

It's not unusual to insult people by identifying them with their body parts. Calling someone a *pr**k* is a commonplace insult, but we reserve use of the expression for males of a particular character, and not for men in general. *C**t*, on the other hand, is not only a term filled with contempt and disdain, but it is applied indiscriminately, regardless of the person's character, insulting not only the person toward whom the remark is aimed, but all women everywhere.

Words Fail

Man has not only spoken ill of the *c**t* but has also described it in glowingly romantic terms. According to Karen Horney, the noted psychiatrist, this makes very good sense. Both approaches reflect man's deep-seated dread of the female *genitalia;* each in a different way helps allay this fear. By making little of the *c**t*, he convinces himself that there is nothing to fear from so mean an object. Through idealization he insures the unlikelihood of harm from so divine a being.

And we have no shortage of superlatives to describe it. We have everything from the *dearest bodily part* (Shakespeare) to the *best part* (Earl of Dorset), the *best in Christendom* (Rochester), and *la belle chose* (Chaucer). For some, it's been just plain out of this world—as in *heaven* (18thC.).

Yet that nagging fear is always there beneath the surface. It's also been *sheer hell* (18thC.) and a *devilish thing* (18thC.); so much so that many would dispense with the entire matter by putting the *Devil into hell* (18thC.).

Some reserved judgment, as did John Donne with the *best-worst part*. Others extolled it as a *masterpiece* and featured it prominently as the *star* (16thC.), depicted ofttimes as *pretty-pretty* (17thC.) and indescribably *quaint,* as in Chaucer's "Miller's Tale": "Full prively he caught her by the *queinte.*"

At its lowest, this *cloven stamp of female distinction* (18th C.) has been reduced to a *suck-and-swallow,* a *man* (or *fool*) *trap,* a *butter boat,* an *oystercatcher,* and *sperm-sucker* (19th C.). At the same time, it's been elevated to a position of power as the *controlling part* (19thC.) and the *regulator* (late 18thC.-19thC.).

It's almost as though they forgot its more mundane functions as the *water box* (19thC.) or *streamstown* (*c.* 1820-90), the *generating* or *brat-getting place* (19thC.), the *nursery,* and the *bath of birth* (early 20thC.).

A Tough Slot to Fill

Oh, the *muff!*
The jolly, jolly *muff*
Give me of *muff* great store
Red, black or brown, divinely rough
I honor and adore.

       —Captain Morris, in Bee's *Dictionary*

Most know the *c∗∗t* best, however, by one of its more conventional aliases. Traditional favorites include the *quim* and the *tail. Quim* (17thC.) originates with the Celtic *cwyn* for "cleft" or "valley" and has that same *cwe* root noted earlier. The *tail* derives from the French *taille* for *"nick"* or *"notch,"* the *vagina* having first turned *tail* during the fourteenth century in Chaucer's "Wife of Bath's Tale." Both have had their ups and downs but there's none more popular than *twat,* the *muff* (both 17th-20thC.), and the *snatch* (20thC.).

Twat's origins are unknown, and it has long been a source of mystery and puzzlement. There was no one more confused than Robert Browning, the poet, who stumbled across the word in an old Royalist rhyme, failed to understand its satiric intent, and came away with the impression that the *twat* was an article of clothing belonging to a nun. He liked the word so much that he proceeded to incorporate it, with that meaning, into a work of his own, "Pippa Passes" (1841).

Editors of the nineteenth-century edition of the Royalist rhymes changed the phrase from an "old nun's *twat*" to "I know not what." As far as we know, Browning's poem continued to make a habit of it. The *twat* also has the dubious distinction of gaining separate entry into the OED even before the *c∗∗t* itself, in the totally male company of the *pr∗∗k* and the *c∗∗k,* who gained access at the same time.

Muff is more aptly likened to clothing ("Lost, lost and can't be found a lady's thing with hair all 'round" — Farmer and Henley),

61

and a popular part of a seventeenth-century bridal toast: "To the well-wearing of your *muff,* mort!" — meaning "To the consummation of your marriage, girl!" Today, *muffs* are out of fashion, but as part of the ever-popular sport of *muff-diving* (cunnilingus, 20thC.), they're still very much an in thing.

Snatch was an illicit or mercenary *copulation* (17thC.) before it got its present meaning. It eventually teamed up with *scratch* (which had become "money" c. 1930); and together they produced the immortal couplet: "No scratch, no *snatch!*" Long before Visa and Bank-Americard, it was "No cash, no *gash.*"

No money
No *coney*

> — Massinger and Decker, *The Virgin
> Martir, A Tragedie,* 1622

More Wise Cracks

We have more than 1,000 terms for the *vulva.* In the inner city you'll hear talk of getting some *trim* (Engl., 16th-18thC., a verb, "to deflower"). Earlier, it was the ever-popular *poon* or *poontang. Poontang* probably made it into the language through Creole via the French *putain* for "prostitute." That, in turn, originated with the Latin *puteus,* the well at which all came to drink their fill. Southern Blacks couldn't care less, always identifying the *poontang* directly with p*ssy.

"Eye that *poontang* there," he said.
"I could eat it with a knife and fork.
Where I come from we call that
kind of stuff 'table p*ssy.'"

> — William Saroyan, *Jim Dandy,* 1947

P*ssycat, P*ssycat, Where Have You Been?

Oh, the ring-a-dang-doo, now what is that?
It's soft and round like a pussycat.
It's covered with fur and split in two,
And that's what they call the ring-a-dang-doo.

> — Anon., 20thC.

It's for that same *p*ssy* that men truly go wild. This is one helluva pet—warm, cuddly, soft, and nice—a real pussycat who can turn into a regular tiger.

Given her profligate nature and her personal appearance, it was only a matter of time before the *p*ssy* became identified with a woman's *private parts*. She first surfaced as a *pusse* in 1662 and is recorded for posterity in a toast of the period: "Aeneas, here's a health to thee, to *pusse* and good company." In the eighteenth century they spoke of her trotting out her *p*ssy* (17th-20thC.) and *giving her p*ssy a taste of cream,* or just *feeding the p*ssy. P*ssy* was temporarily eclipsed in the nineteenth century by *cat, chat,* and *mouser.* Later, we even had a *mousetrap,* but she always remained a little *p*ssy* (19thC.) to those who knew her best. Come the twentieth century she began to make a strong comeback. By 1948 you could find her everywhere, and a very popular *commodity* at that. Alan Lomax cited her in "Mr. Jelly Roll":

> Papa's in jail!
> Mama's on bail!
> The baby's on the corner
> Shouting *p*ssy* for sale!

Her star was now fully ascending. By the seventies, *p*ssy* had reached a new high in popularity. T-shirts proudly proclaimed, "Happiness is a warm *p*ssy,*" and dozens of books and hundreds of assorted icons were produced in its honor. In 1981, after twenty years under lock and key, the only complete Beatles recording never put on sale was finally released. Its title? "Please Leave My Kitten Alone."

Leave It to Beaver

Be kind to animals, kiss a *beaver.*

> —Army saying, 20thC.

The hard-working *beaver* also deserves a tip of the hat. It's he who labors in the shadow of the *p*ssy.* Kilgore Trout, in Kurt Vonnegut's *Breakfast of Champions,* defined a *beaver* as "the photo of a woman not wearing underpants and with her legs far apart so that the growth of her *vagina* could be seen." He then went on to explain that:

> The expression was first used by news photographers who often got to see up women's skirts at accidents, sporting events, and from underneath fire escapes and so on. They needed a code word to yell to other newsmen and friendly policemen and firemen and so on, to let them know what could be seen in case they wanted to see it. The word was this: *"Beaver!"*

Its origins are elusive. One theory is based on guilt by association, *beaver* having once been slang for a *hat* and a *beard,* both of which did time as *c**t.*

Others looked elsewhere, finally finding an answer in women's underwear. When panties first appeared in the sixteenth century, their primary purpose was to protect the wearer from the cold. So, naturally, the first undergarments were made of warm material—flannel, cotton, velvet, and, you guessed it, beaver skin. Given only rare glimpses of reality, you can understand how the confusion arose in man's mind.

You Can Call Me

Such knees, such thighs
And such a *bum*
And such a, such a *modicum.*
> —Cotton, "Scoffer Scofft," 1675

Have you heard the one about the rabbit who washed her thing and couldn't do a hare with it?
> —Anon., *Maledicta*

It was only a matter of time before the *c**t* emerged as its own person. But we have fewer personal names for it than for *pr**k.* Most have only limited usage and none have attained the prominence, popularity, or instant recognition of a *John Thomas,* a *Dick,* or a *Peter.*

There's little rhyme or reason to the names for the *c**t* except for the rhyming cockney slang that gave us *Joe Hunt* ("Don't be such a Joey!") and *Charlie Hunt* ("That bloke's a Charlie!")

However, men spoke fondly of *Miss Laycock* and *Miss Horner*, perhaps of nursery-rhyme fame (both 19thC.), and women of their *Little Sister* (19thC.), their *Granny* (20thC.), and their *Aunt Maria* (before 1903). Intimate relations aside, she's always been a good *chum* (19thC.).

They also knew her as *Madge* (c. 1780) and *Mons Meg* (from the cannon with the huge aperture at Edinburgh Castle) as well as *Mary Jane* (c. 1840) and *Lady Jane* (c. 1850) who, together with *John Thomas*, provided most of the action in *Lady Chatterley's Lover*. But this is also one lady with a good bit of *tomboy* in her. John Taylor, in "The Water Poet" (1643) wrote of her "playing *tomboy* with her *tomboy*."

For the most part, people prefer that she remain anonymous. An old British ballad reminds us, "Such delicate thighs and that shall remain nameless between" (17thC.). There's also *her thing, what-do-you-call-it, what's her name, what's-it's-name*, and *you-know-what* (all 18thC.). In 1772, a fellow named Bridges sadly mused, "I wish I'd never touched her *what-d'ye-callum*."

Well, what d'ye know about that!

Long Time, No C

The *whore* laughs with one eye
and weeps with the other.

—Pietro Arentino, 16thC.

As with the *pr**k*, the *c**t*, when not a whole person, has been made a small part of one. But whereas we displaced the *pr**k* downward, we made things look up for the *c**t*. In the eighteenth century you might have heard an angry fishwife scream, "I'll knock six of your eight eyes out." An ophthalmologist's dream. The other six, as detailed by a lexicographer of the time, included two *bubbies* (also called *big brown eyes* in twentieth-century U.S. Southern slang), the *navel*, the *pope's eyes* (the *a*shole* and the *p*sshole*), and the *c**t*.

In a somewhat upside-down view of the world we saw the *c**t* as the *long eye* (c. 1850), the *nether eye*, the *upright wink*, and the *dumb squint* (all 19thC.). It was further distinguished as the *eye that weeps most when best pleased* (G.A. Stevens). The *long eye* was characteristically shortsighted and often caught by surprise. Seeing his *thing* for the first time often proved to be a real *eye-opener* (19th-20thC.).

Look Ma, No Cavities!

No need to stand there with your mouth wide open. Wipe off that *upright grin* (19thC.)! Not believing in a *mouth that cannot bite* (18th-mid-19thC.), men suffer from the classic male phobia of *vagina dententa,* fearing that when the *penis* is inserted into the *vagina,* it will be bitten off.

Psychiatrists tell us that men who dream of teeth in the *vagina* are expressing a fear of women and emasculation. Those so afflicted might consult their analysts for treatment, but any friendly lexicographer could tell them that they are confusing her *bite* (late 17th-early 19thC.) with the Anglo-Saxon *byht* for the fork of the legs.

On one account you can relax. Your secrets are safe with it. As the *nether mouth* (late 16thC.) it's *the mouth that says no word about it* (18th-mid-19thC.). But don't expect it to express appreciation. It's also *mouth thankless* (mid-16th-early 17thC.) — take, take, take, and never a sign of gratitude.

What's Cookin'?

The standard family fare was *la soupe et le boeuf* (19thC., "beef stew"), the *conjugal ordinary* (19thC.). Some men preferred *being in a woman's beef* (18th-mid-19thC.); later, *in her mutton* (19thC.). It was *mutton* (c. 1670) that truly proved to be his *meat* (late 16thC.), especially when served *laced* (c. 1575-1860), *split,* and *hot* (both 17th-19thC.).

One man's meat is another's *poisson.* For *C-food* (20thC.) fanciers we have a *bit o'fish* (18th-20thC.). *Fish* has long been identified with the *she-thing:* "Two things smell like a fish, and one is a fish." Some, however, might prefer some *oysters* (19thC.), named for their shape and garniture as well as their reputation as an aphrodisiac, to say nothing of our *bearded clams* (20thC.), very close in appearance to the real thing and also a very popular item.

Green with Envy

I was never so scar'd since I
pop'd out of the *parsley bed.*

—Ward, *London Spy,* 1719

I got a sweet woman;
She lives right back of the jail.
She's got a sign on her window
"Good *cabbage* for sale."

—Jelly Roll Morton, "Lowdown Blues"

If it's veggies you fancy, you'll love her *greens.* It used to be
that people *got, gave,* or *had 'em* (19thC.). Both men and women
were *on for their greens,* and men were *forever after 'em. Fresh and
curly greens* were a special delicacy. Men used to swear by them.
"S'help my *greens!*" they used to say.

Either way, if it's *head* you're after, you won't be disappointed if what's in the *grocery basket* (19thC.) turns out to be
cabbage.

Cabbage in nineteenth-century England was the *c**t,*
creating a vegetable fancier known as the *cabbage man,* also
lending an added touch to the French term of endearment, *mon
petit chou,* "my little cabbage."

Somehow, *cabbage,* with the same meaning, found its way
across the Atlantic and into the Black dialect of the 1920s and
'30s and finally made its way to the White community. When
children asked the inevitable question, "Mommy, where did I
come from?" the standard reply was, "I found you under a cabbage leaf." In England, little girls came from under the *parsley
bed* (17thC.) and little boys from under the *nettle* or the *goose-
berry bush. Parsley* came to represent the *pubic hair* and the
parsley bed the *she-thing.* Everyone enjoyed taking a turn in the
parsley bed.

But if *cabbage* and *parsley,* why not a *cauliflower?* Grose recounts an incident in a court of law where a woman used that
vegetable in order to make reference to her *private parts.* Taken
somewhat aback and somewhat amused by so far-reaching a
metaphor, the judge countered by suggesting, "You might as
well have called it an artichoke."

"Not so, my lord," replied she, "for an artichoke has a bottom but a *c**t* and a *cauliflower* have none."

Branching Out

I was never stained but once falling
out of my mother's *plum tree.*

> —*Marriage of Wit and Wisdom,* 1547

What's a meal without fruit? And what better place to look for it than in the *orchard*? The *orchard* has traditionally been symbolic of fertility and virility. There you'll find the *Fruitex vulvaria* (19thC.), the *fruitful vine which bears flowers every four weeks and fruit every nine months* (19thC.). There you might take an *orange* (17thC.) or *shake the plum tree*. The *plum tree*, according to Shakespeare, has long been man's favorite. We are all said to have fallen out of the *plum tree* at birth. A plum is considered the ultimate—hence the connection with the *c**t*. And for a *plum,* no man will hesitate going out on a limb, especially with two strong ones to support him. Every man comes equipped with his own personal *plum-tree shaker.*

For your just desserts, you might want to try a little something from the *sugar basin* (mid 19thC.) or the *hymeneal sweets* (19thC.): a *bit o' jam,* a *cookie* (both 19thC.) or perhaps some *jelly roll* (20thC.). W.C. Handy gave it his own personal endorsement: "I'm most wile about mah *jelly roll!*" Thomas Wolfe also attached very special value to it:

> "What's—what's he going to give you a dollar for?" he muttered, barely audible. *"Jelly roll,"* said Ella Coperning.
>
> —*Look Homeward Angel,* 1929

Going to Pot

My daughter's a girl of reputation, though she has been seen in your company, but she's resolved never more to venture her *pitcher* to the well.

> —William Wycherly, *Love in a Wood,*
> 1672

All that talk of food. But where's a lady to put anything? You can use any old *cannister, pan, bucket, chalice,* or *box,* but look also to the *melting pot* (19thC.), the *mustard pot* (19th-20thC.) and the *honey pot* (18th-19thC.).

If you enjoy fine craftsmanship, you might favor a nicely shaped *pipkin* (17th-19thC.), which is a small earthenware pot, or the magic in *the miraculous pitcher that holds water mouth downward* (mid-18th-19thC.).

However, M'lady's not always been comfortable with the arrangements. Eighteenth-century maidens were heard to complain, "I will not make a *lobster kettle* of my *c**t!*" (c. 1795-1800), a reply that according to Grose was frequently made by the *nymphs* of Portsmouth when requested by a soldier to *grant him a favor.*

Mind Your Business

Woman cannot make living with left leg
Woman cannot make living with right leg
But between them she does all right.

—Pseudo-Oriental wisdom, *c.* 1950s

Inevitably, one comes around to that which puts the food on the table. Ever since Adam made the first entry at *Eve's customhouse,* men have reduced her and *it* to a marketable commodity, speaking of her *business* as the *leading article* and her *stock-in-trade.*

There was more than a hint of this in eighteenth-century England. When a young lass bent over somewhat injudiciously, a true gentleman would avert his glance and gently warn her, "Take care Miss, lest you show your *money.*" Nell Kimball, the Great American Madam, was one who realized its earning potential. Reminded that most women were either unaware of it, or chose not to treat their *money* as such, she quoted her Aunt Letty, "Every girl is sitting on her fortune, if only she knew it."

Saving it for marriage used to enhance a woman's value. It was once said that a woman without a dowry at least possessed a *Cambridge Fortune.* Cambridge was interchangeable with the city or town of your choice. Her wealth consisted of a *windmill*

69

and a *watermill*, the *a*∗*s* and the *c*∗∗*t*, respectively. An Irish inheritance was a *Tipperary Fortune* which included *t*∗*ts* as well, the precursor of today's *well-endowed woman*.

Lovers' Lane

One way to a man's heart is through his stomach, but there is a shorter and more direct route. Admittedly, not one of the smoother routes to travel, it still is one of the more *agreeable ruts of life* (19thC.). In fact, the *vagina* is the one body part of *The Erotic Tongue* that's actually had a street named for it. Peter Freyer, the British authority on prudery, researched a Grope-cuntlane, a street name appearing in London, York, North Hampton, Wells, and Essex in England in the thirteenth and fourteenth centuries. Further study revealed it to be "a common name for a dark and disreputable passage."

As forbidding as it sounds, there's little to fear in taking a walking tour of the area—providing you apply the proper terminology and exercise the necessary discretion in following directions.

Hit the road (17th-20thC.), *take a turn on love lane* (19th-20thC.). Though on first sight it might appear a *blind alley*, it is the *Main Avenue* (both 19th-20thC.). If you don't believe it, check out the *traffic* (19thC. for *sexual* activity). After a brief stretch on *Leather Lane*, proceed with caution, for the *road to paradise* quickly converges into the *road to a christening* (19thC.)—a sudden turn that could lead to disaster. Keep on the *straight and narrow*. At the fork check out all signs. Do not make a mistaken turn onto the *old dirt road* (19th-20thC.), known also as *Hershey-Bar Road* (20thC.).

Going All the Way

At last there's cause for celebration. We've finally come to the *end of the sentimental journey* (18thC.), which also happens to be *home*. The connection goes back to the very last word in Lawrence Sterne's 1786 book, *A Sentimental Journey Through France and Italy*, which ends with "So I stretched out my hand and caught hold of the *fille de chambre's* _____."

It may not look like much, but whether you call it the *thatched house under the hill* (c. 1770-1850) or the *mansion of love* (19thC.), it's there that you'll find the *rest and be thankful* (19thC.-20thC.), and a retreat from the hurly-burly of the outside world.

Your Place or Mine

Please, Mother, Open the door!

> — Cocky boys calling out to the girls,
> early 20thC.

When a door has once been broken open,
It is hard to keep it shut.

> — Anon., 19thC.

With luck, the keeper of the *premises* will *have rooms to let* and be willing to take in a *lodger* (19thC. for a *penis*).

The quality and the location of the rooms vary. Most prefer the *front parlour* or the *front room* with the *front window* (both 19thC.). But you may have to make do with the *front attic* (19thC.) or the *cellar* (Richard Brome). For all, there's the convenient entryway at the *front door* (18thC., John Cleland) or the *portal of love*.

It's the door they're all looking to *get in*. Some sought to force matters by *picking the lock* (18thC.) as well as boasting of it: "Here's the lock of all locks and unlocking the same" (G.A. Stevens, *Songs Comic and Satyrical*, 1788). Many a man applied his *key* (18thC. *penis*) directly, a very special *key* that young girls especially feared, frequently described as the *key that lets a man in and a maid out* (18thC.).

Is This Trip Necessary?

. . . License my roving hands and let them go
Before, behind, between, above, below,
Oh, my America, My Newfoundland.

> — John Donne, "To His Mistress Going
> to Bed"

I wish I was a diamond ring
Upon my Lulu's hand
And everytime she scratched her *a∗s*
I'd see the promised land.

— Anon., *Lulu*, 20thC.

There are men, however, with a quest for adventure. They'd much prefer to idealize and romanticize the *vagina* as a faraway and exotic land to be reached only after a long and difficult voyage. The strangeness of the geography makes it seem distant and remote, perhaps even foreign to them. Only when she *spreads her pretty map* (Alex Comfort, 20thC.) do parts unknown become locatable. The explorer now sees the *Antipodes* (19thC.), the *Midlands* (c. 1820), the *Low Countries* (18th-mid-19thC.), and the *land down under.* The easiest way to find it is to *go south;* it's somewhere *'twixt wind and water* (18th-19thC.).

The entire trip is a pleasurable one. There's pleasure not only in sailing toward foreign parts, but in the ecstasy experienced at the moment of arrival as well as the romance and mystery of exploration.

Once there, the man can discover the romance, color, and charm of nature's *tufted treasure.* Take a dip in the clear, deep pool in the *forest glade* or the *shady spring* (Bridges). View the awesome *hymeneal waterfall* (George Barker), the spectacular *oracular portcullis* (James Reaney), the *living fountain* (Robert Herrick). Retire to the exotic *downy cave, love's pavillion,* and the *mystic grotto* (all 19thC.). Pass through the *postern gate* to the *Elysian Fields* (Herrick). Frolic in *love's playground* (19thC.). Take a turn in the breathtaking *Grove of Eglantine* (Thomas Carew) and the historic *Orchard of the Hesperides* (Christopher Marlowe).

And thanks to the new direct flights and special stopover fares, he can also include in his trip a breathtaking excursion through the *Cyprian Strait* and the *cloven inlet,* round *Cape Horn* or the *Cape of Good Hope* (both 19thC.), while anchoring in majestic *Botany Bay* (19thC.).

How Does Your Garden Grow?

With your warm kisses on my lips,
How could I stay your hand;

The veil was lifted and by faith,
You viewed the *promised land.*

> —Anon., "The Rehearsal," 1895

Her legs opened wide
My eyes I let down steal
Until that I espyed
Dame Nature's Privy Seal

> —Farmer, *Old Songs, Merry Songs,* 1897

The *promised land* features many scenic wonders. Shakespeare's Venus encouraged Adonis to roam in both the high delightful plain and the *sweet bottom grass.*

"I love your hills and I love your dales," John Keats reminded us. It tops a slight incline known as *Mons Veneris* ("Mount of Venus" in Latin), known also as Pill(i)cock Hill (16thC.), *Mount Pleasant* (c. 1880), or *Shooter's Hill* (late 19thC.). It's there you'll find the *green grove,* the *green meadow* (c. 1850), *the (front) garden* (16th-19thC.), often described as a *gentleman's pleasure garden* (19thC.).

Amidst it all you'll see the *beauteous flower* (19thC.), the *flower of chivalry.* If you should check the *bush,* you'll find a *nest in the bush* (18thC.), *a bird's nest* (for both pudendum and pubic hair). It could be that of the *magpie* (18thC.), the *cuckoo* (19th-20thC.), the *goldfinch* (before 1821), the *dove,* and the *phoenix* (c. 1640). A famous *nest* is this. It's the *nest* in the *bush* (18thC.), one widely celebrated in prose, poetry, and drama.

I must another way,
To fetch a ladder, by the which your love
Must climb a *bird's nest* soon when it is dark.

> —Shakespeare, Nurse in *Romeo and Juliet*

Letting Your Hair Down

Here's to America, land of the push,
  Where a bird in the hand is worth two in the *bush.*
But if in that *bush* a fair maiden should stand,
  Then a push in the *bush* is worth two in the hand.

> —Anon., 20thC.

Tired of beating around the *bush* (mid-19thC.)? Looking for closure? John Ruskin found the *bush* an insurmountable obstacle. Because of it he was unable to consummate his marriage on his wedding night, so shocked was he to find his teen-age bride, Effie, sporting a growth of hair above *love's triangle.* Why it was enough to raise the *nether eyebrow* (19th C.). Another sportsman might have taken a *shot over the stubble* or, better yet, *taken a turn in it* (19thC.). Others would have *tickled her scut* (16thC.), long considered her *tufted honor* (17thC., Urquhart). But not John!

Obviously, our Victorian long-hair had never heard about *fluff* (19thC.), the *fleece* (17thC.), the *short-hairs* (20thC.), the *belly-* or *quim-whiskers* (19thC.), the *silent beard* (18thC.), the *twat rug* (19thC.-20thC.), the *snatch thatch* (late 18thC.), the *lady's welcome mat,* or the *c**t curtain.*

> It is not fit the *silent beard* should
> Know how much it is abus'd . . . for
> if it did, it would . . . make open its
> Sluice to the drowning of the low countries
> in an inundation of salt water.
>
> —Sir Thomas Browne, *Works,* 1704

If That Don't Top Everything

> If dresses get much shorter
> Said Mary with a sob,
> I'll have two more cheeks to powder
> And one more place to bob.
>
> —Ditty from the 1920s

They had entirely different problems two hundred years earlier when a smallpox epidemic resulted in considerable fallout in the most exotic places. Thoroughly embarrassed by their baldness, women fashioned artificial hairpieces known as *merkins* (*merkin* also being a long-standing name for the female *genitalia,* 17thC.).

Merkin is still with us today in a different capacity. The name of the President of the United States in *Dr. Strangelove* was Merkin Muffley (*c**t c**t*). A curious turnabout, given that

Presidents have traditionally been seen as *pr**ks* rather than *c**ts*. Interesting too, that a *c**t* should be the only voice of restraint and moderation heard during a time when the world was perched at the brink of destruction. At any rate, the original epidemic passed and the fashion faded, leaving us with such phrases as the *quim wig* and the *ladies' low toupee* (both 19thC.) – and some miscellaneous organs still in charge of the government.

This Bud's for You

The Erotic Tongue would be less than complete if it failed to mention more than the *vagina* or the *vulva*. We haven't even touched upon the *clitoris* (c. 1615), a part which Aristotle considered "the foundation and the fountain of sexual love in the female." Widely recognized as woman's source of *self-pleasure*, we have only a few words to describe it.

The reason, clearly, is that men have never tolerated rivals particularly well, and the *clitoris* (popularly the *clit*, 20thC.) is no exception. At one point they didn't bother with it at all, dismissing it as the *penis muliebris* (19thC., medical terminology meaning "a female *penis*" from the Latin *mulier*, "woman"), thus reducing it to a vestigial organ, a weak homologue of sorts, something about as useful as a man's nipples. For Freud, the *clitoral orgasm* was only a stage of infantile sexuality. Woman's developmental goal was to move from the *clitoral* ("infantile") to the *vaginal* ("mature"). Others practised character assassination upon the word itself. When they came to determine its derivation, etymologists linked the word to the Greek *kleiein*, "to shut or close," implying that something or somebody was being shut out. Wayland Young, in *Eros Denied,* asks us to take a closer look and see if the *clitoris* really does shut or bar access to the vagina, inquiring, "What forced such derivation but that it should be barred or shut." This when they could have chosen *kleitos* for "renowned, splendid, or excellent," or even settled for the somewhat neutral *kleitoris*, "the small hill."

Men's anatomical perspective was also somewhat cock-eyed when they likened it to the *ear-between-the-legs* and the *shame tongue* (direct translation from the German). Others settled upon the nondescript *button* (19thC.) or *little bud* (Edmund Wilson, *Memoirs of Hecate County,* 1951).

As a person, it's played various roles: the *goalie* (20thC.), always keeping his eye on the puck; the *little ploughman,* supervising the proper sowing of the seed; and the *peeping sentinel,* guarding love's treasure against intrusions.

It's also been the solitary adventurer — *the little boy in the boat* (*c.* 1908, Can.) — adrift upon the *open C* (mid-19th-20thC.).

After the grandiloquent terms for the *vulva,* it's quite a letdown. The *clitoris* not only comes up second best but ends up sounding like an outtake from a TV commercial.

Tickle Your Fancy?

The *hymen* (*c.* 1615) comes off somewhat better. We know it best as the *cherry* (20thC.), which describes both the thin membrane stretched across the *vagina* and identifies the bearer with *virginity.* Those who still have it are also described by the fruit, a term that's used for men as well ("He's still *cherry*" or "still got his *cherry,*" even though an anatomical impossibility). *Cherry* was originally a nineteenth-century term for a young girl, a time when it was still believed that all girls were intact. Other terms include the favored *maidenhead,* which preceded the *hymen* (13thC.), the *virgin flower,* the *darling treasure,* the *jewel without price* (all 19thC.), but also, unfortunately, the *perishable commodity* (Cleland).

Hymen himself is a Greek god of marriage who lent his name to that unique membrane. He also gave us "hymns," those special songs sung on the wedding night to invoke his blessings on the marriage and, as some believe, the shrieks of pleasure given off by the bride the moment she bade *hymen* adieu.

Dis-Organization

Women's *organs* have never had an easy time of it. They were always considered something less than, or a variation of, the male's.

Dr. William Acton, a noted Victorian sex quack who made himself known as an authority, published an opus in 1857 entitled *The Functions and Disorders of the Reproductive Organs in Childhood, Youth, Adult Age and Advanced Life Considered in Their Physiological, Social and Moral Relations.* All without a single mention of woman.

The *ovaries* are another case in point. We didn't even know them as such until 1662 when Johannes Van Horne, a Dutch professor of anatomy, tired of the standard references to them as "the female *testicles.*"

Angry over the manner in which women's *organs* have been dealt with? Looking to vent your spleen? OK, but only if you're a man. According to Hippocrates and the ancient Greeks, the spleen was the organ of the body responsible for melancholia, what we now know as depression—in man. When treating a man for depression, the physician would make a small incision in the general area of the spleen and allow the unhealthy vapors to escape. The counterpart to man's melancholia in women was said to be hysteria, from its location in the *hystera*—the womb. No small incisions for her. To rid woman of her hysteria they had to remove the entire womb, an operation that we now know as the hysterectomy.

And that, dear reader, finally brings the *c**t curtain* (19thC.) down.

There is an all-woman, new-wave rock group known as the Slits.

†††

Though the vulva is the proper word for woman's external *genitals* and the proper counterpart to the *penis,* few ever speak or write of it. Instead it's the *vagina,* the internal organ that connects the *uterus* with the outside of the body, which we're always talking about. Many times what people call the *vagina* is really the *vulva.*

Dr. Mildred Ash, a noted psychiatrist, in an article in *Maledicta, The International Journal of Verbal Aggression,* expressed shock at the absence of *vulva* from our vocabulary. She viewed this as not merely an oversight but part of the general deprecation of the female *genitalia,* concluding that women avoid its use because they are ashamed of its "ugliness" and its close association with the obscene *c**t* and because it also reminds them of their lack of a *penis.* Men prefer using the word *vagina* because by reducing it to a hole of sorts, "It enables them to master their fear of people who have no *penis* and do mysterious things like menstruate and have babies."

†††

No ordinary four-letter word, *c**t*'s rather special. It's a "sexually energizing word," one which, according to Partridge, conveys "the sexual pleasure produced by a woman in a man and indeed all that woman-as-sex signifies to a man both physically and spiritually." James Joyce saw it in quite different terms when he described the Dead Sea in *Ulysses* as "the grey sunken *c**t* of the world." However, D.H. Lawrence captured its essence perfectly through Mellors, the game-keeper, in conversation with Constance Chatterley, and it was a touch of poetic justice that the *c**t* was "liberated" by the decision in the *Lady Chatterley* case, making it possible for us to see the word in print once more when the book was finally cleared for publication and distribution in 1959.

"Th'art good *c**t* . . ."
"What is *c**t?*" she said.
". . . *c**t!*"
"It's thee down theer; an' what I get when I'm
i'side thee; it's a' as it is, all on't."

— D. H. Lawrence, *Lady Chatterley's
Lover,* 1928

† † †

Animals have always been symbolic of our basic
drives. And if you had to choose one animal to represent
both *reproduction* and the *vagina,* why not the rabbit?

We know it best in its obsolete form, *con(e)y, cunny,*
or *cunnie* (17thC.), which is also, coincidentally, a dimin-
tive of *c**t. Coney* rhymes with *bunny* (18thC.), a word
that originated in Scotland for the tail of the hare. It was
later shortened to *bun,* which also attained considerable
popularity as the female *genitalia.* Rather than having to
rub a rabbit's foot, sailors in the eighteenth century, prior
to embarking on long voyages, would *touch bun for luck,*
a ritual that proved even more popular than knocking on
wood.

† † †

There was a time when, after a hard day's work, the
man of the house would come home to find his wife with
skirt raised before the fireplace — *warming the old man's
supper* (18thC.). That, however, soon gave way to the
oven (18th-19thC.). *Oven* was very much in vogue as the
*c**t* during the eighteenth and nineteenth centuries.
Some think it originated with the Old English proverb,
"No man will another in the *oven* seek, except that him
selfe have been there before."

But if my *oven* be over-hot
    I dare not thrust it in, dear,
For burning of my *wriggling pole*
    My skill's not wirth a pin, sir.

— D'Urfey, *The Jolly Tradesman,* 1720

Nothin' says lovin' like somethin' from the oven.

— Pillsbury Flour commercial, 1960s

† † †

Aristophanes, in his play *The Peace*, encourages us to:

Now live splendidly together
Free from adversity
Pick your *figs*
May his be large and hard
May hers be sweet.

Since Adam and Eve both reputedly covered their nakedness with a fig leaf, the fig has come to be identified with the *vagina* (19thC.), the *penis,* and even the *act* itself. The appearance of the split fig added further to the case because it so closely resembles the lips (the *labia*) of the *vulva.* It Italy, the *fica* is a common gesture of contempt: thrusting the thumb between the middle and index fingers. Originally, it was used as a good-luck gesture to ward off evil spirits. Today, it's yet another way of saying, "*F**k* you!"

† † †

Jelly roll is a popular Southern Black term. You'll find references to it in many blues songs of the twenties and thirties, as well as in the literature of the period.

We also have some plain *jelly* (19thC.) serving as both *c**t* and an attractive female. Both *jelly* and *jelly roll* have done yeoman service in the Black jazz lexicon as nicknames for men who loved both women and their parts. They both began as Standard English, took on a sexual connotation, and then later merged with elements of African verbal translation. David Dalby, a student of African elements in American English, traced it back to the Mandingo *jeli,* a minstrel who gained much popularity with the women by his delightful use of words and music.

What a dream combo we'd have with Jelly Williams

on bass, Jelly Thompson on guitar, and Jelly Roll Morton on piano. M-m-m-m-m-m!

† † †

Counted among a woman's most precious possessions and the counterpart to a man's *family jewels* was *cupid's ring* (mid-18th-19thC.), also called (Hans) *Carvel's ring* (*c.* 1700), after the medieval doctor who slipped it on one night in his sleep.

According to Grose, the good doctor dreamt of receiving a ring from the Devil which, as long as he wore it, would insure his wife's fidelity. "Hans took the ring . . . and thrust it beyond his joint. 'Tis done,' he cry'd . . . 'What's done, you drunken bear,' cried his wife. 'You've thrust your finger God knows where!'"

FIVE

Spare Parts

MAMMARY LANE

The woman's *breast* nourishes the
child and gladdens the father.
> —The Koran

See Jane Russell shake her tambourines
and drive Cornell Wilde.
> —Tag line for preview of *Hot Blood*,
> 1956

Our treatment of women remains incomplete. While rummaging about through love's attic you'll find the greatest assortment of odds and ends since the Olde Curiosity Shoppe: nicely shaped *jugs* (early 20thC.), hand-crafted *love handles* and *knockers* (both 20thC.), a *pair of* (Cupid's) *kettledrums* (c. 1770-1850), some restful *chest and bedding* (c. 1785, nautical) and, for the autoerotic set, a pair of *headlights* (20thC.).

Upon closer examination, you'll see that this mixed bag from the past consists of nothing more than *breasts.* If it seems like *breasts* have been around forever, you're not far off: They bounced their way into the language about the year 1000, coming from the Indo-European *bhreus,* "to swell or sprout," starting life as an Old English *breost* and a Middle English *brest* before finally settling in to the form we know today.

But it's the *bosom,* a word that appeared about the same time, that's proven more acceptable. According to its ancient Aryan origins, the *bosom's* nothing more than the space between the arms. Nothing much, but you have to admit that it filled the space nicely. Around the middle of the nineteenth century, *breasts* fell out of favor, and "nice" people stopped referring to them. When you were invited out for turkey dinner and you wanted to express your preference for white meat, you always asked for turkey *bosom*, never the *breast*.

Over time, the *breast* came to be perceived as increasingly impolite to the point of being considered savage, and the *bosom* as refined and gentle. *Bosoms* had a brief, wild fling as *bazooms* (mid-20thC.), but ultimately reverted to their conservative character and traditional spelling.

As acceptance of *breasts* declined, other substitutes were tried, including the *top*, the *torso*, and the *chest*. The *chest* was adopted by many, including a twentieth-century ecdysiast who promoted herself and her wares as "Evelyn West and her treasure chest." But such efforts proved a total *bust*, a general term for the upper part of the body including the head, shoulders, and upper chest when speaking of a sculpture, but reduced to the *breasts* when referring to a woman.

Breasts, however, wouldn't take it lying down. They fought back valiantly, finally making a remarkable comeback in the 1920s. Today, they are quasi-respectable. They still occasion a twinge or two when mentioned publicly, but for the most part appear to be holding their own.

Tit for That

In and around the locker room there's little talk of *breasts*, but lots of conversation about *t*ts*. *T*ts* is a charming word that suggests many things. George Carlin once proposed a new crackerlike snack treat from Nabisco—"You can't eat just one!" We prefer *t*ts* as the family dog, small, warm, cuddly, and benign—not unlike the little pooch sitting dutifully with his ear to the RCA phonograph. "Here, *t*ts*!" "Nice *t*ts*!" "G-o-o-o-o-o-o-d *t*ts*!"

Historically, *breasts* began as *teats* (c. 950), not becoming *t*ts* till around the seventeenth century, while later spinning off the likes of *t*tties* (c. 1740) and *diddies* or *diddeys* (c. 1780). Once they referred solely to the *nipples* (c. 1530), but today they describe both soft protuberances situated at the thorax of the female. *T*ts* have been considered vulgar since the nineteenth century. Today it is considered gauche to tell a lady what lovely *t*ts* she has.

83

Lip Service

And tho' I let boobies oft
Finger my *bubbies* who think
When they kiss them that they shall *possess* me.

> —"Wooburn Fair," in Farmer, *Old
> Songs, Merry Songs,* 1897

Call them what you may, to the little sucker born every minute, it's all academic. When he's looking to quench his thirst, he heads straight for the *mountains.*

So there you'll find him, cozying up to the *dairy arrangements* (*c.* 1923), chug-a-lugging at the *baby's public house* (*c.* 1884), or taking lunch at *Café la Mama* (*c.* 1970). Functioning as such they're the *mammary glands* or *nature's fonts,* long used as the *milk bottle,* the *milk shop,* and the *milky way.* They're also the *toora-loorals* (*c.* 1909), as in the Irish lullaby "Toora-loora-loora."

When the service is slow, baby's sure to let you know. The child's cry goes "bu-bu-bu," from which we get the ancient cant word, *bub* for "to drink" as well as *bubbies* (late 17th-20thC.), *bubs* (19thC.), and *boovies, boobies,* and *boobs* (all 19th-20thC.).

More Food for Thought

Then those twins, thy strawberry *teates,*
curled, purled cherrilets . . .

> —Joshua Sylvester, *Miracle of the
> Peace,* 1599

Please let me squeeze your *lemons*
While I'm in your lonesome town
Now, let me squeeze your *lemons,* baby
Until my love *comes down.*

> —Charlie Pickett, "Let Me Squeeze
> Your Lemons," early 20thC.

Young or old, we all need a balanced diet. And what better way to get each day off to a rousing start than with a good breakfast? Our morning menu includes *muffins* (20thC.), *pancakes* (19thC.), or *flapjacks* (20thC.), *dumplings* (*c.* 1709), as well as the specialty of the house, *deux oeufs sur le plat* (20th C., two fried eggs up).

Rounding out our meal, we've got fresh fruit. You can select from *oranges à l'étalage,* (oranges on display), *grapefruit* (20thC.), *watermelons* (H. Allen Smith), *honeydew melons* (20thC.), *clusters of grapes* (Song of Solomon), and a *lovely bunch of cokernuts* (c. 1909). We have no raisins or prunes, but if you look real hard you'll probably spot an occasional *lemon* (20thC.) or two.

It's all *eye-pleasing fruit* (Sir John Suckling, 17thC.), *love's strawberries,* and *apples.* Do we have apples! *Apples tipped with coral berries* (Carew), *ungathered apples* (Wright, 20thC.), *two fair apples, fragrant, sweetly savor'd apples* (Francesco de Barberini, 14thC.), *apple-knockers* (c. 1940s), *twinn'd apples round and small* (Cornelius Gallus), and *fair apples in their prime.* As well as something from the *apple-dumpling shop* (late 18th-19thC.).

Thanks for the Mammaries

The French used to say, *"Jactons d'entrée des Roberts!"* "Dig those boobies!" (*Roberts* has been a nursing-bottle trademark since 1888). American men prefer *whatta pair* (mid-20thC.) and *TNT!* (two nifty t*ts, 20thC.).

But these aren't just ordinary playthings to be casually fondled and then tossed aside. They're a *classy pair,* a *matched set* with a splendid history behind them.

In the 1930s and '40s, they were virtually inseparable as the *twins.* In the nineteenth century, they were *les deux soeurs* (the two sisters, a.k.a. the twin sisters) as distinguished from *les deux frères siamois* (the Siamese twins — i.e., the b*lls). They've been named *Charlies* (c. 1840), after Charles II's many mistresses, who were noted for their opulent *charms,* and *Langtries* (c. 1880-1900), society slang from Lily Langtry, the famous singer and actress, and one of the most beautiful women of her time. Her name became so synonymous with beauty that the most attractive women in the British colonies were addressed as "Mrs. Langtry." *Langtries* first denoted lovely eyes and later made a natural progression to the *breasts.*

In a more contemporary vein, Mae West's pointed remarks are still with us and so is her name as rhyming cockney slang for *breasts.* We also used her name during World War II for life-jackets "that bulged in the right places," twin-turreted tanks, and twin-lobed parachutes that malfunctioned. Other cockney slang for *breasts* includes *Lewis and Witties, town and cities, Jersey cities, Bristol cities* (most commonly referred to as *Bristols*), and *thousand pities* — all rhyming with *t*tties.*

Eventually, *breasts* attained seniority as the *elders* (17thC., Eng.; *c.* 1920, Aust.), bringing to mind the story of the woman who had two tattoos, smiling portraits of two former lovers, one on each breast. How she feared the moment of revelation on her wedding night. But when the disclosure was made, her husband appeared to take it in stride. "I'm so glad you're not upset, dear," said she. "No need to make a fuss," he commented philosophically. "They may be smiling now, but in a few years, what long faces they'll have."

Poetry of the Spheres

A woman has *bosoms*, a *bust*, or a *breast*,
    Those *lily-white swellings* that bulge 'neath her vest
They are *towers of ivory, sheaves of new wheat*,
    In a moment of passion, *ripe apples* to eat.
You may speak of her *nipples* as small rings of fire
    But by Rabelais' beard, she'll throw fifteen fits
If you speak of them roundly as good honest *t*ts.*
                            — "Ode to Those Four-Letter Words"

The poets were especially fond of them, immortalizing them forever in marble and alabaster.

Geographically, they've been *East and West, globes* (*c.* 1860), *hemispheres,* and *points of interest* (both 19thC.). Naturally, *pleasant eminences, chalky cliffs* (both Shakespeare); *mounds of lilies, twin orbs, orbs of snow* (all Cleland); and *nature's fonts,* as well as *two rounded hillocks* (Thomas Heywood, 17th C.), *ivory hills* (Cleland); and *hills of paradise.*

Bustin' Out

. . . They and their ilk [hucksters who exploit love and sex] now turned every billboard and even kiddies' comics into peep shows. Furthermore, it is the upper half of women, the infants' half, that has gotten most of their attention and I sometimes marvel how it is, with all these misdirections sprawled about, that the birthrate has risen so.

— Philip Wylie, *Generation of Vipers,*
1958

Breast interest and competition peaked in the States during the forties and fifties, when sweater girls, pin-ups and movie stars were all bursting at the seams, vying for the honors. It was the heyday of Marilyn Monroe, Sophia Loren, and Silvana Mangano. Howard Hughes used every bit of his God-given engineering genius to design and build a bra for Jane Russell with an uplift rivaling that of his famed aircraft. And teen-age boys spoke enthusiastically about her *gazongas, goonas, snorbs, hooters, wallopies,* and *bazooms.* Big *breasts* were sure winners. At every contest we also had our also-rans; recipients of the booby prize included the *droopers,* the *hangers,* and the *swingers* (all 20thC.), also known as *saddle-bags* (20thC.) and *tobacco-pouches* (Fr. *blagues à tabac*).

Breasts were now an object of passionate concern. In America women rubbed in proteins and got silicone injections (*silicones,* 20thC.); in Europe, they spread on an exotic ointment, a special muck consisting of oysters, caviar, and mud from the bed of the sea. Other approaches were deceptively simple. Joan Rivers' solution was to merely coat the *breasts* with sugar and water, lie naked in the sun, and pray for killer bees.

Front and Center

But behind every pair of *breasts* there was a man. It was men who set the standards for the Breast Betterment League and determined when a pair was ready to face the world. They described women who qualified as *well developed* (19thC.), *(well) stacked* (mid-20thC.), *(well) endowed* or *zaftig* (20thC., Yiddish for "soft" in the right places). Later, they said a woman was *well built* (19th-20thC.). Women of truly outstanding construction received the ultimate compliment: *built like a brick s**thouse* (20thC.). What finer compliment could a woman hope for?

87

Literate men described such women as *buxom. Buxom,* from the Old English *bouen,* "to bow," was once an innocent word applied to both sexes and used to describe a person who was humble, submissive, obedient, tractable, and easily bent, qualities any lord would be happy to find in his peasants. By the sixteenth century the word had begun to be applied specifically to a woman who was a powerfully built field hand. It later made a quantum leap to her appearance, till today it refers to any woman with a shapely *full-bosomed* figure.

Our Cups Runneth Over

Making it to the top: getting to be considered *buxom* or *built like a brick s**thouse* was never easy. You first had to put your *glandular endowments* (19th-20thC.) through a period of rigorous discipline when they were forced to take up temporary residence in a *training bra* (*c.* 1950s). We can only surmise that this was a time when they learned to sit and heel on command. Those that made it reached their final destination, the full *bra* (*c.* 1934) or *bras* (*c.* 1910), more formally known as a *brassiere* (*c.* 1912).

The *bra,* or something like it, has been in use for over 6,000 years but really didn't come into its own until the turn of the century. The first formal application for a patent on the garment was filed on February 12, 1914 by Mary Phelps Jacob, also known as Caresse Crosby, who fashioned a prototype using some ribbons, thread, and two handkerchiefs. After World War I, the donning of the *bra* became synonymous with the chucking of the corset, long considered the restrainer of the female and the mainstay of her oppression. The *bra* allowed women to both liberate their bodies and assume a host of activities, both work and play, previously open only to men.

The word *brassiere* derives from the French *bras,* "arm," and the *braciere,* "arm protector," raising serious questions as to its true contents. The French themselves appear equally squeamish in discussing such matters, referring to the garment as *un soutien gorge,* a support of the throat.

Over the years, we've known the *brassiere* by many names. Originally, it was a *bust bodice* (*c.* 1829), a *B.B.* (*c.* 1920), or a *bust-*

girdle (*c.* 1904). An early manufacturer proudly advertised three basic models: the *Dictator,* which suppressed the masses, the *Salvation Army,* which lifted them up, and the *Yellow Press,* which made mountains out of molehills. More recently, we've had a *booby trap,* a *breast bucket* (20thC. garment-industry expression), a *flopper-stopper,* a *hammock for two,* and an *over-the-shoulder boulder-holder* (all mid-20thC.). *Bras* have also more than held their own. Encouraged by men, women have always tended to exaggerate their *bra-sets* (20thC.) with the aid of *palpitators,* also known as *palpitating bosoms,* and *patent heavers* (all 19thC.), *gay deceivers* (mid-20thC.), and *falsies* (early 20thC.).

As popular as *bras* have been, they momentarily fell out of fashion in the sixties with the *ban-the-bra* movement, during which time they were either burnt or consigned to the trash can. Again, ironically, in the name of liberation.

Please Bare with Us

From the male perspective, banning bras wasn't necessarily a bad thing. Sizing up a woman was always considered easier without her *bra.* Better yet was when she was sporting her *blubbers* (late 18thC.), *flashing* or *displaying her charms* (18th-20thC.), or *airing her dairy* (18thC.). Getting an eyeful, however, has often been a matter of being in the right place at the right time.

Historically, *breasts* have gained their greatest exposure as woman's status in general has grown; the lesser the oppression, the greater the view. The Renaissance blatantly adored, emphasized, and displayed naked *bosoms,* though their revelation was restricted to ladies of nobility and propriety who bared their *bosoms* but were sufficiently modest to mask their faces.

In Victorian England, women bared nothing – even in front of their husbands in the privacy of their own bedrooms. Today, anything goes. Since the second half of the sixties, we've favored the designation *topless* – a trend begun with waitresses, dancers, and shoeshine girls which quickly spread to other sectors. Variations now include *semi-topless* (pasties), and the all-encompassing *topless-bottomless.*

The media continue to feature the *breasts* on *jiggle shows* as part of *T. and A.* (both late '70s) for America's *R. and R.* But we

89

haven't had any new terms recently. Perhaps at long last, the American male's obsession with the *breast* has simply peaked — or better yet, gone flat.

REAL BUMMERS

There was a young lady named Glass
Who had a beautiful *a*∗*s* —
Not round and pink
As you might think
But gray and had ears, and ate grass.

> — Anon., 19thC.

I'm going to whip his _____.

> — Jimmy Carter speaking of Ted Kennedy as reported in *The New York Times,* June 14, 1979

. . . And lastly, we have the parts we share in common.

It was the early days of the "Tonight Show," and Steve Allen was placing his customary "cold" phone call to some unsuspecting party on the outside. The woman on the other end answered with the name of her firm, Big A Cleaners. Allen paused and then smartly inquired, "How much will you charge to clean my big *A?*" The audience roared delightedly.

Everyone knows the big *A*, but it wasn't always an abbreviated version of reality. It came into the world whole as a full-blown *arse* (c. 1000), and was Standard English until the second half of the seventeenth century. However, the word proved so popular that it came to be considered vulgar. It was driven underground and reduced in print to an ar__ or an a__se, occasionally even an _____ or an *a*∗∗∗.

Complicating matters further, people began to confuse the *arse* with the similar-sounding four-legged beast of burden. For years, *a*∗*s* had been a euphemism for the *arse*, but now, it was simply too close for comfort.

Out of this confusion emerged the *A-double scribble* (19thC.) and finally the plain old *A* (c. 1855). For more than two hundred years it functioned in this *half-a*∗*sed* manner. Finally in 1930,

90

with very little fanfare, it was printed again in a book by Frederic Manning entitled *Her Privates We*. The privates, incidentally, referred not to female *genitals* but to Her Majesty's soldiers. No one made a big thing of its return; in fact, hardly anyone cared. The *a∗s* was again whole.

Today, we have come full circle. When push comes to shove and we wish to speak delicately of it, we again fall back on our *arse*. It has now become a euphemism for itself.

Turning Tail

Ever had a piece of *a∗s*?
Turn it over, there's
P∗ssy on the other side.

> —Graffiti, Brown University

Everything should have been perfectly clear. But American men still didn't know which end was up. They chased *tail* with ardor and passion, often settling for partial satisfaction with a *piece of a∗s* (20thC.), a telling commentary both on their mental health and their knowledge of women's anatomy.

This confusion is characteristic of the multifaceted character of the words in *The Erotic Tongue*, which play not one but several parts. Consider not only the *tail*, but the *gig* (or *giggie*), the *keester*, and the *buns*, all of which have at various times stood for different sexual parts. Thoroughly confused by it all, men apparently decided that the only safe way was to treat them all with equal affection.

Steering to the Rear

Ten percent of the people at UNC have hemorrhoids.
The other ninety percent are perfect *a∗s-holes*.

> —Graffiti, University of North
> Carolina

The *a∗s* is a dependable part that holds up its end of things. As the *seat* (19thC.), it certainly knows its place.

It would be wrong, however, to think it just rests there. This is a hard-working part that quietly goes about its business at the orifice, functioning as the *s**t-hole* (19thC.), the *brown bucket* (20thC.), the *dirt road* (early 20thC.), and the *poop-chute* (20thC.). However, there's little recognition paid its work, and no more insulting a remark than being called "a *f**king a*s-hole.*"

Getting Off One's A*s

With an arrow so broad,
He shott him into the *backe-syde.*

> —Joseph Ritson, ed., "Robin Hood,"
> 1795

The entire experience proved so puzzling that some could no longer locate what they were looking for. They looked to the *backside* (16thC.), the *posterior* (c. 1614), the *rear end* (c. 1920s) or the *behind* (described in the OED as something "in the rear of anything moving" or "the rear part of a person or garment").

Not knowing where else to turn, they came up with the *lower back* (late 19thC.). And in 1912, British papers recorded news from South Africa of a certain Lord Methuen who had been wounded in the *fleshy part of the thigh.* Most thought this all very *a*s backward* (or *bass ackward*, both 20thC.), a somewhat strange expression used to describe something that's askew or out of sync. So too with the expression itself, *a*s-forward* being a much more accurate description of the condition.

Global Perspective

I've had it up to my *keister* with these leaks to the press.

> —Ronald Reagan, summer of 1983. His
> speech-writer substituted *keister* for
> "tush."

The *a*s* was soon totally alien to us. From France we borrowed the *derriere*, made especially popular by women's magazines in the late nineteenth century. From German, via the Yiddish, we came up with the *tochis* (early 19thC., also *tochus, tochos, tochis, tokus,* etc.), affectionately referred to as the *tush* or the *tushie(y)* (both 20thC.).

The Germans also saved our *rump* (since mid-15thC.), from

rumpf, "the trunk of the body." But it's the Italians we can thank for the *labonza* (mid-20thC.), a word popularized by Jackie Gleason as an *a∗s,* though in the original Italian it meant a stomach.

It was the *keester* (also *keister, keyster, kiester, kister*) (mid-19thC.), however, that truly got us into Dutch, from *keest,* "kernel" or "core" — the best part of anything. A contentious group of wordsmiths has argued that it originated with the Yiddish through the German *kiste,* "box, chest, or basket." They made the connection either through the round, basketlike shape or — and this is really reaching for it — went back to a time when sneak-thieves used the orifice as a place in which to hide stolen items, giving us the practical side of the ever-popular suggestion, "You know what you can do with it!"

Everybody may love somebody's *a∗s* but, like Rodney Dangerfield, it "simply gets no respect." People kick *a∗s* and call it stupid. There's something about it that just does not sit right. In the anatomical hierarchy it is considered the dregs, the pits, if not the absolute *bottom.*

The Bottom Line

There seems to be no end to the calumny. When it was time for Shakespeare to make the weaver in *Midsummer Night's Dream* into an *a∗s,* what did he call him but *Bottom.* No matter, *Bottom*'s tops in our book. As *b∗lls* are the repository of courage, the *bottom* is the seat of endurance. In eighteenth- and nineteenth-century England, it was synonymous with grit and perserverance, and good soldiers were often described as having "a great deal of *bottom.*"

It may well be our lowest part, but *bottom* comes directly from the old English for "ground" or "the soil" and, according to its Indo-European roots, means "to place firmly and securely." When you rest on your *bottom,* you're on pretty solid ground.

That's more than we can say for the Soviet Foreign Minister who, at the Vienna Summit Conference several years ago, attempted to use the word in a toast to the wife of the U.S. Secretary of State — without a translator. "To a gracious lady," said he. "Up your *bottom.*"

Esquire magazine hit rock bottom in 1943-44 when the Postmaster General threatened to curtail its circulation for printing such suggestive words as *backside, bottom,* and *bawdy house. Bottom* needs no defense. We've known it as the *sitting part of man* since 1794. Its distinguished progeny include *botty* (19thC.), *b.t.m.* (late 19thC.), and the *booty,* as in the 1984 disco hit, "Shake Your *Booty*!"

A Bum Rap

Despite the *bottom*'s excellent lineage and its deserving a fair shake, most people still treat it as nothing but a no-good *bum.* The *bum*'s been with us since the late fourteenth century, but around 1790 it fell into disrespect, and since 1840 it has been made to feel especially unwelcome in England. When an Al Jolson film opened there in 1930, the Lord Chancellor, Britain's public censor, had it retitled, "Hallelujah, I'm a Tramp!"

The American tramp, however, had nothing to do with the English *bum.* The British *bum* has been with us as an *a*∗*s* since the late fourteenth century and its origins are thought to be onomatopoeic. (It couldn't be a contraction of *bottom,* which wasn't used in that sense until later.) The American *bum,* as hobo, goes back to the German *bommeln,* "to loaf or loiter" and the *bummler,* "an idler or loafer," who didn't appear here until the first major wave of German immigration during the 1850s.

Only occasionally do the two converge as when you "give someone the bum's rush," picking up a loiterer or trouble-maker by the seat of his pants and throwing him off the premises. That's also a *bummer,* a real bad experience (*c.* 1960s), and a possible tie-in with the earlier *bummler.* John Ciardi passes on an intriguing bit of folk etymology suggested by *Musical Heritage Magazine* (May 2, 1977), attributing *bummer's* origin to the famed eighteenth-century organ-maker, Johann Jakob Bommer, "whose organs were so much admired they gave rise to the expression 'It's a real Bommer.'"

Unfortunately, so's the explanation.

The Real Bad A∗s

Bums are also people. Among our more famous *bums,* we

have the notorious *Roby Douglas,* a mythical nineteenth-century nautical figure noted for his "one eye and a stinking breath," as well as *Gluteus Maximus,* "the notorious blowhard Roman general." People were also hostile to *Heinie,* from the amalgam of Heinrich and *hind end,* used in a derogatory fashion to designate a German soldier or a person of German descent during World Wars I and II. Such nuisances were often considered a *pain in the Frances* (19th-20thC.). When the pain became especially severe, you might even find yourself with your *a∗s in a sling* (mid-20thC.).

The standard response to such discomfort is, "Ask my *Nancy!*" (c. 1810-1910). This, however, is not an especially effective recommendation since *Nancy* is generally not capable of answering back, although on occasion *Brother Round Mouth* speaks (c. 1810-70).

Let's Face It

Appearances notwithstanding, how could anyone dispute the *a∗s*'s fine disposition? Just look at that *Sunday face* (c. 1860), decked out with its *broad smile* and its *vertical grin* (18thC.). Few will ever forget that classic mouth, those *two fine cheeks* (mid-18thC.), and *ne'er a nose* (c. 1750).

Some would liken its roundness to a *moon* (both as a noun and a verb, mid-20th C.), as when an avid female fan of the New York Yankees in the summer of 1980 *mooned* for the players on the team bus — showing her "admiration" for them.

Still can't see it? Obviously a problem with your *blind eye* (18thC.). Check it out through the *monocular eyeglass* (c. 1860-1910). Foresight is flawed, but hindsight is always 20/20.

Sitting Pretty

You could *tickle my Toby!* (c. 1675) or *kiss my blind cheeks* (17th-20thC.) if a closer look doesn't show our *tush* to be really friendly, and none more so than our dear *Fanny.* In England she was originally a *c∗∗t* via Fanny Hill, the high-flying heroine of John Cleland's raunchy eighteenth-century novel, *Memoirs of a Woman of Pleasure.*

In America, however, *Fanny* has always been the *butt* of all our jokes. Our *Fanny* derives from *fundament* (13thC. for *bottom*), and she was shortened and punned successfully into *funniment*, *fun*, *funny*, and at last *Fanny*. But there was nothing funny about her problems in the States. As late as 1929, *Fanny* found herself on B.F. Keith's list of forbidden expressions that vaudeville performers were not allowed to use on the stage. Instead, they preferred *the part that went over the fence last*, *the caboose*, and *where the sun never shines*.

Today, she's out from under that cloud. She is well respected, accepted by all, and travels in the best of circles together with the *tush* and the *derriere*.

The Other Cheek

Still displeased with the choices? You can always fall back on your *prat* (16thC.), a fine word which originated with the Old English *praet* for "prank," which, in addition to being an *a*s*, also doubled as a *vagina* during the nineteenth century. It was from the first meaning that many a vaudevillian and silent film star developed his pratfalls, building entire comedy routines about them. There being no better way to guarantee a laugh than by falling on one's *a*s*.

Show biz also gave us the *bippy* (mid-20thC.), made famous by Steve Allen from "bipinnate": having two parts equally distributed on the sides of a common axis. It was a sure winner. As Allen might have remarked:

"Bet your sweet *bippy*?"
"I'll see you and raise you two cheeks."

The End

"In what part of her body stands Ireland?"
"Marry, Sir, in the buttocks. I found it out by the bogs" [latrine].

—Shakespeare, *Comedy of Errors*

But as they say, the *end* is near. As the sun sets on beautiful *Spice Island* (c. 1810-50) and the *moon* begins to rise, we weigh anchor from *Dilberry Creek*, also known as *Stinkhole Bay*, and set sail for the *Hinterland* and the *Western End*.

It's no easy feat to negotiate the *Windward Passage,* what with those treacherous gale-force winds. But ours is a sturdy vessel, wide in the *bow, poop,* and *stern* (late 16thC.), with the requisite *porthole* and an extraordinary *fantail* for the overhanging portion of the *stern,* from which some think we got our *Fanny* — all very nautical, but nice.

It's with a touch of sadness that we leave behind those magnificent promontories that, "plump, smooth and prominent, form'd luxuriant tracts of luxuriant snow that luxuriantly fill the eye . . ." (Cleland), *pleasant eminences* (Shakespeare) that have encouraged us all to scale new heights.

In the tradition of good service, older terms for *breasts* include the *dugs* (*c.* 1530), from the Danish *daegge,* and the Swedish *daegga,* "to suckle a child." *Dugs* long represented *teats* or *nipples;* now the OED considers their use as applied to a woman "contemptuous." The *paps* (*c.* 1200) also had their day, originating with the first sounds made by a baby, identified with its call for food and its main source of nourishment, the mother's *breasts. Pap* later became synonymous with a food that was soft or liquid, providing us with the word for something of very little substance, "pap," as well as a name for the food itself, Pablum. This is to say nothing of the baby's end product, soft *s**t,* or *poppycock.*

† † †

We've also got our animal friends such as *cat's head, cats and ditties* (rhyming cockney slang) as well as the *two young roes,* from the Song of Solomon. Can't see it? A few years ago a story made the rounds of a young woman in a bikini who was bathing in the surf when a particularly violent wave hit her and swept off the top of her bathing suit. To avoid embarrassment, she embraced her nakedness with both arms. As she was making her way to shore, a young boy stopped her and innocently inquired, "Lady, those sure are cute little puppies. You suppose I could have the one with the pink nose?"

† † †

Décolletage or *cleavage* became high fashion in seventeenth-century France, where it was even given a special name, "the well of sanctification or dedication." We later knew it as the *mammaelar trench* (19thC.) and the *great divide* (20thC.).

† † †

Samuel Johnson included *arse* in his *Dictionary of the English Language* (1755) and so did Francis Grose, in his *Classical Dictionary of the Vulgar Tongue* (1785), but the last writer to spell *arse* in full until 1930 was Jonathan Swift, in his *Battle of the Books* (1704), when the spider asked the fly, "Do you think I have nothing else to do in the devil's name, but to mend and repair after your *arse?*"

When someone asked Dr. Johnson its meaning, he referred to it as the part on which we sit. His questioner responded, "Do you mean a chair, Doctor?" You too can sit on it, dear reader, as the *sit-me-down* (19thC.), the *sit-upon* (19thC.), the *rumble seat* (c. 1920s), the *seat of honor, shame,* and *vengeance* as well as the plain old *seat* (all 19thC.), there being no better place for your favorite *flesh-cushions* (Cleland).

† † †

The *tail* (14thC.) comes from the Indo-European, describing an appendage at the rear end of an animal. In England, it began life as a *pr**k,* evolved into an *a*s* during the fourteenth century, and later became a *c**t* and a taboo expression around 1750. In the States, *tail* quickly made an *a*s* of itself.

Gig took an alternative route, starting off as a *wanton* (17th-18thC.), reaching midlife (19th-20thC.) as a *rectum,* as in *"Up your giggie!"* and toward the middle of the twentieth century began to settle in as a *vagina.*

Other multi-sexual words include the *keester* (*c**t,* early 20thC., *a*s,* mid-20thC.), and the *bun. Bun* did itself proud as the *c**t* early on (late 17thC.), coming as it did from the *bunny,* but in the plural as an *a*s* it probably derived from the bakery shelf and its relationship to *tarts* and other assorted pastries.

In the singular, however, *bun* still refers to the *c**t,* even as a bakery item. Including the hot-cross buns, which some put the sign of the cross on, to help soften their erotic character. But what's a *bun* anyway without dough, without which we couldn't get off our *duff* (mid-20thC.). The *gh* in dough was once pronounced like an *f,* and the word itself meant the soft and spongy part of anything.

† † †

The medical profession has always treated the *a∗s* less as a whole than by its component parts: the *anus* (since mid-17thC.), the posterior opening of the alimentary canal; the *rectum* (since mid-16thC.), the large end of the bowel which connects to the *anus;* and the *buttocks* (14thC.). The *buttocks* especially took their lumps – *butt,* the bottom, the thicker end of anything, a swelling caused by the Indo-European *bhau,* "a bruise."

† † †

Gluteus maximus is the largest of the muscles in the buttocks, the others being *medius* and *minimus* and the province of your average M.D. Any internal questions should be referred to your *proctologist.* A Brown University medical sociologist reports that proctologists are commonly referred to in the profession as *Rear Admirals.* Coincidentally, Dr. Reinhold Aman, editor of *Maledicta,* adds that when former President Jimmy Carter was treated for a hemorrhoidal condition in 1978, the attending physician was Dr. William Lukash, a real *Rear Admiral* in the U.S. Navy.

SIX

Different Strokes

WARNING

*This chapter is about masturbation and could be
dangerous to your health.*

As this branch of uncleanliness, viz., Sinning with a
person's own Self, is the most general of any Sin of Im-
purity . . . instructions concerning it are the most
wanted in the world to awaken the Guilty, and deter
the Innocent and Unwary from falling into it, through
Inadvertence or Ignorance.

> — *The Crime of Onan or the heinous Vice
> of Self-Defilement with all its Dismal
> Consequences,* 1724

The mother of the household stands outside the bathroom
door hyperventilating. A gentle knock. No response. Knocking
escalates into a rapid rhythmic tempo, becomes a pounding, finally degenerates into a series of irregular thuds. A shrill scream
and the all too familiar refrain, "What are you doing in there?"

Inside, oblivious to it all and comfortably ensconced against
the outside world, is you-know-who doing *you-know-what.*

Little boy sits on the lavatory pan,
Gently caressing his little old man.
Flip, flop, into the tank,
Christopher Robin is having a *whank.*

> — Anon., 20thC.

Swinging Single

"With whom did you first do it?"
"I was alone at the time."

— Woody Allen

The parts can be a whole lot of fun when put together properly, but individually they're also a source of enjoyment.

Playing with oneself (18th-20thC.) is a worthwhile activity for both sexes and one of the most rewarding of all the sexual practices. In terms of orgasmic efficacy, it seldom fails us. Alfred Kinsey reported that 95 percent of the time it is successful, with 75 percent of the participants attaining *climax* (20thC.) in less than four minutes. Yet some consider it as *wasting time* (20thC.), as does Richard Spears (*Slang and Euphemism*), who arbitrarily lumped all 127 synonyms for the act under that heading.

Detractors apparently didn't realize its potential as the source of real *self-pleasure* (20thC.) and the ultimate expression of *self-love* (20thC.). Why, even the Germans consider it *selbst befriedigung,* satisfaction of self by self.

Self-love? Why not? George Carlin tried it and so enjoyed the pleasure of his company that he sent himself flowers afterward.

The Yanks Are Coming

Love thy neighbor as thyself.
What am I supposed to do — *jerk him off,* too?

— Rodney Dangerfield, 1982

Most men who *play with themselves* generally *jerk off* (19th-20thC.). The basic all-American *jerk-off* consists of a motion that is quick and suddenly arrested, a stop, a sudden pull, throw, thrust, or twist: one, two, cha-cha-cha. You *bring it up by hand, bring it down by hand,* and *bring it off by hand* (all 19thC.). For variation, you may *jerk jelly, jerk juice,* or *jerk iron* (all 19thC.), as you are disposed.

In second place we have the *jack-off,* from *Jack,* an old personification of the male organ. The British, on the other hand, mostly *whank off* (19th-20thC.), also *wank, wank off, whang off,* and *whank.* No one really knows where the *whank* comes from, though a good guess might be a combination of *whack* and *bang*.

Alexander Portnoy, Crown Prince of the *hand-job* (20thC.), favored none of the above, preferring instead to *whack off* (20thC.). Portnoy's *whack-offs* are of legendary proportions. He soloed at fifteen on the 151 bus from New York. They still talk about his famed three-finger *hand-job* with staccato half-inch strokes up from the base.

Success didn't come easy for Portnoy. It took hours of hard work, determination, discipline, and practice, to say nothing of an understanding mother.

> Now this time don't flush, do you hear me, Alex? I have to see what's in the bowl.
>
> — Philip Roth, Mother Portnoy in *Portnoy's Complaint*, 1967

Doing It by the Book

> The good thing about *masturbation* is you don't have to dress up for it.
>
> — Truman Capote

Though *masturpation* had a brief fling in 1621, officially it's *masturbation* (*c.* 1766) — one of those elusive words that etymologists can't seem to get a grip on. Some think it originates with *manus,* Latin for "hand," and *stupare,* for "defile," hence "to defile by hand." A nice theory for moralists, but one which would give us *manustrapation,* and a chorus of st-t-t-tuttering acned teenagers. Others, including the authors of the venerable Oxford English Dictionary, found its roots in *mastitubari,* which they translate as "to disturb the male member," though some believe that it is the seed (*mas*) that is disturbed. Either way, a simple act appears to have left the entire scholarly community in a highly agitated state.

The World's First Jerks

Masturbation has a long and distinguished history, and we're at no loss for words to describe it. Ancient Egyptian papyri reveal how Atum-Ra created the universe when he *"frigged with his fist and took the pleasure of emission."* He is said to have cried out, "I was the one who *f**ked with my fist* and *milked with my hand."*

Self-manipulation (19th-20thC.) was sanctified among the Egyptians and was an important part of their rituals. True believers were encouraged to engage in the practice to provide food for the gods and to ensure a fertile land.

According to Gordon Rattray Taylor's *Sex in History,* rivers were an especially important part of the gods' work. The sacred Nile represented the *masturbatory ejaculation* of the god Usiris, who controlled the rise and fall of the river by *"alternate continuous manipulation and regurgitation of his gushing genitory."* But the Nile was not unique. For devout Hindus, the Ganges flowed from the throbbing head of the divine *lingam,* as did the Sea of Soma. And among the Assyrians and the Babylonians there was a particular deity who was noted for having *"fertilized the fertile crescent with his superfructiferous seed by a torrential act of self-stimulation."*

It was an exciting time when man literally had the whole world in his hands.

Crafty Southpaws

The Greeks and Romans also felt especially comfortable with the practice. Juvenal, Diogenes, Laertius, Ovid, Scioppius, Pliny, and Aristophanes all wrote freely and openly on the topic, and there was seemingly little stigma attached to it. But the right hand apparently didn't know what the left hand was doing, and *masturbation* soon came to be considered *sinister.* That's Latin for "the left hand," the hand most closely associated with *masturbation* and other "unclean practices," such as wiping after *defecation.*

Any wonder that the word has come down to us through the years associated with evil doings, or that left-handed baseball pitchers are considered particularly flaky?

Waste Not

But for the best source of *masturbation* lore, you have to turn to the Old Testament. There you'll find the story of the granddaddy of them all, the man who allegedly started the practice, the person many consider *Mister Masturbator:* Onan.

Ironically, though his name is closely identified with *self-manipulation,* the truth as revealed in Genesis 38:9 is that he never once raised a hand on his own behalf.

Onan and Er were both sons of Judah. One day, God got so upset with Er's behavior that he upped and slew him, leaving Er's widow alone and unattended. Hating to see a good woman barren and going to waste, and in keeping with the Levite tradition, Judah turned to Onan and said, *"Go in unto* thy brother's wife and marry her, and *raise up seed* to thy brother." *A bit of home gardening,* as they say in the trade.

For God's sake, Onan *went in unto* his brother's wife, which also translates as he *fallowed her field,* but knowing that the seed should not be his, *left her unseeded after plowing,* i.e., he spilled it on the ground. Medieval rabbinical scholars described the act as *threshing within and winnowing without.* Masters and Johnson call it *coitus interruptus.* Whichever, what he did proved so displeasing that the Lord slew him on the spot. And mistakenly, Onan's boo-boo came down to us through the centuries as the *solitary evil.*

Onanism (18th-20thC.) was man's first somewhat unoriginal sin: both a fall from grace and a nasty spill.

Bible Thumpers

Masturbation never sat well with the ancient Jews. *Self-abuse* (early 18thC.) was the basis for the banishment of Ishmael, and God caused the great flood in part because of the actions of Noah's contemporaries who *spilled their semen on trees and rocks* and constantly *abused their fountains.*

The act once even brought down the house. While a crowd of thousands watched, Samson, captive of the Philistines, was forced *to make sport of himself.* Pained, blinded, and humiliated, his last words to Yahweh were, "May I be avenged to the Philistines for the *draining of my fountain."*

Samson had let it all hang out. Accordingly, he is described in ancient Hebrew as a *sâhug,* a *phallus-beater,* a term also found in Job 12:4 and Jeremiah 20:7. This translates also as a "laughing stock." Our contemporary equivalent is a *jerk* — one whose brains have been addled through *masturbation*.

Good to the Last Drop

It was no laughing matter to the Jews. Friends of the Foetus — the contemporary anti-abortionists who mark life from the moment of conception — have nothing on their Hebraic precursors, who considered the *seed* as the beginning of life.

This led to a number of rabbinical prohibitions against behavior likely to lead to *masturbation*. Males were advised not to touch the *penis* while urinating. They were also warned against wearing tight pants, riding bareback, having lascivious daydreams, and looking at either one's own sexual *member* or that of another. It was also strongly recommended that a boy sleep on his side rather than face up.

With all these restrictions, is it any wonder that Jewish boys aren't any good with their hands? Or that in nineteenth-century England they referred to the practice as *cynic friction, keeping down the census,* and *simple infanticide?*

God'll Get You for That

If God had intended us not to *masturbate*, He would have made our arms shorter.

— George Carlin

Never to be outdone by Judaism, Roman Catholicism made sexuality its special concern. In the seventh century, Theodore of Canterbury issued a penitential for offenders against morality in which he recorded a variety of forbidden practices, including *masturbation*. By the twelfth century, the Church's anti-sex campaign was in high gear.

Saint Thomas Aquinas helped matters by arranging the sins hierarchically, creating a "top forty" of sexuality. Though *masturbation* trailed far behind the other *unnatural vices,* it outranked in seriousness *fornication,* an offense deemed more serious than murder. The penitential codes contained twenty-five paragraphs on the topic of *self-abuse* by lay people and even more for cases when the sin was performed by the clergy. As far as *rape, adultery,* and *incest* were concerned, it was no contest. *Masturbation* was the winner, hands down.

Doing It Religiously

Almost as if in reprisal, people began striking back at the Church through language. *Boxing the Jesuit and getting cockroaches* is an anticlerical expression dating back to the eighteenth century. It originated with sailors and was defined by a lexicographer of the times as "a crime much practiced by the reverend fathers." It was yet another way of saying that man cannot live by a fistful of Hail Marys alone. To box is to enclose, as with one's hand. No one really knows, however, why the Jesuits were associated with such activity. Speculation is that it was their high standing in the Church and their propensity for manipulation.

As to cockroaches (perhaps nothing more than a dreadful pun on c**k), why not? If God can visit boils, locusts, famines and the like upon us, cockroaches are certainly not beyond Him. Cockroaches may well be an important first sign. Check with your friends. Do they show any of the primary symptoms? Has hair begun to grow on their palms? Have they started going bald? Are their eyes bloodshot; their brains going soft?

Getting cockroaches merely clinches the diagnosis. Reach out to your friends. Plead with them to stop before it's too late. Encourage them to drop Dear Abby a line. Have them see their clergymen, seek out professional help, or, if the condition persists, an exterminator of their choice.

A Penance for Your Thoughts

Some were so angered by the Church's attitude that they turned violent. They even went so far as to *shoot the bishop* (19thC.), a form of mayhem also known as a *wet dream* (19thC.), which the Church deemed a serious offense. The penalty for *shooting the bishop* was singing seven penitential psalms, to be done immediately after rising from the debauched state, followed by another thirty in the morning. If the offense occurred while falling asleep in church, the guilty party was required to

107

sing the entire psalter. No provision appears to have been made for those of us who are tone deaf.

Night Time Is the Right Time

Man who go to bed with problem in hand wake up in the morning with solution at his finger tips.

— Teen-age babble, mid-20thC.

It was only an *involuntary seminal emission* (19thC.), but when the evening air is thick with activity, you're talking about a case of *nocturnal pollution* (17th-19thC.) and perhaps the need for an environmental impact statement.

Claude Francois Lallemand, a nineteenth-century professor of medicine, cited the practice as causing the genitals to deteriorate, the spermatozoa to decrease in number and vigor, and the muscles, particularly the heart, to weaken. "All sensations decrease, sight is endangered, the mind is threatened, and the usual end result is idiocy and death."

A contemporary of his, British scientist Sir William Acton, assured us that although widespread and out of hand, *pollution* could be controlled. His program: a cold-water enema at bedtime and cauterization of the uretha with silver nitrate, and, when nothing else worked, tying a cord around the *penis* before retiring. The patient should simply think of himself as being at the end of his rope.

Vice for the Lovelorn

The world took a major stride toward sexual enlightenment when authorities began to treat *masturbation* as an appropriate subject for medicine and physiology. We even had new terms for the practice, such as *autoeroticism* (also *autoerotism,* 19th-20thC., popularized by Havelock Ellis), *manual orgasm* and *ipsation* (both 19thC.), making it more a technical than an antitheological exercise.

But though the experts thought they had separated sexual behavior from theology, and introduced it as a subject for scientific study, it still remained a moral issue, a *vice, secret and solitary.*

Misspent Youth

Parents soon joined the Church and the authorities in trying to curb the practice. Mothers and fathers considered it their sworn duty to prevent their children from *throwing the tantrum* (17thC.) and *going off with their marbles.* Father strapped his son's *privates* into a small metal cage prior to bedding him down for the night, so as to insure a hands-off policy. Just in case, Dad kept the key close by if nature should inopportunely call in the middle of the night. More elaborate cages came equipped with accessories – spikes which surrounded the perimeter or tiny bells which went off should an *erection* occur.

Harriet Beecher Stowe warned parents "that certain parts of the body are not to be touched except for purpose of cleanliness, and that the most dreadful suffering comes from disobeying these commands" (from her book on domestic science, designed "to help American women maintain Economical, Healthful, Beautiful and Christian Homes"). Victorian nannies admonished their charges, "If you play with it, it will fall off." But the beat went on. Kids continued to practice *paw-paw tricks* and *pinch the cat.*

A hundred years later, American children were still playing at *pocket pool.* There was simply no suppressing it. In the 1940s, a favorite children's radio program was "The Buster Brown Radio Show." It featured Froggy, the gremlin, who, upon the request, "Plunk your magic twanger, Froggy," would transport us all to storyland. Little did they know that *plunking one's twanger* was part of a tradition that has been carrying kids on erotic journeys since the seventeenth century.

Present Arms

Little boys grow up into big boys, and the military was right there to pick up where Mom and Dad left off. *Mounting a corporal and four* (late 18thC. for the thumb and four fingers) has always been a *soldier's joy* (19thC.), but army rules prohibited the recruit from playing with his *weapon.*

By the twentieth century sergeants began disrupting *the blanket drill,* greeting the dawning of each day with "Hands off c**ks, feet in socks!" Also, "Drop your c**ks and grab your socks"), favorites both in this man's army and the R.A.F. There's nothing like military discipline to make men come clean.

Pound for Pound

You can lick our chops, but you can't beat our meat.

—Sign in a butcher shop, Providence,
Rhode Island, 1980

If talk of weaponry has you nervous, remember, *masturbation* is a rough business. It is the practice of *self-abuse* (early 18thC.), and most consider man's approach to the subject as anything but gentle. Some would even characterize it as downright heavy-handed. Over the years, man has *pulled it* (19th-20thC.), *beat it* (20thC.), *shook it up* (19thC.), *flogged it* (20thC., Aust.), *pounded it* (20thC.), *whacked it* (20thC.), and *tossed it off* (late 18th-20thC.).

"When the flesh rebels against the spirit," asked a monk of his Prior, "What do you do?" "I take my breviary and read it through," he replied. "And I," said a sanctified frater, "jump into cold water." "For my part," observed a young fellow listening in, "I settle the matter at once without ceremony: I knock the brains out of the evil one."

—Sexual humor from Victorian England

Manual Arts

Man has also been known to *pull his wire* (19th-20thC.), *pump his pickle* (20thC., Can.), or *jerk his gherkin* (mid-20thC.). But for the novice, a little rub'll do you. At the end of sixteenth century he started in *frigging* (from the Latin *friccare*, "to rub"), one of the oldest and most durable expressions for the act.

English boys were still using the term far into the eighteenth century. One student later reminisced of "fanciful delights . . . *frigging* in the school *necessary.*"

Beastly Behavior

Many chose to consign such roughhousing to the barnyard.

There, *bird in hand,* a man might *fight* or *jerk his turkey* (19thC.) or *dash his doodle. Doodle* (mid-18thC.) is a child's appellation for a *c∗∗k,* derived from the sound of crowing, "cock-a-doodle-doo." A *doodle-sack* is the likely female repository for said *doodle.* A *doodle-dasher* is a man given to habitual *self-manipulation.*

C.B.'ers today compound the mayhem by *choking the chicken.* Anyway you look at it, that's still using your *doodle,* ole buddy!

Once having put such fowl play behind him, a young man could also *come his mutton* (18thC.), *mutton* being one of those great all-purpose words for both male and female sex organs. *Coming one's mutton* has been a popular sport for lonely winter nights, though a form of recreation that farmers acknowledge only sheepishly.

Today, there's a whole new, exciting world outside the farm. Everything is now fair game, including *flogging the dolphin* (20thC.).

Why the poor dolphin? Why pick on it? Was it a matter of shape? Native intelligence? Leaping ability? Was it an accident or was it done on porpoise? No one knows.

But if you can *flog the dolphin,* there's no reason why you can't also *gallop the antelope* (20thC.).

The origin of the latter remains especially obscure. We know from the mating habits of the antelope that when a stag is frustrated in his efforts to win a female, he *masturbates* by rubbing his antlers rhythmically against a tree, often as much as three or four times daily. Truly *horny!* Though this sheds new light on the *stag party* and *stag films* (both 20thC.), it still leaves us very much in the dark on *galloping the antelope.*

Hold Everything!

When all else fails, you can always

> *Beat the pup*
> *Stroke the lizard*
> *Pump the python*
> *Peel the eel*

So dear reader, why not try your hand at it?

Slam the seal
Blast the bear
_____the_____
_____the_____
_____the_____

CAUTION

If your momma doesn't get you, Greenpeace may.

Poetry in Motion

Others sought to lend a defter touch, hoping to capture the rhythmic nature of the act. They encouraged us to *beat the meat, slam the ham,* and *flog the dog* (all mid-20thC.).

And if alliteration turns you on, you can always *paddle the pick, pound the pud,* and *pull the pudding.* If that doesn't suit you, *pull the pick* and *paddle the pudding.* No need to stop there! Why not also *paddle the pick, pull the pud,* and *pound the pudding*? Far better than lifting that barge and toting that bale.

Few can handle their meter better than Allen Ginsberg:

Pope my parts
Pop my pot
Poke my pap
Pit my plum.

– from "Fie My Fum"

Having One's Hand Full

Tired of *playing solitaire* (20thC.)? Nobody said you had to do it alone.

Ordinarily a do-it-yourself proposition, the game can also be played by two, as in *chopsticks* (20thC., U.S.), after the piano exercise of the same name in which hands are crossed over. Three or more persons constitute a *circle jerk* (20thC., U.S.), the original *theater in the round.*

Those fearful of taking their lives in their hands can always find outside help. You can turn to *Second-Hand Rose* or your friendly *fricatrice.* She's descended from the Ladies of Lesbos, whom Catullus described as standing at crossways and in alleys "to *jerk off* the high-souled sons of Rome."

In Merrie England, a female *masturbator* of men was called a *shagstress* or a *milk-woman* (both 18thC.). The price list in a particular eighteenth-century *brothel* featured a bargain two-guinea job by "a young, agreeable person, sociable, with a white skin and soft hand. Polly Nimblewrist from Oxford or Jenny Speedyhand from Mayfair." Today? Get thee to a massage parlor and ask for a *local.* It needn't be costly; you may *spend* whatever you like.

Lady Be Good

And what of women? A whole chapter and hardly a mention of the fairer sex.

Both men and women *play with themselves* (18th-20thC.). Though the language of *self-help* (20thC.) is expressive, you'll find only a few isolated phrases describing women engaged in the activity. Rare examples include to *jill off* (as opposed to *jack off*), *tickle the clitty,* and indulge in *rubbin' nubbin.*

Historically, few people have taken female *masturbation* seriously. There's little reference to the practice in Judaism, and Roman Catholic manuals of sexual ethics that treat male *masturbation* as "a grave moral disorder" simply dismiss female efforts as acts of mere *lewdness.*

It's been a well kept-secret.

In 1846, Mary Gove Nichols, a lecturer on hygiene, shocked her audience by publicly revealing that women also did it. In 1877, Dr. John Harvey Kellogg of Battle Creek, Michigan, brother of the man who introduced modern breakfast foods to the world, snapped and crackled with indignation as he popped the question, "Do you know what your children are doing?" He then provided thirty-nine telltale signs to help parents determine if their young ones were into *vice.* For girls, those which were particularly telling included lack of breast development; pimples on the face or, especially, on the forehead; fingernail biting; eating clay, slate, pencils, plaster, chalk, and other indigestibles; and habitually moist, cold hands.

Other critics warned of even more dire consequences: the

grave, the madhouse, or, worse yet, the *brothel*. There were caveats galore, but we had precious few phrases to describe the sin itself.

Is it that for a woman, sex without a man was inconceivable and hence . . . well . . . uh . . . not conceivable? Or was it because men, who for so long controlled the written word, deliberately excluded that which did not flatter their king-size egos?

If you'd believe man, this delicate creature's sensibilities exist on a higher plane. Her life's joy is in pleasing him. She is either his sweet madonna, or his very own *whore*. There's no way she could enjoy existence apart from him. As for seeking sexual pleasure? And without him? Absurd! Finding it by herself? *B*lls!*

At long last, women have begun taking matters into their own hands. But man has been slow to come around, finding it especially difficult to accept the idea of women's *self-pleasure*. He is now on the spot. Though groping for an answer, he still can't put his finger on it.

The Final Stroke: Good Vibes

Help is on the way. Recent years have seen the introduction of technology to *masturbation* with *vibrators* (also called *cordless massagers*) and an entire array of *sexual aids*. Women who employ them are said to *catch a buzz*. But, as they say, "You ain't seen nothin' yet" – Not until you've tried *Accu-jac*, the trade name for a device that in time should, deservedly, become generic, and surely nothing to shake a stick at.

The marriage of technology and the time-proven art promises to carry us all to new heights of *self-pleasure*. We have seen the future, but it is clearly out of our hands.

The medieval *Zohar,* or *Book of Splendor,* the guide to orthodox Jewish mysticism, defined a man's participation in a sexual act without the benefit of a woman as the penultimate no-no, citing *wet dreams* and *onanistic practices* as grave sins. It asked the question, "What brings man to grips with himself?" and answers, "The Devil made him do it!"

The Devil indeed! For the *Zohar* says the evil spirits of the night encouraged such practices because every escaped seed provided one of them with bodily form. When a man finally died, all those midnight rides caught up with him. The little demonic bastards he had sired swarmed about him like wild bees, crying out, "You are our father!" They tug and pluck at the dead man, causing pain enough to remind him and God of his sins.

Moral: In a world perched at the brink of self-destruction and drowned in self-despair, man's individual woes are nothing but a drop in the bucket.

† † †

Saint Thomas Aquinas made a major distinction between *natural* and *unnatural vices.* The latter were the worst and included, in descending order of gravity, *sodomy, fellatio, cunnilingus, pederasty,* and, finally, *masturbation.* Aquinas treated *masturbation* as *uncleanness* or *effeminacy* and described it as "procuring pollution without any *copulation* for the sake of *veneral pleasure.*" He considered it the least grievous of all the *unnatural vices,* "as it merely omits connections with another." As usual, the Church was thinking babies, new customers; sex exclusively for pleasure was clearly unacceptable.

† † †

Shakespeare hinted at the consequences of *masturbation* by referring to it as the means of *weakness and debility (As You Like It).* Not much later, scientists and medical men such as William Andrus Alcott cited the proven effects of indulging in the practice of *self-pollution* (early 17th-19thC.). Their litany of resultant ills included St. Vitus' dance, idiocy, apoplexy, blindness, consumption, and hypochondria.

† † †

Krafft-Ebing (*Psychopathia Sexualis,* 1886) saw the *secret vice* as the essential cause of most sexual deviation. "It despoils the unyielding bud of perfume and beauty and leaves behind only the coarse, animal desire for sexual satisfaction."

Paolo Mantegazza, the anthropologist, did him one better:

> This nauseous stench of *solitary vice* continues to contaminate every vein of our body social. It is an odor of moral decay, a moldy sexual smell on all sides with thousands of young men and girls spilling in the sheets or in dark passageways mankind's sovereign.

But for a Dr. Herbert (*Fundamentals in Sexual Ethics,* 1920) it was simply *the vice,* as if there were no other worthy of consideration. "It plucks the flower before the fruit has ripened, and when the true need comes, goes out empty."

Freud was later to take it less seriously, likening the activity to something akin to thumb-sucking.

A best-seller in 1983 was *Liberating Masturbation: A Meditation on Self-Love,* by Betty Dodson. This underground classic has sold more than 130,000 copies and generated over a half-million dollars' worth of business. The author has held countless workshops in *sex* showing women how "to claim their *orgasms.*" ("That one over there . . . that's mine!")

It's women like Ms. Dodson who have shown the way from *self-abuse* to *self-love.* Her workshops have proven so popular that she is now holding them for men as well. Eschewing the *quickie,* she treats *masturbation* as a ritual of sorts.

† † †

Accu-jac features an "external mode" for men that powers a clear, pliant sheath which slides up and down the *penis* and an "internal mode" that powers a six-inch *dildo* whose speed and length of stroke can be controlled. It's all completely automatic, with a control panel that provides the option of varying the length of the stroke or depth of penetration as well as the speed of the airflow and alternating massage. The unit can be used by one person or up to four simultaneously, depending on the model and the options, and you may select the male sleeves from six different shapes and nine different sizes and from two different *dildos* for the internal mode.

The *penis* has always faced stiff competition from the *dildo* as a noun (17th-20thC.) and as a verb (17th-18thC.), meaning to arouse a woman by digitation and fondling of her privates.

Partridge thinks the *dildo* originates with the Italian *diletto*, "delight." The OED cites a *dildo* as a particular kind of tree or shrub with cylindrical form.

Dildos were once made of ivory, glass, porcelain, and wood, often beautifully decorated and dressed with handsome leather covers. Some also came with a leather squeeze bag which one would fill with tree sap. Today, they are made of soft latex with a rubber squeeze bulb.

They've gone by many names. In the nineteenth century we knew them as *bientateurs* (Fr., "do-gooders"), a *godemiche* (from the Latin, "I enjoy myself"), and a *consolateur* (of which there is little to be said).

SEVEN

Act One

Contemporary theatre at its finest. A turgid melodrama in one lascivious act, featuring *the sweet young thing* and *Mr. Right.* See him overcome by *passion* and seized by unbridled *lust.* Watch the hitherto unsullied damsel fight to retain her honor.

FOR MATURE AUDIENCES

Now that we have properly named *IT,* and also mastered the parts, it's time we finally got our *act* together. So let's *get it on* (*c.* 1970s, counterculture) or, as the British say, let's *have it off* (20thC.). A bit of high drama and low comedy. We begin with the chief actors in the piece and the forces that move them, then go on to the preliminaries, the *act* itself, variations thereof, and finally the results.

Thank Heaven for Little Girls

'Tisn't beauty, so to speak, nor good talk necessarily. It's just *it.* Some women'll stay in a man's memory if they once walk down a street.

> —Rudyard Kipling, *Traffics and Discoveries,* 1904

On center stage we have a *knock-out* (*c.* 1940s), the *sweet young thing*—a real *eyeful* (*c.* 1920s), an *armful* (*c.* 1930s), a *cutie* (*c.* 1919), a *real stunner* (*c.* 1862), and a *good looker* (*c.* 1894). She's got *bedroom eyes, plenty of dissa and datta,* and is just o-o-o-zing *S.A.*—*sex appeal* (*c.* 1920s-40s).

118

The sounds you hear as she enters the room are: *"oomph"* (a sexual moan), *"unh, unh"* (Partridge suggests a bull's mating bellow), *"boing boing"* (ringing his bell), *"zing"* (go the strings of my heart) and *"va-va-va-voom!"* all courtesy of the forties. Or *"I say, what a smasher!"* (c. 1945, Eng.).

Some would simply suggest that she has plenty of *it*. *It* first caught the public's fancy during the twenties, when it was made popular by Clara Bow, the original *it* girl, star of the 1927 film *It*, based on a best-selling book of the same name by Elinor Glyn.

In short, she's a real *doll* (since c. 1904) — that is, if you don't care about her past. A *doll* was a common *harlot* through the seventeenth and early eighteenth centuries, and both *doll* and *dolly* occasionally served as *mistress* and *slattern* right through the nineteenth century.

But don't get the wrong idea. This is *a nice girl*, one *so innocent that she thinks f**king is a town in China* (c. 1940). She's as pure as the driven snow, as *straight* (c. 1868) as they come, an *article of virtue* (c. 1850-1914), a *square Jane and no nonsense* (c. 1925, Aust.), a *proper bit of frock* (c. 1873-1910), who *draws the line at tick* (c. 1909, tick being the cloth casing of the mattress and the pillow). Self-control's her thing, and it's highly unlikely you'll ever find her ticked off. She's sui generis, the last of a vanishing species — the kind they just don't *make* anymore.

Mr. Everything

Ideally, he's *tall, dark, and handsome* (late 1920s-'50s), words that perfectly describe Caesar Romero, who starred in a film with that title in 1941 and who quickly became the standard by which teen-age bobby-soxers judged their acned suitors. Earlier, the same words were used by female movie buffs when speaking of Rudolph Valentino, who was really short, dark, and handsome, but apparently ten feet tall to his admirers. More recently, he's a *hunk*, something akin to the female *piece*.

There's little else to say. As Stuart Berg Flexner noted in *I Hear America Talking*, women tend to talk much less about men than men do about women, unless the guy's an out-and-out *seducer*, of which we will say more later. So for now, let's simply write him off as *the boy next door*, popularized by Judy Garland

119

who sang his praises in the 1947 film *Meet Me in St. Louis.* She's hoping he's *Mr. Right* (*c.* 1940), until his actions prove her wrong.

Does She or Doesn't She?

I used to be Snow White
but I drifted.

— Mae West

Our young man doesn't want much — only a nice girl. But at times, he's not really sure. Prior to the eighteenth century, a *nice* girl was one who was foolish or stupid. Later, when irony was in vogue, she became a *good girl* (a *wanton* wench, late 17th-18thC.), then a *perfect lady* (*c.* 1880, a *harlot*), or a *thorough good-natured wench* (19thC.), which, according to Grose, meant "a female who being asked to sit down will lie down." *Nice* today means coy, shy, and Ivory-pure, generally considered good, except in the inner city, where she can also be *bad.* Every man would like to marry a *nice* girl; as far as the others are concerned, "*f**k* 'em!" The *nice* girl has only one thing in mind, wondering when *that certain someone* will pop the question.

Unfortunately, the only question he has in mind is: Is she *easy* (since 17thC.), *loose* (since 15thC.), *fast* (18thC.), *swift* (late 19th-20thC.), *speedy* (*c.* 1923), *light* (14thC.), or *convenient* (19thC.)? Does she *go all the way* (mid-20thC.), the *whole route* (19th-20thC.), or the *limit* (*c.* 1916)? Once we have the answer to that question, we have established what is called a *reputation* (since 18thC.).

Every girl has been warned to *watch out for her reputation* (19th-20thC.). Traditional warnings include, *"Don't do anything I wouldn't do,"* originally a farewell send-off in the armed services (*c.* 1939-45) for the man blessed with a pass and headed for *a dirty weekend.* Its impact, however, has been blunted when coming from a mother with a brood of five hanging on her arm. Well, there's always, *"Be good! If you can't be good, be careful"* (from the song of the same name, *c.* 1907), *or at least be sanitary, buy a pram, name it after me,* and *remember the date.*

One *slip-up* and it's all over. Once she's got a *rep,* forget it!

Watch for her soon appearing on the wall of a bathroom stall near you. *For a good time call* . . .

Let's Fall in Love

Julia: Wouldst thou, then counsel me to fall in love?
Lucetta: Ay Madam, so you *stumble* not
  unheedfully.

> — Shakespeare, *Two Gentlemen of Verona*

But life has its peaks and valleys, love its *ups and downs* (19thC.). Those who *scale the heights of connubial bliss* (19thC.) prematurely often *tread the shoe awry* (16th-20thC.), which results in the inevitable *slip(-up)* (18thC.).

Shakespeare's women were forever *tripping, stumbling,* and *tumbling.* In the nineteenth century a woman *did a flop* (from *c.* 1875) or a *turn on her back* (19thC.). Men once *flopped a Judy* (*c.* 1875), Judy being a standard name for a woman, especially one of loose morals. Today women simply *go down* (19th-20thC.). There's no mistaking the *fallen woman.* The next time you see one, pick her up.

Fallen women are *made*; they're not born that way. This is the story of one such unfortunate soul for whom *push came to shove* (19thC.). *Did she fall or was she pushed* (19th-20thC.)? An obvious *pushover* (*c.* 1925), some say. Draw your own conclusions.

Itching for It

Others think the problem is our young man. He suffers from a chronic affliction known as the *galloping gonads, blue balls,* or *hot nuts* (all mid-20thC.), leaving him forever *rooty* (mid-20thC.), *randy* (since 18thC.), *humpy* (mid-20thC.), *juicy* (19thC.), *itchy* (19thC.), *hairy* (19thC.), and *horny* (19th-20thC.) – the seven dwarfs of lechdom.

His *horniness* derives from the ancient horned gods of fertility and procreation, such as Pan and Dionysus, as well as the *instrument* on which he plays his tune. As for *hairy,* our locks have long been identified with virility and strength, as in the story of Samson. Hair has also been considered a highly erotic stimulant and, because of this, many cultures have taken great pains to cover the head. Others have adopted even more radical measures. Shaving of the head has often been linked to castration, and has symbolized control of libidinous desires, as with those who take an oath of chastity upon joining a religious order.

In language, *hair* was most active as a metaphor during the nineteenth century. We had men feeling *hairy* (c. 1860, *having a must*) and looking everywhere for a *bit of hair* or for a woman with *hair to sell*. All they wanted was to *take a turn in haircourt* or *get a haircut* so as to relieve the urgency. A crewcut? A little trim behind the ears? Take it all off? The Puritans introduced the modern short haircut to the world as well as their suffocating sexual strictures. Given the results, isn't it time we all let our hair down?

That Certain Feeling

When I'm good, I'm very good, but
when I'm bad, I'm better.
> —Mae West

The man is not always alone, of course. She's *amative* (early 17thC.), *hot* (since 16thC.), *hot and bothered* (20thC.), *hot-assed* (since 19thC.), *got hot pants* (since early 20thC.), and is *hot in the biscuit* (early 20thC.). You might also say she's got *peas in the pot* (late 19thC.) or that she's *full of beans*. Beans were once considered an aphrodisiac, a theory which unfortunately proved to be so much hot air. But this time you can be sure: she's definitely *dripping for it* (c. 1910).

It was once considered unnatural for a woman to feel that way. In "The Merchant's Tale," Chaucer describes an aroused woman as acting *mannish,* as if *amorous* were a condition that only men might feel.

Henry Fielding, in *Tom Jones* (1750), however, saw her *coming.*

I dare to swear the wench was willing as he, for she was not always a forward kind of body. And when wenches are so *coming,* young men are not so much to

122

be blamed, neither for to be sure they do no more than what is natural.

So the feeling is mutual. They both have an *itch* (17th-20thC.) and feel the *urge, accesnsus libidine*; they're definitely *sexually aroused* and know *lust* (since 19thC.) in their hearts. They are literally starved for affection.

Galloping Gourmets

'Tis not a year or two shows us a man;
They are all but stomachs, and we all but food;
They eat us hungrily, and when they are full,
They belch us.
— Shakespeare, *Othello*

A hearty *appetite* often signals lascivious craving. *Appetite* derives from the Latin *apetere*, "to seek or desire eagerly." We have both *raging appetites (Troilus and Cressida)* and *bestial appetites in charge of lust (Richard III)*. Men often pursue a woman as a *fine dinner*, jitterbug and student slang (from the thirties for an attractive girl); a *picnic*, a peak sexual experience or one easily attained (from student and military use in the forties); or a *barbecue* (c. 1925), an exceptionally attractive female, from the Black community, as in the song "Struttin' with Some *Barbecue*." In England, *"boys call meal after her"* (c. 1970-75, Liverpool), while in the States she's been *P.E.E.P. (perfectly elegant, eating p*ssy, mid-20thC.).

Whatever form it took, the traditional meal was characterized by certain time-honored customs, grace being the standard ritual by which we gave thanks for what we were about to receive; hence, *grace before meat* (19th-20thC.), a kiss or any other activity leading up to the main course. *Dinner without grace* (19thC.) was sex without marriage — apparently a relationship without a prayer. There were always those without patience who wished to dispense with the preliminaries and have a *bit on the fork* (19thC.) immediately. They often were sent home hungry. Those who showed the proper etiquette were always rewarded with a little something from the table.

The Wayward Buss

. . . He was proper, tall, and handsome, and everything
was right. He could *lie* with a pretty girl and *kiss* her
twelve times a night.

— "You Remember the Nuts," Irish
broadside ballad, 1870

It all begins with a *come-hither look* (c. 1920), then a friendly
kiss, perhaps a buss on the cheek, or a *smack at her mums*
(19thC.) — nothing more than a *smooch* (since 19thC.), also a
smoodge, smooge, smouch, or *smouge*), or an innocent peck, an act
of *osculation,* from *oscula,* Latin for "little mouth." What concerns
us is what teen-agers on the West Coast today call *sucking
face* — a practice sure to leave its mark, a lasting impression
known to kids as a *hickey* (c. 1930), a word derived from "doo-
hickey," a whachamacallit of sorts. Equally tasteless is the
notorious *soul kiss* (20thC. Black U.S.) or *French kiss* (20thC.),
brought back by the American Expeditionary Force after World
War I, an act so unspeakable as to leave us tongue-tied.

Nobody really knows why we began kissing. Some link kissing to food and nurturing or identify it with breathing and life
itself, treating the commingling of the lips as the joining of life
forces. The word was first recorded in the language around the
tenth century as a *cosse,* close enough to both a curse and a cuss
as to make us nervous. Most consider the word "kiss" to be onomatopoeic, since it sounds like the action it describes.

Unbeknown to most, *kissing* is an X-rated activity. It has
long stood for the *sexual favor* itself, especially in literature from
the seventeenth to the nineteenth century. So the next time
you're reading from that period and you come across a couple
kissing, remember they're probably really not kissing but doing
you-know-what. When the handsome lad *kyssed* the sweet young
lass hello, she could probably kiss it good-bye.

In his work on the history of *sex,* Rabbi Brasch traces the X
symbol for a kiss to the sign for two mouths kissing: ><, going
back to the time when illiterates signed legal documents with an
X and then kissed the paper to lend it even greater veracity.
Before long, the kiss was fully identified with the mark.

In the fifties, we validated our affection by a string of X's at

124

the end of a letter, a stamp posted upside down on the envelope, and *SWAHAAK* ("sealed with a hug and a kiss") on the back.

Feeling Out the Situation

Drifting down the stream of izzen,
They were seated in the stern,
And she had her hand on hizzen,
And he had his hand on hern.

— Anon., "Hizzen and Hern," 20thC.

One thing quickly leads to another. In Colonial times, when privacy was hard to come by and warmth was at a premium, there was a practice called *bundling*. The parties bedded down together fully clothed for some small talk and some sanctioned *hanky-panky,* (originally some sleight-of-hand), but between them was inserted a "bedding board" to insure that most of the proprieties were met. In earlier times in Europe, they used a "chastity sword," guaranteed to keep cutting up to a minimum.

By the nineteenth century, all barriers had fallen, and a man and woman showed themselves to be *lovey-dovey* (c. 1870) by *spooning* (c. 1831) — engaging in silly and sentimental endearments leading to the couple resting comfortably in one another's arms like two spoons, an innocent enough practice, but one likely to end with her *on the old fork* (late 19thC.). Many saw this as nothing more than *lally-gagging* (c. 1860, a *lally* being a tongue), an expression that also came to mean wasting one's time, which it no doubt was for some. But things heated up with some *sparking* (18th-19thC.), *spunking up* (c. 1840), and *rotten-logging* (early 20thC.). All deal with attempts to start a fire, "spunk" and "rotten logs" referring to the tinder and other materials necessary to get the fire going — the spark referring, of course, to that which sets it off — i.e., the right mix of sweet talk, a bit of *billing and cooing* (19thC.), some *fumbling* (16th-20thC.), *tickling* (16thC.), *messing* (c. 1873) and *mucking about* (c. 1880), and some *fooling around* (c. 1880). Whatever, there'll *be no rushing up the petticoats straight* (c. 1850), at least not without the appropriate preliminary blandishments.

125

Taking Hold of Things

I like to wake up each morning feeling a new man.
— Jean Harlow

You're only as old as the woman you feel.
— Groucho Marx

The twentieth century has featured *petting,* which was originally just a caress or two, and *necking.* According to Groucho Marx, whoever called it *necking* must have been a poor judge of anatomy. Both words entered the language around the same time (1905-10), with *necking* (also *giraffing*) becoming especially *heavy* during World Wars I and II. *Petting* was deemed to be the more acceptable of the two and the one more publicly discussed, though in practice it was often difficult to distinguish one from the other. Teen-age practioners often made arbitrary distinctions based on whether the action occurred above or below the waist and whether it happened clothed or unclothed.

Back to our young couple: he appears to be *making out* (mid-20thC.), all right. He's now *practicing in the Milky Way* (19th-20thC.), *getting a touch-up* (18thC.), and *copping a cheap feel* (20thC.). Next comes the realization of a boyhood dream: *getting bare t∗t* (mid-20thC.) and living to tell about it, a feat writ even larger by the need of overcoming the ultimate challenge — learning to unlatch the demonic *bra.* He's now *making time* (20thC.), hoping *to wind up the clock* (c. 1760).

Till that magic moment, he can try his hand at some *canoodling* (mid-19th-20thC.) or some *firkytoodling* (18th-19thC.). *Canoodling?* "A sly kiss and a squeeze, and the pressure of the foot or so, and a variety of harmless endearing blandishments known to our American cousins (who are greater adepts at sweet-hearting)" (George Sala, *Twice Around the Clock,* 1859).

Firkytoodling? "What do you think you're doing?" she might ask. "Just *diddling about*" (20thC., Can.), says he, indulging in some *foreplay* or a bit of *sexual expression* (20thC.). Eric Partridge would explain to her that *firkytoodling* is "indulging in physically intimate endearments, especially in those provocative caresses which constitute the normal preliminaries to the *sexual congress,*" what we today might call *genital pleasuring.*

Put yet another way, he's *taking (manual) liberties, exploring her frilleries* (c. 1888-1914), *making free of the house* (20thC.) — including *playing at stink-finger* (mid-19th-20thC.), *tipping the long finger* (19thC.), and *playing the harp.* He has now *felt her pulse* (c. 1648-50) and *tickled her fancy* (20thC.), and they're going at it *hot and heavy* (20thC.). Soon they have reached the highest stage of the *sensate-focus exercise* (c. 1982-83).

"Stop, no you mustn't."
"Oh, come on baby, where've you been?"

Getting Down to Basics

I went in the morning to a private place with the housemaid and we bathed in our *birthday soot.*

> — Tobias Smollet, *Humphrey Clinker,*
> 1771

They have now shed their inhibitions and more. They've *peeled* (since late 18thC.) and *disrobed* (since c. 1794). You might now consider them *bare* (before 10thC.) or *naked,* though most people would consider that indelicate. *Naked* is a good English word and it's been around since the ninth century, but somehow we came to prefer being *nude,* a relative newcomer (that's been with us only since 1873), derived from the Latin *nudus* and, ironically, a close cousin of *naked.*

Naked has always given moralists cause to shiver. In the Bible, when one saw another's *nakedness,* it meant to see the *privy parts,* as in Genesis 9:22, "And Ham saw the nakedness of his father." The truth is *naked* or *bare,* never *nude,* but often dangerous.

Statues (and beaches), on the other hand, are *nude,* all very harmless. Bodies that are fixed in position seldom if ever interact, so there is little risk in their being *nude.* If you still can't distinguish between *naked* and *nude,* try standing stark *nude.*

There's an awful lot of euphemistic deception involved in going *bare-assed* (20thC.). We speak of being *au naturel* (20thC.) or in *the altogether* (since c. 1894) when we're really feeling unnatural in the untogether.

And though we are *without a stitch,* we also like to cultivate the illusion of being dressed, like the Emperor with his new clothes. It began with Jonathan Swift and his *birthday gear* (*c.* 1731), inspiring the *birthday soot* (suit) as well as a host of lesser imitators including *birthday attire* (*c.* 1860), *nature's garb* (19thC.), *Adam and Eve's togs* (*c.* 1909), and an *angel's suit* (19th-20thC.). The original *birthday suit* was the splendid suit of clothes specially ordered to be worn on a sovereign's birthday.

Today when we *air our pores* (20thC.) we're mostly *in the buff* (19th-20thC.). But once they used to *go in buff* (17th-late 19thC.) and *buff it* (*c.* 1850). *Buff* derives from the buffalos and their treated hides. When we're *in the buff,* we're dressed in nothing but our own hide — making devotees of nude bathing, *buff-buffs.*

C'est la Guerre

Yet ever as he greedily asay'd
To touch those dainties, she the harpy pla'd
And every limb did as a soldier stout
Defend the *fort,* and keep the *foeman* out.

> — Christopher Marlowe, *Hero and Leander,* 1598

Make love, not war.

> — Gershon Legman, 1963

Naked aggression soon makes itself felt. The unstable truce, the shaky cease-fire, collapses. Make no mistake about it — this is war!

Operations begin with reconnoitering by the *wandering-hand brigade* (*WHB,* late 19th-20thC.), including foreign elements: *Russian hands and Roman fingers* (mid-20thC.). He makes his advances. The *breastworks are assailed* (16thC.) and *Fort Monjoy* comes under *seige* (16thC.). The *encounter* (16thC.) is a brief one. It is simply no contest; *Adam's arsenal* (late 19thC.) proves too strong. He *batters down her portcullis* (17thC., a fortress or gateway) and *deals* her several *damaging blows.* He *invades* (17th-19thC.) and *conquers* (16th-20th). She *yields* or *surrenders.* This is followed by *possession* (17thC.) and *occupation* (16th-early 19thC.).

Possession is thought by some to constitute nine-tenths of the law, a common male fallacy. *Occupying* a woman (16thC.-early 19thC.), though highly popular in practice, was considered obscene in both spoken and written form during the seventeenth and eighteenth centuries, and its absence from the language is specifically noted in the OED. Better that they had sunk swords into ploughshares.

> Fighting for peace is like *f**king* for *virginity*.
>
> — Anon., 1983-84

Coming Attractions

> Then off he earlier *came*
> and blusht for shame so soon
> that he had endit.
>
> — "Walking in Meadow Green," in
> *Bishop Percy's Loose Songs,* 1650

> *Plaisir d'amour ne dure qu'un instant;*
> *chagrin d'amour dure toute une vie.*
>
> The pleasure of love lasts no more than an instant;
> the regret of love lasts a lifetime.
>
> — French epigram

O-o-o-o-ps! You mean that's all there is to it, a *momentary trick* (Shakespeare)? He *discharged, let go* (19th-20thC.), *shot his great stones* (c. 1604, Thomas Dekker), *his wad, his load* (both mid-20thC.). Sometimes he just *shot* or *shot off.* He *came his cocoa* (20thC.), *melted* (17thC.), *dropped his load* (20thC.), *gave his gravy* (19th-20thC.), *jetted his juice* (19th-20thC.), and just plain *ejaculated* (since c. 1578).

Sic transit gloria. Some men *come* (17th-20thC.), others *go* (20thC.). *Coming* or *going,* it's all the same. Of *come,* itself a euphemism for *spend* and a word that people at one time found offensive, Partridge wrote, "how if the fact is to be expressed non-euphemistically, could one express it otherwise with such terse simplicity?"

Because the expenditure is generally considered worthwhile, most enjoy *spending it* (the favorite nineteenth-century term), though there are some who prefer putting something away for a rainy day. Grose wrote of those men "who made a coffeehouse of a woman's **** . . . go in and out and *spend* nothing." General Jack Ripper in *Dr. Strangelove* was so disposed: "I do not avoid women . . . but I deny them my life essence." You, too, might want to test your *mettle* (17th-20thC.) or show *no spunk* (19thC.) by exercising a little self-discipline.

> Priapus squeez'd, one snowball did emit.
>
> — Rochester, *Works*, 1718

Not a Bang but a Whimper

> Nice guys finish last.
>
> — Leo Durocher

And what of her? What's she doing while all this is going on? Not much, according to *The Erotic Tongue*. Man's interest in her end of things is evidenced by the paucity of phrases and expressions we have to describe her *orgasm* (early 19thC.-20thC.) or *climax* (20thC.), apart from her *coming,* which she shares with him. Perhaps with your assistance we can do more than just:

Make her chimney smoke
Pop her cork
Flip her switch

_____ her _____
_____ her _____
_____ her _____

The Real Stuff

> He rumbl'd and jumbl'd me o'er and o'er. Till I found he had almost wasted the store of his *pudding.*
>
> — "From Twelve Years Old" in *Wit and Mirth,* 1682

You could say she's *taken the starch out of him* (mid-19th-20thC.), or, in a more exotic vein, taken some *thrice-decoted blood* (Marlowe), the *lewd infusion* (Rochester), or some *Cyprus sap* (c. 1611).

The *oil's* especially important, but great care is required in

130

its handling. As Rochester reminded us, "Too hasty zeal my hopes did spoil. Pressing to feed her lamp, I spilt my *oil*" (*The Imperfect Enjoyment,* 17thC.). He also has to *get his oil changed* (20thC.) regularly to keep love's vehicle in good running condition.

Popularly, we know it best as *come* or *cum* (c. 1923), *gism* or *jism* (20thC. from *orgasm*); practically, *father-stuff* (Walt Whitman) and *baby juice* (19thC.). *Pudding's* also nice, though Fletcher (*Beggar's Bush,* 1622) would "give her cold *jelly* to take up her belly." In Israel — where else? — they still *give milk for honey.* We have *hot milk* (19th-20thC.), *buttermilk,* and *seminal milk* (Whitman, c. 1860).

Most popular of all is *cream* (since 19thC.). Traditionally, men have *dished out the cream* (19thC.) while women *had a go at the creamstick* (18th-20thC.), leaving teen-age boys *creaming in their jeans* (20thC.). Which of us has not been encouraged by the lady on TV to "Come on and cream me!" Or had his curiosity piqued by items such as the following:

> STRAWBERRIES and cream are a delectable dream for the true gormet [sic]. I'm a yummy 29 yr 5 ft 11 strawberry blonde seeking generous gents to make a delicious tasteful memory with. P.O. box ---, Salem, N.H. 03078. Can Travel.
>
> —*Boston Phoenix,* July 13, 1982

Cry Babies

That's it! *It's* all over. But no tears, please. Apparently King David wept enough for all of us. According to a Talmudic interpretation of the Old Testament (Psalms 6:6), David found himself so extended by his eighteen wives that he tried *copulating* by day rather than by night in hopes of cutting down on his desires, but with only limited success:

> I am tired of my moaning; every night I flood my bed with *tears.* I soak my couch with my *weeping.* My strength is exhausted through my groaning all the day long; my *moisture* is dried up like the drought of sum-

mer. I am poured out like water; my *moisture* is evaporated as by the heat of the hot season; I am weary of my *weeping*.

Making Conversation

"Years from now . . . when you talk about this . . . – and you will – . . . be kind." Gently she brings the boy's hands towards her opened blouse as the lights slowly dim out . . . and the curtain falls.

– Robert Anderson, *Tea and Sympathy*

Will you respect me in the morning?
– Anon.

The job's complete but there's still much to talk about. If he's kind as well as literate and subtle, he'll say he *took her* (C.P. Snow's favorite), *had her* (16th-20thC.) and thoroughly *enjoyed her*; a *good time* (17thC.) was had by all.

From yet another perspective, he simply *saw her* (19thC.) and *made eyes at her* (19thC.), expressions that originated with the *ladies of the streets*. When a contemporary man and woman *make eyes at one another*, it's inevitable that they end up *seeing* each other. What we really mean to say is that they are *f**king*. Alan Sherman, for one, never understood how we managed to confuse *copulation* with vision, asking, "Have you ever heard of a *f**king*-eye dog?"

When a man gets into the locker room, all ambiguity vanishes. There he *scored* (mid-20thC.), *got into* (18th-20thC.), *put in* (19thC.), *put it in* and *had it in* (late 19thC.). He also *made* her and *made it with her*, two popular expressions that seem as if they've been around forever, but in fact have been with us only since about 1918. They both helped make her what she is today – *an easy make*. More frequently he'll say, *"I laid her"* or *"I got laid,"* also recent expressions that date from about 1930, though man has been *lying with a woman* for more than six hundred years. It's always been hard work in the land Down Under. Unlike their American counterparts, men there look forward to a *lay-off* (20thC. Aust.).

One Good Turn Deserves Another

Worst of all, he *screwed* her, meaning he not only *f**ked* her, but also took advantage of her and cheated her. Every woman must learn how to have *sexual intercourse* without getting *screwed*.

Screw as a slang expression for *copulate* has been around only since the nineteenth century. But a century earlier, it could be found in Grose's *Dictionary* as a noun (*female screw*, or plain *screw*) for a *harlot*. The word itself is of Latin origin, from *scrofa*, "a sow" (the threads of a screw bearing marked similarity to a sow's tail), which in turn was influenced by *scrobis*, "a ditch" (*vulva* in Latin). Add the two together and what do you get but a sow's tail in a ditch.

A *screw* was once slang for a skeleton key (*c.* 1795), perhaps the origin of its present usage as a turnkey, a guard in a prison or jail. In England, around 1859, it came to mean wages or salary. According to Hugh Rawson, it was a time when a person could say with pride, "I get a good weekly screw."

Would we could say the same today! As the Middle Ages featured the search for the Holy Grail, the twentieth century has been dominated by the pursuit of the ultimate *screw*.

Violators Will Be Towed

"Well *that's* gone!" as the girl said to the sailor in the park when she lost her certificate from the Billerica Sunday School.

— Anon., *Pink 'Un and Pelican*, 1898

For her, it was quite another matter. She did a *backfall*, a *spread* (since late 17thC.), *did* or *had a bottom-wetter* (19th-20thC.), got her *leg lifted* and *lay with her feet uppermost* (19th-20thC.).

At least it was once fun, an *act of pleasure*, as when the Duchess of Marlborough recorded in her diary how the Duke "had *pleasured* me thrice in his boots." Then the feeling was mutual. The first time around, the pleasure and the initiative were all his, as when she *succumbed to his blandishments* and *lost her honor*. You could even say that she had been *ravished, defiled,*

or *violated* (all since 15thC.). To be *violated* was once pretty serious business—a *fate worse than death* (19thC.). But today
Woody Allen can recount how he once dreamt that his former
wife had been arrested for having *sex* with another man, but he
slept peacefully, knowing it could not have been a moving *viola-
tion.*

Man: Use it *or* lose it.
Woman: Use it *and* lose it.

Breaking Faith

If I still had a *cherry,*
it would have been pushed
back so far I could use
it for a tail-light.

—Nell Kimball, *Nell Kimball: Her Life
as an American Madam,* 1970

Still our young girl has *had it.* More than her heart has been
broken. Also *Judy's tea cup* (19th-20thC.), her *pipkin*
(17th-19thC.), her *ring. Her pitcher's cracked* (19thC.), and there's
no repairing her precious china. Still, it's not as bad as it's
cracked up to be. You could even say things are looking up. She's
gone star-gazing on her back (mid-19thC.). She's *seen the wolf* (Fr. *a
vu le loup*) and the *elephant* (c. 1875). Young innocents ever since
Red Riding Hood have been warned not to *have eyes for* or *make
eyes at the wolf.* As to pachyderm sighting, God knows why
anyone would have seen an elephant under the circumstances.

As *a first edition* (Oscar Wilde), she has *lost her cherry*
(20thC.). Perhaps we should send flowers for the occasion. Having also been *deflowered* (since 14thC.), she could surely use a
few extras. Flowers have traditionally been the perfect symbol
for blood, fertility, and delicacy, dating back to Greek mythology when Hades *seduced* Persephone, who was gathering
flowers, causing them to fall from her apron. Brides have traditionally tossed their bouquets away after the ceremony, and in
the eighteenth century, when virginity was in flower, a favorite
surgical operation of the time was called *rearranging the
crumpled blossoms of the rose.* Reportedly, it became so popular a

procedure that many women underwent several floral arrangements.

Today, there is little need for it. Ours is a time when the bloom is definitely off the rose.

The Spirit of Compromise

At first glance, it appears that he got the best of it, and that f**king is a somewhat one-sided thing. To square matters somewhat you might want to make a *settlement in tail* (19thC.).

He gets *a bit of snug for a bit of stiff* (19th-20thC., *stiff* also meaning money)

She gives *mutton for beef* (19th-20thC.)

She gives *juice for jelly* (19th-20thC.)

He gives *a bit of hard for a bit of soft* (mid-19th-20thC.)

Remember, though – all trades are final.

In 1976 President Jimmy Carter admitted in an interview with *Playboy* magazine to looking on lots of women with *lust,* having "committed *adultery* in my heart many times." But that's OK, according to the U.S. Court of Appeals for the Ninth Circuit, which in 1984 declared *lust* not to be *prurient interest* ("a shameful and morbid interest in nudity, sex, or excretion"), in striking down a Washington State law that declared as obscene that which "incited *lust.*"

In the words of the court:

We do not think that Carter was describing a shameful or morbid interest; rather, he was obviously expressing a healthy, wholesome, human reaction common to millions of well-adjusted persons in our society. Certainly, we think it clear that this is how the country understood his remark, and how the term "lust" is generally perceived today.

Later in the opinion, the court observed that

If the arousal of good, old-fashioned, healthy lust is equated with an appeal to "prurient interest," it might be necessary to hale into court our leading couturiers, perfumers, and manufacturers of soft drinks, soap suds, and automobiles, as well as mainstream stage, movie, and television producers. Only by distinguishing between the arousal of sexual instincts and the perversion of those instincts . . . can we ever hope to safeguard from state intrusion the already dim and uncertain boundary that surrounds expressions protected by the First Amendment.

† † †

The origin of *canoodle?* Partridge says it comes from "cannie" in the sense of gentle and "noodle," to play the fool, hence to gently play the fool. Others look to the canoe, for the shape of the *vulva* (We do have the *little man in the boat* as the *clitoris.*) plus *doodle*, "to digitate," leaving us *fingering the clit*. It's not a totally unreasonable premise, given that we also *talk to the canoe driver* (20thC. for *cunnilingus*).

Firkytoodle derives from *firk*, to *f∗∗k*, and the *toodles*, a boy's *virilia*, hence to *f∗∗k* around with another's *privates*.

† † †

With *getting it off* (10thC.), the British reduced an epochal moment to a hygienic happening – getting the *dirty water off his chest* (early 20thC.), coming clean, as it were. Americans, meanwhile, *get their rocks off* or *get their cookies off* (mid-20thC.).

It could have been a *flash in the pan* (18th-20thC., *coition* sans *emission*). The English also called it a *dry bob* (c. 1660-1930); the French, *avaler le poisson sans sauce* (19thC.), "to devour the fish without sauce."

If it's security you relish, you can bank on it in the California Repository for Germinal Choice. Deposits, though, are limited to the *sperm* of eminent donors such as Nobel Prize winners. Federal regulations require substantial penalties for early withdrawal.

For the stuff of which dreams are made: *fetch* (late 19thC.), *gravy* (mid-18th-20thC.), *juice* (20thC.), *letchwater* (18thC.), *melted butter* (18th-20thC.), *roe* (c. 1850), *seed* (since 13thC.), *spermatic juice* (Rochester), *spume* (17thC.), *starch* (19thC.), *tail juice* (19thC.), *tail water*, *tread*, and just plain *stuff* (17th-20thC.). For the man who has everything: *love liquor*, *love's nectar*, *white honey*, and *baume de vie* (all 19thC.).

† † †

According to Gordon Rattray Taylor's *Sex in History*, the Romans distinguished between *virgo*, "an unmarried woman, " and *virgo intacta*, "a woman who had never known a man."

Ditto for the Greeks, to whom a virgin was a woman who had opted for personal autonomy instead of submitting herself to the narrow caged life of marriage. It was the married woman, who, in selling her independence, had lost her *virginity.* The only way to restore it was *to sleep with* a god.

Men are said to have *copped a cherry* (since the early 20thC., *cop* meaning "to steal," since the eighteenth century). We also have the *cherry orchard* (a girl's dormitory 20thC., with apologies to Chekhov) and a *virgin Coke,* Coca-Cola with a dash of cherry in it. Life has, however, not always been a bowl of cherries. They once *trimmed the buff* (c. 1772) and *docked her* (since 16thC.).

EIGHT

Let Me Count the Ways

Suppose eating, not sex, were the taboo of our century? Suppose it was illegal for more than two people to eat together and suppose even they had to get a license for it and eat in secret while children were fed alone in dark closets? Suppose our billboards and newspaper ads, movies, and books and art devoted themselves to pictures of food—but never to one glimpse of anybody eating? . . . Wouldn't it result in secret, general passions to try esoteric foods? And wouldn't people like to get together, law or none, and talk about the tabooed subject?

— Philip Wylie, *Opus 21*, 1949

Chastity: the most unnatural of the sexual perversions.

— Aldous Huxley

Sex often takes a turn. It could be a slight turn from the norm—a diversion (from the Latin *di* and *vertere*) or a complete U-turn away from that which is normal (from *per* and *vertere*)— making it a *perversion* of sorts.

According to Alfred Kinsey, a large number of people treat any kind of *sex* other than that involving a single man atop a single woman as abnormal. Other groups are less judgmental, treating such varied activity as creative and healthy.

Think you'd like *a spot of perving* (*c.* 1925, Aust.)? Fine. But only in moderation. As Voltaire reminded us upon declining a second invitation to an orgy, "Once a philosopher, twice a *pervert*."

139

Let Them Eat Cake

Hot roll with cream?

> —Cheeky lad asking a woman to f**k,
> 19th-20thC.

Baker, not today.

> —Housewife's reply to soldier paying
> undesired court, c. 1885-1915

Everyone needs a break from the ordinary and the commonplace. An old blues song celebrated the wife who provided *"cornbread* for her husband and *biscuits* for her back-door man." Both *cornbread* and *shortnin' bread* were Southern Black expressions for "coarse, undistinguished, and routine sex" (J.L. Dillard, *American Talk*). The French used to refer to *le pain quotidien,* the daily bread, for *the act of kind.* But *biscuits* (wordly women), apart from the *cold biscuit* (dull, perhaps unattractive, and only a leftover at that), stood for out-of-the-ordinary sexual activity. Many a *hot biscuit* has been known to *get it on* with the *biscuit roller,* one especially adept at the practice. Given man's predilection for *buns, biscuits,* and *muffins,* clearly he cannot live by bread alone.

The Straight Up-and-Up

Tired of the daily *grind* (19th-20thC.), bored with doing the *horizontalize* (c. 1845)? Not to worry. We've got more ways of *doing IT* than Heinz has pickles.

You can try it *spoon fashion* (19thC.), where the bowl of one rests in the other. Or if you're really game, you can attempt a *perpendicular* (mid-19thC.), also known as an *upright grand* (c. 1925). It's nothing more than *the old three-penny bit* (late 18th-20thC.) — what the girls on the corner used to feature as their standing bargain.

Though a somewhat shaky proposition, your standard *knee-trembler* (c. 1860) was also a *quickie* (20thC.), and the perfect answer to the *man on the run.* Ever a favorite of the pros, it has failed to catch on at home. According to Kinsey, only 4 percent of married women say that they would stand for it.

Can You Top This

Studies by Shere Hite and by Masters and Johnson show that today more and more women are also unwilling to take it lying down. In a world in which everyone assumes that the best person always comes out on top, the favorite way of *doing IT* has traditionally been *the momma-pappa position* or *the conjugal ordinary* (18th-19thC.). This is also referred to as the *missionary position* (19thC.), from what the missionaries gave the natives. Some also knew it as *figura veneris prima,* literally the primary or essential position for making love.

But turnabout is fair play, and with the reversal of traditional roles and women now in high places, *the dragon* is now *riding* (or *upon*) *St. George* (late 17th–mid-19thC.). *IT* has also been described as *making bishops,* because of the commonly held belief that a child thus conceived was destined to hold high office in the Church.

Why Don't We Do It in the Road?

Pet lovers, or those who are so inclined, generally enjoy *doing IT dog-fashion* (*Lassie-fashion,* 20thC., U.S.), or *dog-ways* (late 19thC.). Back in medieval times, they knew it as *more canino,* a practice condemned by the Church because it was considered too pleasurable and a backward practice (*coiting a posteriori*).

Impatient to get on with it? You might try *having a dog's marriage* (19thC.) or *making a dog's match of it* (19th-20thC.) – *doing IT* by the wayside, down and dirty. *IT,* however, just might take longer than you think. Dogs have been known to be linked together for hours on end after the *sexual act.* The *penis* swells, and the muscles of the female contract, locking the *penis* within. This insures them that not till death will they part.

IT's a tough act to follow, but you could possibly try *doing a dog's rig* (mid-18th – 19thC.), defined by Grose as *"sexual intercourse* to exhaustion followed by back-to-back indifference."

You Beast, You!

Although the dog has a firm hold on man's loyalty, other animals also set a fine example. In ancient India, the Kamasutra (the laws of love) of Pandit Vatsyayana described 84 different postures (of which there were over 700 variations), all named after various animals such as cows, mules, donkeys, cats, dogs, tigers, and frogs. Couples were encouraged to imitate the sound of the animals being mimicked to further enhance their pleasure.

"With a moo-moo here, a moo-moo there . . . everywhere a moo-moo."

Beastly Behavior

Some were inclined to take *IT* literally, what we call *bestiality* or *zoophilia* (also *zooerasty* and *zoolagnia,* from the Greek *zoon* for "animal"). It was once a ceremonial, part of religious worship in a number of cultures, including that of ancient Greece. Currently, it's practiced most in the countryside where, according to Kinsey, as many as 17 percent of rural males have experienced *orgasm* at least once with an animal.

Though its meaning is eminently clear, *bestiality* has also on occasion been confused with other "unnatural" practices, such as *buggery.* In the English town of Dunsberry, in 1642, a young servant named Thomas Granger was found guilty of commiting *buggery* with a mare, a cow, two goats, five sheep, two calves, and a turkey. Someone (perhaps a pig) squealed, and although there were problems of making positive identification, the animals were singled out and rounded up for execution, to be burned in a giant pit. When they finally got around to Granger, they found him well hung for his crimes.

Few look on bestiality kindly (except for *voyeurs,* when the animal's partner is a woman). Generally, the act and its participants are treated with contempt and disdain. In parts of South America, to call someone a *sheep-f**ker* is pretty serious business, not unlike an allegation of homosexuality in Oscar Wilde's day.

Pardon Our French

The French, they are a peculiar race
They fight with their feet and they *f**k* with their face.
— Anon., "Hinky Dinky Parley Vous," *c* WWI

I say, hey lover, what're we gonna do?
An he jes look down.
I say, Yoo-hoo pretty baby, you wanna
French? Haff an' haff?
How bout jest a *straight?*
I say twenty berries an you *alla roun'*
the mothafuggin world.

> —Robert Gover, Kitten in *One Hundred
> Dollar Misunderstanding,* 1961

The practice which, according to surveys by Sandra Kahn and by *Playboy,* ranks most popular among men, is *oral sex* (20thC.).

A favored activity through the ages, it was first heard of on American shores as an exotic Gallic sport brought home by our fighting men upon their return from World War I. They discovered it in France, and those good people, pious and Puritanical folk, found themselves once more identified with things considered lewd, illicit, and downright naughty (as with the postcard and the kiss).

Because the practice often loses something in translation, you'll probably need the services of a trained *linguist* (20thC.), someone who really knows *French,* also *Frenching, French culture,* or *the French way.* If you don't know where to turn, the want ads offer all kinds of assistance:

FR tutor
Beautiful blonde woman sks worthy gent
4 private lessons under my affluent [sic] tongue
SASE, Box 8154

> —*Grassroots,* March, 1978

In the United States, *French* traditionally was not spoken in the home, and men hoping to experience a foreign tongue generally had to look elsewhere. Fortunately, there were those who were quick to pick up on the demand. As the noted Detroit madam, Silver-Tongue Jean, remarked, "The *Johns* wanted it so we gave it to them. I think it also saved a lot of girls from contracting VD." Jean herself was a legend at the sport, openly boasting that there wasn't a man she couldn't lick.

Sex Rears Its Ugly Head

Blow's just a figure of speech.

— Anon., 20thC.

The professionals helped forge a common tongue. A man now had his *joint copped,* had some *derby,* or had his *hat nailed to the ceiling.* More frequently, men spoke of being *blown* or having a *blow job* (all since early 20thC.).

The pros were very responsive to the clients' requests. The girls stopped giving customers a piece of their minds and started *giving head* (since mid-20thC.) instead. *Giving head,* however, wasn't always a clear signal for *oral sex;* some took it to mean traditional *copulation.* Why *giving head* should also stand for *straight sex* is a cause of confusion and bewilderment. Psychologists tell us that it's a classic case of displacement of the birthplace, not a bad theory when you consider that Athena sprang full-blown from the brow of Zeus, and Rabelais' Gargantua emerged through his mother's ear. To the remnants of the counterculture it will forever remain a *mindf**k* of sorts.

Loose Lips

During the nineteenth century they used to *gamahuche* (also *gamaroosh* and *gamaruche*), possibly from the French *hucher,* "to purse one's lips," and *gams,* from the Italian for "legs." Today, psychologists, lawyers, journalists, educators, and talking heads on TV all favor Latin — a language noted for its remarkable cleansing power. When Latin's in, dirt's out, leaving filthy words sparkling clean.

Those very same people who would be shocked to hear of a woman *eating a man* (20thC.), find it quite proper that she *fellate.* They seem not at all disturbed by the fact that *fellatio* (also *fellation* and *fellatorism*) comes from the low Latin word for "suck" and was used by the Romans in the most obscene sense. Less familiar, and hence even less objectionable, are the *fellator* (male receiver) and the *fellatrice* (female receiver). They're really nothing more than your basic *c**ks**kers* (since 19thC.), known in more genteel quarters as *corksackers* (since mid-20thC.).

You'd have to go back to ancient Egypt to find the all-time great *fellatrice,* Cleopatra, who was referred to by the Greeks as "Merichane," or "gaper," the wide-mouthed one who allegedly gaped wide for some ten thousand men.

Currently, while some *fellate,* others get their licks in with *penilingus,* literally "tonguing the penis," a construction parallel to *cunnilingus,* its flip-side sister activity. Most folks, though, prefer linking *fellatio* and *cunnilingus* together, forgoing good grammar for good taste.

Word of Mouth

Lick *Dick* in '72.

—Bumper sticker, Presidential election, 1972

Generally considered in even worse taste has been the notion of one man *tonguing* another. They could, however, *wear the kilts* (20thC.) and *do a bagpipe (c.* 1785), although even Grose considered that a piece of bestiality "too filthy for explanation."

But it was music to the ears of the *piccolo player* or *fluter* (early 20thC.), who also *did a tune* (20thC.). It took years of practice for the world to accept him as an accomplished performer. Today, he's no longer just your ordinary *blow boy* (20thC.), he's now *Lord of the Flies* (1980s). You'll recognize him by his T-shirt with the rooster-shaped lollipop on it.

Ne regrettez pas. If you've got it, *flute* it.

Boy Eats Girl

There's yet another side to *oral sex,* one sure to bring men to their knees. A Chinese empress, Wu Hu of the T'ang dynasty, used to insist that all visitors to the royal court pay homage to her by an act known as the *licking of the lotus stamen.* Today, we're somewhat less poetic when practicing *cunnilingus* or *licking twat* (17thC.). It's all a matter of direction. When man's the active partner, he *heads south* (20thC.). While down there he can engage in some *muff-* or *pearl-diving* (20thC.) or just *talk to the canoe driver* (20thC.).

Either the man or the woman can extend the trip down *south*

145

(also *Dixie,* early 20thC.) by going *around the world* (since mid-20thC.), affording further opportunity to explore the international body politic.

Lickety-Split

Stay Healthy—
Eat your Honey

—Bumper sticker, *c.* 1982

Q. What is eighty-two, wrinkled, and eats Ginger?
A. Fred Astaire.

Such a trip also presents an opportunity for some novel culinary fare. It's but a short trip down *below 14th Street* (mid-20thC.) to grab a bite. Eating and *oral sex* have long been synonymous for both sexes. In this case, it's the *face man* who favors *eating out,* opting for a *box lunch,* a *furburger,* or a bit of *hair pie* when dining with the *C-food mamma* (all since mid-20thC.).

Eating at home has now become an accepted and refined routine, giving one little reason to go out for exotic fare. This is not to say that there still aren't those who enjoy an occasional snack between meals.

"*Eat* me!"
"I want a meal, not a snack."

Swing Your Partners

We didn't take to a varied diet overnight, but once we developed a taste for it, we *swung* right in.

America first began to swing in the forties—to music. Swing was the big-band sound of the period, and when they told you to "Swing and sway with Sammy Kaye," you did so feeling comfortable that you were part of the current musical craze. After a while, swinging identified those who were knowledgeable and into the latest fads. It was the yardstick against which all things were measured. Duke Ellington reminded us, "It don't mean a thing if it ain't got that swing." And Frank Sinatra pointed us in the right direction with his "Songs for Swinging Lovers" (1956), expanding upon a sexual theme just vaguely referred to earlier.

Swinging and *sex* have always had a historical relationship reflecting the sexual fashions of the period: *f**king* (16th-17thC.), *necking* and *petting* (early 20thC.), and *homosexuality* (briefly, mid-20thC.). Each had its moment to *swing*. Around 1953, a phenomenon called *wife swapping* was reported in the suburbs. During the early to mid-sixties, *swinging couples* or *swingers* became the subject of serious study by sociologists as well as a common male fantasy. But there was little need to limit *swinging* to married folks, and it expanded to include any kind of innovative sex with multiple partners, rendering all other definitions obsolete. The *swinging single* was now upon us.

Cast of Thousands

The kids also *swung* right in, joining in pursuit of their favorite rock stars, offering their bodies in service to the muse. In tribute to their talents, Frank Zappa, of the Mothers of Invention, dubbed them *groupies*. But as Germaine Greer pointed out, the name had just the opposite effect from what was intended; in less than six months the term was considered an insult.

Of more lasting consequence was a specialized squad called the *plastercasters*. Armed with an ample supply of plaster of Paris and nothing more than their nimble fingers to guide them, they made replicas of the *private parts* of the stars they had *f**ked*. Their consummate skill and artistry earned them and the performers a permanent place in the history of sexual practices.

Stop It, I Love It

Miss DuCane
Strict Governess
Corrective Training
> — Window sign, Victorian England

B/D. Slaves wanted. If you think
being spanked would be fun,
write P.O. Box 214.
> — *Boston Phoenix*, July 13, 1982

The beat continued with some *B/D* (mid-20thC.) – a little *bondage and discipline,* courtesy of Ritter Leopold von Sacher-Masoch (1836-95), the man who put the *M* in *S and M* (*sado-masochism*).

A historian, dramatist, and novelist, Masoch loved children and cats, but his real penchant was for older and stronger women who could maltreat him physically and help scourge and subdue his animal lusts. Virtually all his books reflect this passion, and they always include at least one powerful and moving passage in which a woman in furs whips a pleasured male into a state of ecstasy.

> "Wonderful woman!" I cried. . . "Whip me," I begged,
> "Whip me without pity."

It wasn't Masoch, however, who discovered sexual pleasure from self-inflicted pain. You'll find it in early pagan rites as well as in the Christian mysticism of suffering. Masoch merely captured it so well that he inspired Krafft-Ebing, in *Psychopathia Sexualis,* to name it after him.

Masochists today love being treated like slaves, little boys, animals, or lifeless objects such as doormats. You'll find them in the personal columns under *English* (also *English guidance, acts,* or *culture*) from the British affection for the rod – spanking and flagellation long having been a staple of the English sexual life. The French have always treated *masochism* as *le vice anglaise.* Look for terms like *dominant, submissive, B/D,* and *S and M.* Furs are now out but leather's in, especially high boots, together with fish-net stockings and garter belts, the basic accoutrements of the practice. Whips, chains, and riding crops are optional.

The Whip, the Whip, Anything but . . .

Masochism is only one side of *algolagnia* (from the Greek *algos,* "pain," and *lagneia,* "voluptuousness"), the sexual urge tied to pain and that which causes it. *Sadism* is the other. But unlike *masochists, sadists* give rather than receive, deriving their pleasure from humiliating or physically harming another or from merely watching another experience pain.

Sadism, of course, was inspired by the Count Donatien

Alphonse Francois de Sade (1740-1814), one of the great philosophers and scientific minds of the eighteenth century. De Sade held God, virtue, and convention in equal contempt and spent most of his life in prison, twenty-seven years in eleven different institutions. He had many passions and few inhibitions. His greatest hangup was whipping a naked woman strung from the ceiling while he was being *masturbated* by his servant. *Sadism* today has fallen on bad times. The word simply connotes cruelty and abuse without the sexual flair of the "Divine Marquis."

"Why do you hang around with that *sadist*?
"Beats me."

— Kliban

The Wild Bunch

Male *swingers* who assert themselves through a polymorphic sexual abandon in which the line between the sexes dissolves, to the delight of all.

— Gore Vidal, *Myra Breckinridge,* 1968

If you can't beat 'em, you can always join 'em — in some *group sex*. What better way to meet new people and *make* new friends?

There's certainly no easier way to forge new relationships than through your neighborhood *daisy chain* (mid-20thC.). We knew it once as a group of well-connected male *homosexuals* joined through *anal intercourse,* but over time, it's come to represent *heterosexual* sport and to include oral activities as well. However, as Gershon Legman, who has been called the high mathematician of *oral-genital sex,* points out, no *daisy chain's* complete without some *homosexual* participation; otherwise, it might not add up.

It's also part of *Greek* and *Roman culture* (20thC.), because of the Greek *orgia,* the secret rites of worship and the frolicsome and bawdy processions held in honor of Venus, Bacchus, Priapus, and the other good-time gods. The *bacchanalia* or Roman *orgies* (since *c.* 1589) were especially noted for their sexual excesses, so much so they were finally halted by law. You don't have to be in Rome, however, to do as the Romans did. The Japanese also used to promote teamwork and interdependency in a game called *crossing the valley*. The girls would stretch out in a line from one end of the room to the other, while the boys would *f**k* each in turn, the object of the game being to *cross the valley* without *coming*.

Any Number Can Play

How do I love thee? Two's company, three's a *troilism*, where the third party functions either as a spectator or with specific *oral* or *genital* tasks to perform. One man by himself with two or more women was once considered as near heaven as he'd ever get, hence he was said *to lie in state* (c. 1780-1850); more discreet and personal arrangements created a *ménage à trois*, literally, a family of three. The other way around, two guys and a gal, made for a *cluster f**k* or a *club sandwich* (mid-20thC.).

It was plain hard work for the lone gal having to pull her weight as well as that of her friends while *pulling the train* (mid-20thC.), a succession of men who, like a string of boxcars, had to be coupled and uncoupled. Unfortunately, it was a *choo-choo* or *chuga-chuga* (20thC.) that seldom put anyone back on track.

Most times, when it entailed one gal and more than two guys, it approached a *gang bang* (or *shag*), also a rhythmic procession known as a *bunch punch* or a *team cream* (all 20thC.), an act seldom voluntary on the female's part. Many considered it a case of *gang rape*, from the Latin *rapere*, "to seize or carry off."

Gay Abandon

"How long have you been *gay*?"
"I ain't *gay*," said she astonished.
"Yes you are."
"No I ain't."
"You let men [*make love* to you], don't you?"
"Yes, but I ain't *gay*."
"What do you call *gay*?"
"Why the gals who come out regular of a night, dressed up, they get their livings by it," she said.

—Anon., *My Secret Life*, 1888

150

THOUSANDS MOURN AT *GAY* FUNERAL

— Headline in San Francisco
newspaper cited in *Detroit Free Press,*
August 27, 1979

Gay does have its cheery side, as in the *gay* life — life in the fast lane. Feeling *gay?* It once meant you were *amorous.* Look for the *gay woman* in literature from Chaucer to Shakespeare and right on through the nineteenth century. She was *gay in the arse, groins,* or *legs* and often spent much of her time in a *gay house.* Even today, in England, we have the *gay girl,* a hard-working *flat-backer* trying to turn an honest shilling. The *gaying instrument* (19thC.)? The male *member,* without which it wouldn't be possible *to gay it.*

The word *gay* has had a number of lesser connotations apart from its primary definition of "bright, lively," but its meaning as *sexually loose* and *dissipated* has proved most popular and enduring. Although there exists much controversy among scholars, the word most likely derives from the Old English *gāl* for *lewd* and *lascivious* (which also gave us *quite a gal,* a nineteenth-century British term for a *prostitute*) rather than the more obvious *gai,* from Provence in southeastern France, a word which earlier referred to courtly love and its literature.

Gay did not become associated with *simulsex* (early 20thC.) activity until the early part of the twentieth century, and then it was primarily underground. It didn't go public with this meaning until 1925, with the *gay boy* in Australia, and 1935 in the United States in the film *Bringing Up Baby,* in which Cary Grant donned a dress and commented how he had gone *gay.* Between 1955 and 1960, it captured everyone's fancy, culminating in the joyous outburst of the seventies.

Scores of *gays* celebrated by *coming out of the closet,* like a thousand clowns emerging from the tiny car at the circus. Others merely *dropped their hairpins,* admitting to having been *in the closet.* The sexual landscape was crowded with born-again *gays* as well as *pretenders to the throne* (would-be *queens?*).

Today, *gay* or some word close to it, is used in more than a dozen countries in the same sense as in English. We now have *gay* bars, *gay* boutiques, and *gay* publications. Madison Avenue

151

has awakened to the word's full commercial potential, and wordsmiths have begun to retool the language. It was probably only a matter of time before "the gay old dog" became an aged *homo* and "the gay blade," a means of removing unwanted body hair.

> Damned silly . . . A term which made us into frivolous idiots – sort of bliss-ninnies.
>
> – Christopher Isherwood

Vice Versa

Our hearts weren't always young and *gay*. Earlier they spoke in hushed whispers of *the love that dare not speak its name,* from the poem written by Alfred Lord Douglas to Oscar Wilde, introduced by the prosecution as prime evidence at Wilde's trial, and the centerpiece of his eloquent and brilliant defense. However, few knew what else to call it, because of the general scarcity of terms that existed at the time.

Some had him *doing a detrimental* (early 20thC.) or *the other* (*c.* 1925, *homosexuality* as a criminal offense as opposed to *prostitution*). They said *he didn't care much for members of the opposite sex* (c. 1925). He's *epicene* (early 20thC.) or a *member of the third sex* (20thC.). Today he's mostly *versatile,* or of a *different sexual orientation,* or even *bisexual* (because it's more acceptable).

A Man's Man

In 1869 a Hungarian physician named Karoly Maria Benkert coined the word *homosexual.* It was a curious (dare we say "queer"?) blend of Greek (*homos*) and Latin (*sexus*), meaning "same sex." Lots of people were confused, thinking it meant "lover of men." Others were downright uncomfortable with the merger. Havelock Ellis was furious, calling it "a barbarously hybrid word." There have since been numerous attempts either to make the word philologically pure or to find substitutes for it.

Scholars approached it from both ends, first creating the *homogenic,* the *homoerotic,* and the *homophile,* and then the *simulsexual* and the *isosexual.* Some made their feelings even clearer with the *controsexual,* or by cutting him down to size as a *homo* (also *homie, c.* 1925).

As the word became increasingly identified with men, it also inspired the *feminosexual* for women so inclined, but by doing so, created a whole new problem. If men were to be called *homosexuals* and women, *feminosexuals,* what would we call them collectively? From this emerged the *intersexuals.*

Our most current entry is the proposed *herosexual,* who sounds as if he came out of a telephone booth rather than the closet. America, however, is not quite ready for that one.

Is it any wonder that we finally returned to the *homosexual,* the worst of all possible words – save all others?

A Clothes Call

Here's to the maid of bashful fifteen
Likewise to the widow of fifty
Here's to the wild and extravagant *quean*
And also to her who is thrifty.

– Toast, 19th C.

Gays may have been unnamed and unloved, but they were seldom unsightly. Clothes always made the man *one of those,* and special dress was at one time de rigueur. Henry III of France (1551-1589), probably the most notorious royal *homosexual* in history, loved to deck himself out in outrageous attire, transforming his royal majesty into what we would call today a *screaming queen* (20thC.)

The *queen* has had a glorious and colorful career. She started as an *easy woman* and a *prostitute,* "a flaunting woman of loose morals if not practice" (Grose). During the nineteenth century she evolved into a man with girlish manners and carriage; a century later, she became a *queen,* surfacing publicly as a highly conspicuous and garishly attired *homosexual.*

Even in the melee of *queen*fares, painted eyes, bodies in *drag* – even then she stood out from all the others . . . a *queen* perched on a stool like a startled white owl: a man with bleached, burned-out hair and a painted face dominated to the point of absolute impossibility by the

153

largest, widest, darkest eyes I have ever seen, pointed into two enormous tadpoles, slanting to the very edges of her temples.

... Her dress, short, reaches her knees, the legs crossed so that the purple spike-heeled shoes coming to a long point; like those of a witch, protrude on either side of the stool: one foot swinging back and forth, impatiently, recklessly, constantly like a pendulum.

... A *queen.*

A flamboyant, flagrant, flashy *queen.* A *queen* in absurdly grotesque, clumsy *drag.*

— John Rechy, *City of Night*

A Dressing Down

In late nineteenth-century America, they simply *tied one on.* Havelock Ellis tells of *inverts* of the time employing red neckties to identify themselves to fellow *fairies,* a practice especially favored by male *prostitutes* out for a *cruise* (early 20thC.). They also used to appear *in drag* (c. 1850), from the long gown brushing against the floor, creating the *swish* (also *swishy,* early 20thC.), originally a term for a man with an especially effeminate gait. During the second half of the nineteenth century they used to *go on drag* and to *flash drag. To do* or *wear* the *drag* was to wear women's clothes for "immoral" purposes.

Most today would consider it all very *camp* since c. 1920), from the Italian *campeggiare,* to stand out from a background. *Camp* was also once a *brothel* and a gathering place for *homosexual* males. Would you, we ask, still send this boy to *camp?*

Dressing up draws mixed reviews and is especially annoying to *transvestites* (*cross-dressers*) or *TVs* (mid-20thC.), who feel it gives them a bad name. Most *TVs* enjoy getting into a woman's pants but prefer that she not be in them at the time. *Cross-dressing*'s always been a kick for them as well as for the *TV* viewer. The practice goes back to Greek mythology. Achilles loved to deck himself out on occasion (high heels?), and Hercules once dressed himself in the clothing of Queen Omphale. It was a tight fit. He squeezed into her girdle and split the sleeves of her gown, but the result proved so convincing that Pan tried to *put the make* on him. Hercules was so incensed that he threw Pan across the room—from which moment, Pan swore never again to have anything to do with clothes.

Stranger Than Life

For something truly different we offer *deviants, degenerates* (both since late 19thC.), *oddballs, weirdos, freaks* (all since mid-19thC.), and *preverts* (*Dr. Strangelove*).

Most people believe that if you're not *straight,* you must be *bent* (19th-20thC., Eng.), *kinky* (*c.* 1920, for a *homosexual*; since *c.* 1960 for any kind of exotic, way-out sex), or *twisted* (mid-20thC.). Joe Six-pack considered them all a bunch of *f**kin'*: *queers, fruits, fairies,* and *faggots.*

A *queer* (*c.* 1920) was once slang for counterfeit money. It didn't gain currency as a *homosexual* until 1925, when the connection was made public in *Variety,* the theatrical trade journal. Today, with both inflation and gaiety raging everywhere, being "as queer as a three-dollar bill" seems to have become an established fact. Some people think "queer" to be a polite term. Most *homosexuals* consider it a "curdling epithet."

Fruit of the Loom

Who is that *fruit?*

—Ty Cobb on meeting Bill Tilden

California: Home of Fruits and Nuts

—Bumper sticker, 1982

Some *fruit's* definitely forbidden. Both the U.S. *fruit* and the Brittish *fruiterer* (also early 20thC., U.S.) derive from the youthful fruit dealers in fourteenth-century England and their predilection for *oral sex* as well as other sexual activity considered beyond the norm. The female *fruitesters* go back as far as Chaucer. Along the way, your *fruit's* been a *loose* and *easy woman,* later a man of similar morals, and even a verb meaning to *f**k.*

By the middle of the twentieth century, inner-city Blacks

were *fruiting* – cool *dudes galavanting* about town in their quest for *a piece of a∗s.*

Fruit is often depicted as ripe and easy for the picking. Like *gay, sucker,* and *dupe,* all of which have also been synonymous with *homosexuality,* he has also been characterized as an unknowing tool – the person who's easily influenced and victimized.

In 1912 *fruit* began its stint as a weird and off-beat person. More recently, we joined its promiscuous nature to its odd and eccentric character, producing the contemporary *fruit.*

A Grimm Reminder

In the beginning, God created fairies and they *made* men.

> – John Rechy, *City of Night,* 1962

If there's an air of unreality to it all, it must be the good *fairy.* Starting life around 1880 in the States as an attractive girl, the *fairy,* in early twentieth-century England, had become a debauched and hideous woman often reeling with drink, soon to hit rock bottom as a *lady of the night.* The *fairy's* been *one of them* only since 1924 in England and since 1949 in the U.S., although some record his presence as early as 1908. Teen-agers still recount the classic *fairy*tale, which originated about that time, of the lost tourist who inquiried of the stranger, "Where can I find the Twelfth Street ferry?" And the famous response, done with a lisp and a flourish: "Thpeaking."

A Class Act

I want to live out my life as the one who wrote *The Murder Game,* not as the *faggot* who killed his wife.

> – Ira Levin, *The Deathtrap,* 1980

Like the *fairy,* the *faggot* (c. 1930, also *faggart*) has also been a term of contempt for an old and dissipated woman (16th-19thC.) as well as a *prostitute* (19th-20thC.) – social outcasts all. In its abbreviated form we know it as a *fag* (early 20thC.: your *three-letter man*) and as *agfay* (mid-20thC.) in pig Latin.

The *faggot* began life as nothing more than "a bag of sticks," (14thC., Fr.), the small bundle of twigs and branches placed under the feet of the heretic who was to be burned at the stake. According to Bailey (1728), the faggot was once a proper symbol of recantation. The heretic who escaped the stake was required either to bear a faggot or to wear an imitation on the sleeve as a badge. This was at a time when the Church often confused religious dissent with both social nonconformity and sexual deviance (three vices for the price of one). It was then but a simple leap of faith to identify the lost soul with the instrument by which he was put to death. The Vatican no longer burns *faggots*, encouraging us to face *homosexuality* with "objectivity" and with the "understanding" one would show such a "disorder."

We also find the *faggot*'s origins in the British public (what we call "private") schools. Boys from the upper forms traditionally forced weak and submissive underclassmen to perform mean and humiliating tasks. The work was often so demanding as to leave them fatigued or "fagged," a complaint so frequently heard that the younger lads were transformed into *fags* or *faggots* in the eyes of their tormenters.

> Bob Trotter, the diminutive *fag* of the studio, . . . ran all the young men's errands and fetched them apples and oranges.
>
> — William Thackeray, *Newcomes*, 1855

Odd Man Out

When lord St. Clancey became a *nancy*
It did not please the family fancy.
And so in order to protect him
They did inscribe upon his *rectum*:
All commoners must now drive steerage;
This *a∗shole* is reserved for peerage.

> — Quoted by Leonard Ashley in
> *Maledicta*, winter, 1980

They may not have been so crazy about *faggot*, but they were just wilde about Oscar, who in this case happens to be Oscar Wilde, British writer and wit (1854-1900), and the most celebrated *homosexual* of the nineteenth century. He bequeathed us *Oscar* (late 19th-20thC.) for males caught *oscarizing* or thought to be *a bit on the Wilde side.*

People's names, both male and female, have always been favored. On the feminine side you might try *Nancy* (c. 1820), *Miss Nancy* (c. 1880), *Nance* (19th-20thC.), *Molly* (18th-20thC.), *Mary Anne* (c. 1890), *Alice, Flo, Sissie, Jesse, Margery* (c. 1850-1900), *Bessie, Beaulah* (both 20thC.), and a *John and Joan* (18th-mid-19thC.). Currently, *Mary*'s a grand old name, as is *Mable,* two Stateside favorites, while *Mavis* does her thing in England.

You'd think the names normal enough, but in some quarters, they're still seen as a strange bunch — of flowers: *daffodils* (England since c. 1945), *buttercups, lilies, ivies, roses, violets* (all 20thC.), and of course everybody's favorite — *pansies* (since c. 1930) — making, we suppose, those who are slow to reveal themselves late bloomers of sorts.

In England, they've all gone *pouf.* A *pouf* (or *poufter*) was once a would-be actor or a term for a silly fellow. No one's really sure of its origin. One can only surmise that the word is an affectation of sorts, a variation of "poof" or "pooh," as in, "Pooh! I couldn't care less!"

Global Penetration

Irish by birth
Greek by injection

— Anon., 20thC.

Thoroughly foreign to most, it's still probably *Greek* to you, as part of *Greek culture, the Greek way,* and the *Greek fashion* (all mid-20thC.), or just plain *Gr.,* as in the personal columns.

There is nothing parochial about the practice. Its appeal is definitely global. Shakespeare named it the *Italian habit.* The French, who have always been suspicious of Germans, came up with *le vice allemand.*

Shortly thereafter, the Christian world discovered a *Turkish culture* in which men *turked each other.* The Turks took the prize for their reputed excellence in the sport and for their invention of the fly, an open crotch in front of the pants and a flap in the rear, allowing for ready access both fore and aft.

It was all part of the war of the words in which men shot off their mouths rather than their guns. Could it be that the United States passed up a potentially powerful new weapon in the Cold War when it failed to introduce the world to *commie culture,* losing one of those rare opportunities to truly stick it to the Russians?

Tails of Two Cities

Mum, me *bum*'s numb.
                                    — Anon., 20thC.

Talking turkey, you're also talking *sodomy,* derived from Sodom and Gomorrah, the twin-sin cities of the Old Testament (Genesis 19:24) with a reputation for abandoned sexuality and a special fondness for the practice of *coitus per anum.*

Sodom's link with the *bum-f**k* (mid-20thC.) comes directly from the Old Testament and the experience of the two angels whom God dispatched to the city. The decision had been made to destroy Sodom and Gomorrah for their wicked ways but, out of deference to Abraham, God agrees to spare the cities if ten good men can be found. The angels are sent to conduct the search. Upon their arrival, they secure lodging in Lot's house, but soon a curious and angry mob of townsmen gather outside, demanding to know the strangers.

The entire story as well as the origin of *sodomy* turns on this incident and on the word "know." As noted earlier, in addition to its more innocent usage, to *know* someone in the Old Testament often meant to *f**k* that person. What we don't know for sure is whether the Sodomites only wanted to get acquainted with the angels, or had other things in mind. Philo of Alexandria took it in the worst possible way and it was his interpretation that was later adopted by the Church fathers, firmly establishing the link between Sodom and the nasty act.

There are those scholars who feel that the city's reputation has been unnecessarily sullied, and that charges of *anal intercourse* as a common practice there may be nothing more than — you should pardon the expression — a *bum* rap. They point out that there are 943 recorded "knows" in the Old Testament and that only 15 have any sexual meaning. But they fail to answer why the men of Sodom were so determined to *know* the strangers, and why Lot offered them instead a chance to *know* his daughters who had not yet *known* any man. Also unanswered is what so angered a just and merciful God that He struck them blind and later destroyed the city with fire and brimstone. No one seems to know the gospel truth.

Be that as it may, He finally did get the boys out of Sodom, though He never did quite succeed in getting Sodom out of the boys. It left us with a *ream* of *sodomists* (since *c.* 1785) and *sods* (late 19th-early 20thC.). *Sodomy* now serves as a general, catch-all term for any form of non-*orthogenic sex,* i.e., that of a non-procreative nature. It includes everything from *anal copulation* to *lesbian* acts, *mutual masturbation, analingus, bestiality, exhibitionism,* and *taking indecent liberties with a minor.* In this country, most states still have laws on their books against *sodomy* — whatever it may mean. New York's definition of the crime includes *oral copulation,* leading one critic to remark as to how the legislators apparently did not know heads from tails.

What's Buggin' You?

Love means not having
to say you're sore.
— Anon., 20thC.

Sodomy, did, however make believers of some. Witness the *Albigensians,* a medieval religious sect with a reputation for abstaining from any sexual practices that might result in procreation. They were in fact so repelled by *the act* that they not only avoided *IT* but also shunned any food *IT* engendered, including meat, eggs, cheese, and milk. Their beliefs somewhat limited their options, forcing them to create new outlets for their sexual drive, forging a lasting bond between them and the *unnatural vice* (19thC.). Because they originated in Bulgaria, they came to be known as *Bulgars* or *buggers* and their practice, as *buggery* (16th-20thC.).

Some scholars discount the Bulgarian connection, finding *buggery's* origins instead in Sir Robert Le Bougre, the famous Inquisitor, and the unnatural pleasure he derived from the suffering he inflicted upon his victims as well as the nature of the confessions he extracted – admissions of both sexual and religious deviance, *buggery* being a common charge of the time.

Buggery's never been popularly received. British schoolboys once spoke of the three *B*'s of public-school life: birching, boredom, and *buggery*. It was once treated as an *abominable crime* and a *gross indecency* which, under England's Criminal Law Amendment Act of 1885, meant four years of hard labor for Oscar Wilde. Yet today, we know it best as a term of surprise: "Well I'll be *buggered!*" as well as one of affection: "You little *bugger*, you!"

Child's Play

"Kid stuff," you say! Not when it involves the young; it then becomes *child abuse* (1970s-80s). The Greeks called it *pedophilia* (from *pais*, "child," and *philos*, "loving"), describing the sexual attraction of an older person to a child.

Those who preferred sending a boy to do a man's job committed *pederasty* (since 14thC.), an Anglicized version of the Greek *paiderasty*, again from *pais*, "boy" and *erastes*, "lover." The tradition goes back to Ganymede (16thC.), Zeus's cup bearer, who waited upon his master and attended to his every need. In Latin, he became *catamitus*, our *catamite* (16th-20thC.), currently defined as any young boy used for "immoral purposes."

Pederasty's still actively practiced today. It comes in the guise of the *chicken queen* and the *chicken hawk*, a.k.a. *Colonel Sanders* (all 20thC.), *cruising* about, waiting for the right moment to swoop down from above and steal away a fresh young *chicken* (20thC.), who may have strayed from the roost.

Lady's Choice

Angry young woman
They call me a *dyke;*
Don't know much about it
I just know what I like.

–"Theme song" of the *lesbian* movement, *c.* 1982

The Criminal Law Amendment Act of 1885 under which Oscar Wilde was convicted made no mention of female *homosex-*

uality out of deference to the sensitivities of Her Majesty, Queen Victoria. Members of Parliament later sought to smuggle it in as part of the working definition of *gross indecency,* but it never made it past the House of Lords, primarily because they couldn't imagine what it was that two women might possibly be up to.

This same male vanity and ignorance, combined with male control of words, helps explain the somewhat impoverished state of language pertaining to female *homosexuals* and the dearth of terms to describe the members of the *sisterhood* (20thC.) or their activities.

The one word which everyone knows, however, is *lesbian* (*c.* 1896) or one of its many variations: *Leslie, les, lez, lesbo,* and *lesbyterian.* The lesbian and her friends all come from the Island of Lesbos, where the famed Greek poetess Sappho founded and directed her famous school for girls. Sappho's poetry was beautifully crafted and reveals a special depth of feeling and intimacy for women, much of it directed to her pupils. Because of that, she herself has also been associated with the movement (*Sapphists,* 20thC.).

There are historians, however, who are convinced that Sappho was *straight,* and her school anything but a hotbed of carnal activity. It's hard to prove. Much of her work is difficult to translate and we have only fragments to work with, most of her writings having been destroyed by Christian zealots who feared its immoral character.

From what we know, the curriculum of the school featured dancing, singing, and instruction in musical instruments, with students also receiving lessons in grace, coquetry, and "womanly" skills. Fragments of lessons which survive show that the school stressed the passive and subordinate aspects of womanhood, with little or no emphasis on encouraging female independence. Students were taught how to lift their skirts in order to show a well-turned ankle, and much emphasis was placed on how a woman should not act proud while looking for a husband. Could these have been your original *lesbians?* Consistent with this, the term originally (17thC.) meant pliant and accommodating; only during the nineteenth century did it begin to take on its present meaning and its association with more assertive, if not militant, behavior.

Guise and Gals

It's the men who have always been diffident and clumsy in treating the subject of *lesbianism* as well as in making proper distinctions. Among the types they did identify were *Amy-Johns* (19thC. pun on Amazons) and *bull dykes* (also *bulls, dykes,* and *dikes*). The *bull* is your sexual aggressor; when joined with the *dyke,* a nineteenth-century term for the female *genitals,* it gave us the "aggressive *hole,*" i.e., the masculine *lesbian.*

Some knew her better as the *butch* (20thC.) or when she *butched it up* (mid-20thC.), from a common nickname fathers once bestowed upon their sons. The name "Butch" told the whole world that he was "all boy," like the firm handshake and eye contact, part of the requisite masculine style. The "butch" was once your manly haircut, very short – the crewcut of the forties. All things butch originated with the butcher, one who was never out of character as a man, making it quite clear where today's *butch* stands.

There's really much more – lots of it being researched, much of it unrecorded, but for now, *Lesbian our way homo* (mid-20thC., U.S. teen-age babble).

The Sweet Bi and Bi

That the whole species or kinde should be *bisexous*
          – Sir T. Browne, 1646

Bi-F wanted by attr cpl. Must be sensitive, intllgt, attr, sincere. No drugs, swingers, kooks, or lessies. Photo and phone to Box ---.
          – Providence *Eagle,* August 24, 1980

If you enjoyed the *lesbian* and her friends, you'll flip over *twixters* and *tweenies* (c. 1909: boyish girls and girlish boys), *ambisexuals* (20thC.: married men who have an occasional *homosexual* fling), and *bisexuals* who in addition to being just plain *bi* are also *double-gaited* and *bi-gaited* (20thC., from horses that both trot and gallop). Woody Allen considers them doubly fortunate, being twice as likely to be asked out on a Saturday night.

What a talented and *versatile* group of performers! They're both *ambidextrous* (said primarily of a woman) and *bilingual,* as is your *preference.* Sports fans thrill watching them *bat from either side,* these *switch hitters* who can *go* or *swing both ways.* If you should hear them singing the body electric, it's *AC/DC,* whatever or whichever turns you on.

"Whatta trip!" you say. Then go *transsexual.* The word "*transsexual,*" like so many others in *The Erotic Tongue,* conveys a special image – this one of rapid movement. Hugo Flesch suggests "a train that carries sexuals across the United States without any hassles." In 1952 the *transsexual* went trans-Atlantic when George (now Christine) Jorgenson underwent the first *sex change,* now called a *gender change,* making it into a grammatical exercise of sorts, ending with a great big question mark.

That Special Something

If you'd rather just watch, you can be a *voyeur* and practice your *scopophilia,* your love of watching others undress and engage in sexual activity.

As a show-off of sorts, you stand exposed as an *exhibitionist.* Displaying one's *genitals* publicly has been described by the clinical community as an act of degeneracy, neuropathy, psychosexual infantilism, and the expression of a pathological and perverted personality. We have *flashers* (20thC.), who will stand for almost anything, and *streakers* (c. 1970), always on the go.

Exhibitionism means literally "to hold forth or hold out" to someone (from the Latin *exhibere: ex,* "out," and *habere,* "to have or hold"). Psychologists are also troubled by inhibitions (holding in). Perhaps it's time they made up their mind.

Still looking for the object of your affection? The *fetish* can be quite fashionable (roots include the Latin *facticius* or *factitius:* "made by art"). The Latin became the Portuguese *fetiço,* a word that Portuguese explorers used to describe amulets bought from African natives with the added meaning of "a charm, sorcery, or something that works by a magical act." It passed into French as a *fétiche* on its way to the English *fetish,* a word which we today identify with any item that generates irrational devotion. Sexual *fetishes* are legend. What have you? Parts of the body? Fabric? High-heeled shoes? Hats? Bicycle seats?

Revolting Matters

There are those who, like Dr. Reuben, cannot accept the following simple fact of so many lives (certainly my own): that it is possible to have a mature sexual *relationship* with a woman on Monday, and a mature sexual *relationship* with a man on Tuesday, and perhaps on Wednesday have both together (admittedly, you have to be in good condition for this).

> — Gore Vidal in rebuttal to Dr. David
> Reuben's review of *Myra Breckinridge*
> in *The New York Review of Books*

The legendary Mrs. Patrick Campbell had few questions or concerns about sexual behavior. She didn't care what we did as long as we didn't do it in the streets and scare the horses.

What would Mrs. Campbell have said now? We've not only taken to the streets but also stormed the gates of constraint, torn down the pillars of convention and trampled the canons of morality underfoot. It's nothing short of a revolution in morals. We call it the *sexual revolution* (1960s). The critics describe it as "simply revolting."

The origins of the *blow job* could be found in the *blow*, who served as a *mistress, concubine,* or *prostitute,* a shortened version of the cant *blowen* (18thC.). But it more likely comes from just putting your lips together and . . . The girls who provided the services were known as *lick-spigots* (18thC.), *mouth whores* (19thC.), *suck-stresses* (19thC.,), and *smokers* (20thC.).

Some preferred *to gam,* as an abbreviation of *gama-huche* or from *Gamiani,* the surname of the heroine of a famous nineteenth-century erotic novel of the same name.

For *cunnilingus,* there's *tipping the velvet* (19th-20thC.) and *muff-barking* (20thC.). *The Sensual Man* suggests *the alternating flame,* where the tongue works its way alternately up the inside of the legs until it reaches its final destination, where it at last expires. Part of a series of recipes to keep one's marriage from burning out.

† † †

The French toasted their own culture during the nineteenth century with *café au lait* (the female *puden-dum*). *Aller au café,* "to go for coffee," and *prendre sa demi-tasse au café des deux colonnes,* "to have coffee at the café of the two columns," was to project one's lips upon the *cup of pleasure* (18thC.) — what to the uninitiated is known as *cunnilingus.*

Avaler les enfants des autres — "to swallow another's children" — was to act as a *fellator* to a woman fresh from the embrace of another man, i.e., to *gamahuche* a *buttered bun.*

Many states still have laws on the books that make it illegal to eat your wife. Some folks adhere to the letter of the law. Others merely pay it lip service.

† † †

It wasn't always easy for men to do it with one another. In nineteenth-century America, when they practiced *orastupration,* you said a mouthful. Today, they have a *picnic* doing it. And that includes not only *tasters, munchers, noshers* (all 20thC.), *nibblers* (early 20thC.), and *gobblers* (19th-20thC.), but *cannibals* and *man-eaters* (both 20thC.) as well.'

† † †

It's not as if there haven't been plenty of colorful expressions for the *homosexual*. *Urnings* may sound like something out of Dr. Seuss, but they really were the creation of a Dr. Karl Heinrich Ulrichs (1825-1895), a nineteenth-century scientist. He was one of the first to try to explain and classify such behavior, calling it *uranism* to describe a condition in which the female soul resided in a male body. The *urnings* and their condition come from the numerous references to Uranus in Plato's *Symposium,* with its idealization of the *homosexual*. Like Plato, the good Doctor always wrote on the topic with both sympathy and understanding.

Urnings, however, never caught on either among Ulrichs' colleagues or within the lay community. And we are now the sadder for it, having lost a colorful and expressive term. Contemporary media would have simply adored it – what with some guy *"urning a living"* and two men *"urning for each other."* With several successful trips already to the moon, it would seem almost natural to anticipate a trip to Uranus.

† † †

For some light reading on the topic of sadism you might curl up with *The experimental lecture by Colonel Sparker on the exciting and voluptuous pleasures to be derived from crushing and humiliating the spirit of a beautiful and modest young lady; and delivered by him in the assembly room of the society of aristocratic flagellants* (late 19thC.).

† † †

Coitus per anum has inspired all kinds of *back-door work* (19th-20thC.), including a *behind the behind*

(20thC.), a *dip in the fudge pot* (mid-20thC.), a *daub of the brush* (mid-20thC.), *99* (20thC.), a *keister-stab* or *bum-f**k* (20thC.), some *pedication,* a *pig-sticking* (early 20thC.), and a *ram job* (mid-20thC.).

Bee identified the practitioner as a *backgammoner* (mid-18th-early 19thC.) or *backgammon player:* "a fellow whose propensities lie out of the natural order of things." We also knew him as a *gentleman of the back door* (18th-20thC.). The active partner or the *inserter* (or *insertee*) is also known as *birdie* (early-mid-20thC.), a *bird-taker* (early 20thC.), *brown-hatter* (early 20thC.), *brownie* (mid-20thC.), *brownie king* or *queen* (mid-20thC.), *bugger* (14th-16thC.), *burgler* (early 20thC.), *cornholer* (20thC. – did they really used to clean the *anus* with corncobs?), *eye-opener* (20thC.), *indorser* (late 18th-early 19thC.), *ingler* (early 17thC.), *inspector of manholes, jockey, reamer* (all early 20thC.), and *stern chaser* (19thC.).

Let's not forget the *gooser* (20thC., Can. for *pederast*). The *goose* has seen it all—from a *finger thrust* to a *pederastic act* (earlier, in 19thC., it was a *prostitute,* and an act of *copulation*). Mencken defined the goose as "a most pugnacious bird often given to nipping the buttocks of humans who offend it." Where to locate the elusive bird? "Bend your knees and touch your toes, and I'll show you where the wild goose goes" (mid-20thC.).

† † †

Socrates *had* his famous pupil Alcibiades. During the latter part of the nineteenth century, they used to say *se laisser Alcibiadiser,* to *play Alcibiades,* for one assuming the passive role in *pederasty.* A distinction soon arose between Socratic love (*amour socratique*) and that of a Platonic variety (*amour platonique*), though it's clear that when Plato wrote of human love in the *Phaedo,* he really meant *homosexual* love. This is further underscored in his other writings. In his *Symposium,* it's love between two men he considered the noblest and most spiritual.

Henry III's favorite boys were called *mignons* (today,

minions). A diarist at the court, Pierre de L'Estoile described them thus:

> These pretty mignons wore their hair pomaded, artificially curled and recurled, flowing back over their little velvet bonnets, like those of *whores* in a *bordello,* and the ruffs of their starched linen shirts were a half-foot long, so that seeing their heads above the ruffs was like seeing Saint John's head upon a platter. The rest of their clothes were made the same way. Their exercises were playing, blaspheming, fencing, and *whoring,* and following their king everywhere.

† † †

Speaking of the *sorority,* we've got the *daughters of Bilitis* (*c.* 1955), from the name of the *lesbian* poet in "Songs of Bilitis" by Pierre Louÿs. As for special words for activities, the best we can do is *tribadism* (16th-20thC.), from the Greek for "to rub," the activity of men most closely associated with it. There are few phrases unique to the *lesbian* community; most have been borrowed from other parts of *The Erotic Tongue.* Some of the better ones are *flat f**k* or *Venus observa femina, vice versa* for mutual *cunnilingus,* and a *she-male,* a recent synonym for a *butch,* thought to be especially popular in women's prisons.

NINE

The Dynamic Duo

If the Lord had not wanted us to be tempted by the flesh, why did he make us of flesh – why not burlap, or Jell-O?

— Marty Feldman, *In God We Trust,*
1980

Sex as the world's greatest act may be fine theater, but most people still consider it a game in which competitors with finely honed skills are pitted against each other. The stakes are high, the action, fast-paced. A program's essential: you can't tell the players without one.

How you play the game depends largely on how you look at it. Seasoned male practitioners see as its primary objective *getting into her pants* (mid-20thC.), a challenge made all the more difficult by her being in them at the same time. Once he has *got it on* successfully, he is said to have *scored.* Points are awarded both for technical proficiency and artistic impression.

Your One and Only

We all are mortal men and frail,
And oft are guided by the *tail.*

— Bridges, *Burlesque Humor,* 1774

It's all in the approach. We once knew it as the *three F's* (19thC.): *f**k, fun, and a footrace,* in reference to a wild time and a *lewd* person. More recently it's *the four-F method* (c. 1890): *find, feel, f**k, and forget,* though we later thoughtfully added " 'em" to the expression. The editors of *The American Thesaurus of Slang* (1953) coyly recorded it as *find 'em, feel 'em, frig 'em, and forget 'em.*

The game's leading scorer is the legendary a*sman (mid-20thC.). The *a*sman* cometh but sayeth little. A deep conversation consists primarily of *"getting much?"* or *"getting any?"* His reputation speaks for itself. His credo: *"I've seen more a*s than a toilet seat."*

Here's Looking at You!

Put a bag over her head
You don't have to *f**k* the bag.
— Anon., 20thC.

Put a flag over her face and *f**k* for Old Glory.
— Anon., 20thC.

His limited perspective comes of *looking at every woman through the hole in his pr**k* (late 19th-20thC.). He used to look for a *fast filly* (early 17thC.); today it's the *fox* (1960s, U.S. Black slang). But more than likely he'll come home with a *dog* or a *bow-wow* (mid-20thC.) on his arm. Even a *pig* (mid-20thC.) isn't out of the question. His philosophy is: *"All petticoats are sisters in the dark"* (18thC.). An equal-opportunity employer, he's not concerned with age. As for older women: *"They don't swell, won't tell, and are as grateful as hell"* (20thC.). His general assessment of most females: *"I wouldn't kick her out of bed for eating crackers"* (mid-20thC.).

Mr. Everything

He only answered by gracious nods and approbation, whilst he *looked goats and monkeys* at me.
— Cleland, *Fanny Hill,* 1749

There's no avoiding him. The *a*sman* is everywhere — perched on street corners or just strolling down the highways and byways of life. Today, he frequents the singles bar. Years ago he slithered about as a *parlor snake* (c. 1915) and a *lounge-lizard* (c. 1912). *Leching* always brings out the animal in him; it brings out several in fact: the *young stud* (19thC.), the *old goat,* the *town bull* (both 16thC.), the *game-cock* (19thC.), the *gay dog* (1920s), and the *tomcat* (19thC.), just to name a few. But let's not forget the *wolf,* who first entered the lexicon as a *homosexual* around World War I, quickly established his manhood, and emerged from World War II as a *WFC* (wolf, first class) – your classic *lech* (*c.* 1918) on the *prowl* (17th-20thC.).

For many years we thought him *gallant,* polite and attentive to women. His roots (*galer*), however, also show him having a good time; *galer* comes from the old High German *geil,* "wanton," with ties to the Anglo-Saxon *gāl,* the source of *gay* – making for a gala occasion at that.

French *gallants* were always reputed to be extraordinary lovers, though not everyone has been impressed by their sexual prowess. During the Franco-Prussian War (1870-71), an English *demimondaine* visiting Paris wrote of these same *gallants,* "The tripe-colored *mousquetaires* who infest this capital are not capable of making anything heave except my stomache."

The Man for All Seasons

They [men] want only one thing.
　　　　　　　　　　　　– Anon.

In a short time he had established himself as a *philanderer* (17thC.), originally a female lover of men, later a lover, and finally a male flirt; a *libertine* (16thC., from the Roman deity, Liber, a god of fertility, whose annual celebration featured a giant wooden *phallus* carted about the countryside, followed by a crowd of drunken revelers who later crowned it with a wreath); and a *rake* (16thC. – you'd have to "rake hell to find another like him").

He was now an integral part of the Western literary tradition, and we identified him with the greatest: *Lothario, Casanova,* and *Don Juan.* This isn't just your average Romeo we're talking about.

Faint Preys

In striking contrast to his female counterpart, the *a∗sman* has had few harsh words said about him. Most thought the *lecher* (since 12thC.) pretty bad, but nonetheless found him acceptable. Even the vile *rapist* – his name has never been considered obscene.

This is not to say we haven't kidded the *a∗sman* on occasion. *The answer to a maiden's prayer* (19th-20thC.), they used to say – *God's gift to women* (20thC.), satisfaction guaranteed. You had only to return the unused portion for a full refund. Some say he's not worth a *pendejo* – "a pubic hair" in Spanish.

So's Your Father

He's so tough they have to take a wrench to loosen his *nuts* at night so he can sleep.

– Anon., 20thC.

The day of the *a∗sman* is now over. We no longer consider him *gallant*, not even a *smooth article* (*c.* 1913), or a *smoothie* (*c.* 1915). He's still *macho*, from the Spanish *machismo* for exaggerated masculine pride, and a *real cool dude* (mid-20thC.). The *dude*, who entered the language in 1883 as a term of ridicule for a dandy or swell, was derived from the German *dudenkopf*, a "drowsy head." This left him a fool *dawdling about*.

Macho does not prove mucho.

– Zsa Zsa Gabor

What in Creation?

So God created man in His own image, in the image of God created He him; male and female created He them.

– Genesis 1:27

And Adam said, This is now bone of my bones, and flesh of my flesh.

– Adam, on seeing Eve, Genesis 2:23

The *a∗sman's* not just anybody's fool. He's primarily woman's. She's his chief competitor and arch foe, and every bit as good at playing the game.

The contest goes back to Year One, to the world's first woman, and a *fallen woman* at that. Her name was *Lilith.* "What

173

of Eve?" you ask. Contrary to the conventional wisdom, Eve, Adam's helpmate, was but a poor second — falsely represented as number one by the same folks who brought you the rest of the Western intellectual tradition. But because few males celebrate *Lilith* as an ideal type of womanhood, she has been successfully exorcised from scripture and erased from the consciousness of contemporary men and women.

You won't find her story in the Old Testament despite what appear to be two conflicting accounts of the creation of woman. The popular version can be found in Chapter 2 of Genesis — woman as "sparerib." It is a humiliating story in which she is fashioned almost as a divine afterthought out of an insignificant portion of the masculine frame in order to comply with Adam's need for amusement. This account is the one that has come to be accepted as gospel. Less well known, however, is the untold story referred to in Chapter 1 of Genesis, in which Woman is created simultaneously with Man, each reflecting in equal measure the glory of the divine original. It's a tale that appears to have gotten lost in the telling, and it's time to set the record straight.

Medieval scholars used *Lilith* to help reconcile the apparent contradiction by citing her as the first woman in Adam's life, the woman mentioned in Chapter 1. *Lilith* and Adam — a match made in heaven. Though literally created for each other, they're in trouble from the very outset. Adam insists on exercising his male prerogative and tries to dominate the household. *Lilith* refuses to be subservient, believing herself Adam's equal, since they have been created in the same manner.

Angry and hurt, Adam is beside himself. Things come to a head when she refuses to lie beneath him — to assume the recumbent or passive posture during *intercourse*. This really gets his back up and sets the stage for a confrontation between the first male chauvinist pig and the first liberated woman. Adam has had it, and he cries out to God in his agony. *Lilith* simply packs up and leaves. She declines paradise and a subordinate role for the right to assert her own identity, and establishes a life of her own. *Lilith* thus bears witness for all womanhood and its future burdens of submission.

But an uppity woman is a *fallen woman*. It's only a matter of time before *Lilith* becomes history's first *good-time girl*. She settles down in the notorious Red Sea region, an area populated by evil spirits and other devilish creatures. There her passion for equality blossoms into a fullblown demonic career. She consorts with various and sundry lascivious spirits of the night and generates "lillum," ass-haunched devil-children, at the prodigious rate of one hundred per day.

At Adam's request, God dispatches a trio of angels to bring her back. He strikes dead a number of her progeny and threatens worse. But *Lilith* is adamant and refuses to return. Why trade her exciting new life by the Red Sea for a mundane role as an honest housewife? God finally gives up, and the angels return empty-handed, but God pacifies Adam by creating Eve as a proper stay-at-home mate.

Rabbinical tradition has *Lilith* consorting again with Adam — returning to him both during the period of 130 years when he is separated from Eve following their expulsion from the Garden of Eden, and also during the time when, after Abel was murdered, Adam decides to have no further relations with Eve. From Adam's and Lilith's unholy *union,* in which it is said that Adam's "generative powers were misused and misdirected," comes a variety of demons, or *Shedim,* who rove about the world plaguing mankind.

As time goes on the *Lilith* myth becomes even more elaborately embroidered, and *Lilith,* the forerunner of equal rights, is eclipsed completely by *Lilith,* Queen of the Underworld. What ensues is the most sweeping and devasting character assassination in history. Aspersions begin to be circulated as to her origin. It is said by some that she was created not from pure dust, as was Adam, but from filth and sediment. Others identify her as one of the wives of Sammael, or Satan; being of a wild and passionate nature, she had deserted her demonic spouse in order to take up with Adam.

She is depicted as heading up a retinue of evil spirits and destroying angels — taking to the skies each night, screeching her hatred of mankind and vowing vengeance for the contemptible manner in which she was and continues to be treated by the Adams of the world. She terrifies households and poses a special threat to the children therein. She is further charged with provoking men to commit the gravest of sins — participation in a sexual act without the benefit of a woman. (Would you have it *nocturnal pollution?*) As the quintessential *other woman,* she's your original home-wrecker, actively working to destroy the family unit of which she cannot be a part.

So there's your *Lilith:* Everyman's fantasy, Woman as Man would like her — but totally out of his reach and class.

Isn't it time that her name was cleared and that she was returned to the language, synonymous with the independence of spirit, intelligence, and free will that she represents?

Lilith, won't you please come home?

Who Was That Lady?

Phryne had talents for mankind;
Open she was and unconfined,
Like some free port of trade:
Merchants unloaded here their freight,
And agents from each foreign state
here first their entry made.

— Alexander Pope, *Phryne,* early 18thC.

Wives for child-bearing,
Hetaerae for companionship,
Slaves for lust.

— Demosthenes

Lilith was only the first in a long line of historical figures whose names have become synonymous with the highest virtues of the oldest vice. The Old Testament provided us with the deceitful *Delilah* as well as the utterly shameless *Jezebel* (II Kings 9:33): "And he said, Throw her down. So they threw her down." Ancient Greece and Rome likewise made significant contributions.

She was at her very best as a *hetaera* (literally, "companion or woman friend") and considered among the most treasured assets of the Athenian city-state. Renowned for their beauty, many *hetaerae* were also famous for their intellectual capabilities, their quick wit and repartee, and the considerable political and economic influence they wielded. Relationships with *hetaerae* were often lasting, and *liaisons* were not merely sexual.

The more famous include Thäis, the Athenian *courtesan* and

mistress of Alexander the Great and Ptolemy; *Aspasia,* mistress of Pericles; and *Phryne,* who was charged with impiety by the state and was defended by one of her *lovers,* the orator Hyperides, who secured her acquittal by exhibiting her partially in the *nude,* the *naked* truth ultimately winning out.

They continued their activity in one form or another through the centuries. One born of sufficiently high social class who was also discriminating about whom she bedded down with was likely to be viewed with envy and grudging respect. People spoke of her as a *woman of the world, a woman of pleasure,* or, at the very worst, an *adventuress.* A favorite of the nineteenth century was the *demimondaine* (sometimes shortened to just *mondaine* or *demi*), a phrase invented by Alexandre Dumas the younger to refer to a woman of doubtful reputation and social standing who occupied the half-world or half-society on the outskirts of the established order. Though many were uncomfortable with her uncertain status, others took to her for her services, believing half aloof better than none.

Fallout

The tree of knowledge stood – ah! yes, it stood.
Past tense, you see – and while the past was good,
The present need was great, without a doubt
And pretty Eve began to fret and pout.
She wept and sighed and said, "I see it all,
For here was life and there, alas! the fall."

— Anon., "The Fall of Man"

In Adam's fall we all took quite a tumble, but women fell hardest. The aforementioned ladies lost society's respect in the process, leaving them all *promiscuous. Promiscuous* comes from the Latin *pro* and *miscere,* "in favor of mixing it up." Both men and women mix well, but only women are thought *promiscuous* – for doing what men do all the time.

The Broad-based Experience

A woman without respect is just another *broad* (c. 1925). *"Have you ever been abroad?"* (mid-20thC., teen-age boy struggling to make conversation). Originally a term for a *mistress* or a *prostitute, broad* is now a catch-all term of contempt. We're not terribly sure about her origins. Much speculation centers on the *bawd* (14th-17thC., *"procurer,"* 18thC., *"procuress"*), who made her way up through the ranks. The word may have its roots in the German *bald,* meaning bold. Partridge found her "broad in the beams," i.e., "broad where a broad should be broad" ("Honey Bun" in *South Pacific*). *Broad* also implies a certain latitude in matters personal. After all, she was once a *lady of expansive sensibilities* (19thC.).

Making Do

Let us eat, drink, and *make* merry
for tomorrow Mary may reform.

—Anon., 1920's

When better men are made,
Vassar women will *make* them.

—Wall hanging, Vassar College, 1960's

This girl has definitely *been there* (19th-20thC.), abroad? She's *on the make* and *puts out* (both 20thC., U.S.) — though the British have a better sense of direction as a *put-in* (19thC.) — and is said to be *merry-legged* (19thC.), *nimble-hipped* (19th-20thC.), *on the flutter* (c. 1875), and *willing to pay a bill on sight* (c. 1820-1910). *Easy* (17thC.) does it. She's an *easy lay* (17thC.), and an *easy make* (20thC.). She's got the *rabbit habit* and is *hopping for it* (both 20thC.).

The Heat of the Moment

When Gods have *hot backs,*
What shall poor men do?

—Shakespeare, *Merry Wives of Windsor*

An itching *c**t* feels no shame.

—Anon., mid-18th-20thC.

The *heat is on* (19th-20thC., said of a woman who is *sexually* excited), and some like it hot. The *fire-box* (c. 1900-15, a man of unceasing passion), is a *fiery lot* (c. 1840-1900, "a fast man"), and there's simply no cooling his ardor. This *broad* is *as warm as they make them* (c. 1909); in fact, *there's a fire down below* (mid-20thC.). She's got *a bad case of the hots* (20thC.), *a hot back*, and *a hot-bot* (also *Miss Hotbot* or *Lady Hotbot*, c. 1920). She's a *hot sketch, hot stuff* (20thC.), *a hot biscuit* (1930s), *hotter than a red firewagon, hotter'n a Fourth-of-July hoedown* (both 20thC.), *hot as a firecracker* (c. 1910), to the point of being downright explosive, a regular *bangster* (19thC.) — she's your *blonde bombshell with the great gams* (1940s).

Do You Take This Man?

In school they voted her most likely to conceive. Her picture in the yearbook was horizontal.

— Rodney Dangerfield

Out of the novice category and fast approaching professional status, she's now a full-fledged *nympho*, a truncated *nymphomaniac*, suffering from an insatiable *sex drive*, also called *erotomania, furor feminus*, or *hot pants*. The original *nymphs* of Greek mythology were the eternal brides of the streams and forests known to cavort with *satyrs*. Latin assisted us with the word *nubilis*, which is related to *nymph*, giving us not only our *nubile* maiden, but also making her ripe for the *nuptials*.

Their Finest Hour

The *town bull* (17thC.) and the *common cow* (19th-20thC.) — destined for each other. *She's got an itch in her belly to pay with the scarlet hue* (c. 1720, D'Urfey), and he's just dying to *get it on. Don't fight it, it's bigger than both of us* (mid-20thC.).

The dénouement? Faster than a speeding bullet... *"Wham-bam-thank-you-ma'am"* (20thC.), a phrase which began life in the Black community around 1895 as *bip-bam*, from a popular song of the times. Once considered a descriptive term expressing gratitude after *lovemaking*, it now connotes a rapid and uninvolved sexual *encounter* — a fine thank-you if ever you heard one.

Down and Dirty

In the language used to speak of women, dirtiness and sex have gone together, while men have gotten off scot-free. Words which describe her as slovenly and untidy make her seem immoral as well, the inference being that sloppy women are as derelict in their morals as they are in appearance.

There is none dirtier than the *slut* (14thC.) or *slattern* (17thC.), unless it's the *draggle-tail* (16thC.) or the *drabble-tail* (19thC., literally "one who dirties the hem of her skirt"), often synonymous with the *bob-tail* (17th-18thC., Grose, "one who plays with her tail"), and the *cock-tail* (19th-20thC.), who also put it to professional use.

Our ordinary *floosie* (or *floosey*, or *floozie*, *c.* 1940) is not without prospects for redemption. Her origins go back to her proper name, Florence (17th-early 19thC.). Florence meant a girl who has been tousled and ruffled, and once meant sloppily dressed. But around 1935 she began to clean up her act; "flossy" entered the language, meaning "to dress up or to refurbish," giving us a new and improved *floosy*, finely decked out and ready to party.

Word spread quickly from the popular song, "The Flat-Foot Floogie with the Floy-Floy" (*c.* 1938), and she became a special favorite of Navy men, helping establish her present reputation as a bubble-headed, fun-loving *accessible* simp.

A Class by Herself

But her reputation still remained suspect as a *woman of a certain class* (19thC.). *Bunters* (18th-19thC.) picked up the rags from the streets; *scrubbers* (early 20thC.) cleaned and washed; and *doxies* (16th-18thC., from the Dutch *docke*, a "*doll* or *dolly*, a *mistress* or *prostitute*") accompanied those who begged for a living. The *trollop* (17th-19thC.) was coarse and vulgar. Today everyone knows the *tramp* for what she is. Class distinctions always made it easy to identify her, though *the hoity-toity wench* (late 17th-early 19thC.) still didn't know her place.

It was traditional to not only treat lower-class women like dirt, but to further characterize them as *lewd*. *Lewd* once referred to anyone not belonging to the holy orders, hence unlearned and unteachable. Being *lewd* made a woman rude and artless, which some deemed characteristic of the lower classes. Her ignorance and rude manners were then accepted as conclusive evidence of *lascivious* and *unchaste* behavior, the meaning which we associate with *lewd* today.

The language has claimed many an innocent victim in this fashion. The *hussy* (early 16thC.) started offf as a simple phonetic reduction of "housewife" but soon came to mean a country woman, a lower-class bumpkin, and finally (19th-20thC.) a temptress and seductress, which, when preceded by "brazen" or "shameless," made the "housewife" the threat to the family she is.

Bits and Pieces

A chapter of chambermaids, *green gowns,* and *old
hats . . .*

—Sterne, *Tristam Shandy,* 1760

Man has always had difficulty dealing with woman as a total entity, requiring that he pursue her a little at a time. This has forever made her attractive to him as *bits, pieces, chippies,* and *hunks* (20thC., also used by a woman speaking of a man).

In Victorian times, they made every little bit count, including a *fresh bit* (c. 1840, a beginner, or a new mistress), a *bit of crumb* (c. 1880, a pretty, plump girl, similar to the Yiddish *zaftig,* 20thC.), as well as a *bit of skin, stuff* (mid-19th-20thC.), or *goods* (c. 1860) — which they hoped would also *be a bit of all right* (20thC., one who was both attractive and obliging).

Settling for relatively modest increments, they only wanted to *tear off a piece* (19thC.). Who or what wasn't material. It could be a *fine piece of dry goods,* some *fluff* (20thC.), *a bit of frock* (c. 1875-1910, attractive and well dressed), or *as pretty a piece of muslin as you'd wish to see* (19thC.). In the eighteenth century, they *labored leather* (18thC., one very young). Shortly thereafter, they ran after *calico* (1880-1920, U.S.).

Men still *chase skirt* today, but a piece of dacron or polyester just doesn't have the same feel to it.

Winging It

It takes a tough man to *make* a tender *chicken*.

— Frank Perdue, TV commercial
c. 1976

With several coated *quails* and *laced muttons* waggishly singing.

— Rabelais, Peter Motteux, trans., 1708

We now consider such talk passé and, worse yet, sexist. It's also sexist to call a woman a *chick* and a sure way to ruffle her feathers. Though *chick* and *chick-a-biddy* (*c.* 1785) were once innocent terms of endearment for a young girl, our more recent *chicks* have generally been "slick," especially when accompanied by cats deemed "hip" and "cool" (1940s).

Few remember the *chicken fancier* or *pullet-squeezer looking to strop his beak* (*c.* 1830). As a *womanizer* that "likes 'em young," he was one who always had his eye on the *virgin pullet*, "a young woman, though often trod, has never laid" (Bee, *c.* 1820-70); failing that, any *game pullet* (late 18th-19thC.), one guaranteeing a good *lay*, would do. *Quail* (17thC.) was also considered a fine game bird, in this instance not unrelated to the Celtic *caile*, "a girl." A *covey* of same (late 17thC.-early 19thC.) referred to a well-filled *bawdy house*. We later had *San Quentin quail* (mid-20thC., a.k.a. *jail bait*), whose pursuit was not without risk, often landing not the bird, but the fancier, in the "cage."

Smile When You Say That

"When I use a word," Humpty Dumpty said in a rather scornful tone, "it means just what I choose it to mean. Neither more nor less." "The question is," said Alice, "whether you can make words mean so many different things." "The question is," said Humpty Dumpty, "who is to be master. That is all."

— Lewis Carroll, *Alice in Wonderland*

Women tried to be cheerful throughout the ordeal. The *minx* (16thC.) was pert and cheeky, and men took it to mean she was *wanton*. *Wanton* (13thC.) had always implied a certain lack of discipline, but by the sixteenth century it described any *lewd* and *immoral* person, most likely a woman.

The *chippy* (also *chippie*, 1880s) should have seen it coming. Begining life as a somewhat impudent lass noted for her short-ness of temper, she quickly began her descent. We soon knew her as a *dance-hall girl,* then one *given to amorous dalliance,* and finally as a *semipro,* "one who would just as soon give it away as charge for it." The origin of the word may be the chirping sound she made to attract passing males, or the treatment of her as just another *piece* – a small chip(py) off the old block.

Men consider any female who makes them uncomfortable, either by appearance or manners, to be fair game. Our con-dolences to the poor lass who is ill kempt, doing menial work, is spirited and independent – obviously an *easy mark.*

Over the years we've known the *a*sman* as:

Amorist (16thC.)
Ballocker (19thC.)
Basher (20thC.)
Bed-presser (17thC.)
Belly-bumper (late 17thC.)
Bird's nester (19thC.)
Carnalite (late 16thC.)
Chimney sweep (19thC.)
Cocksmith (20thC.)
Dolly mopper (19thC.)
Faggoteer (19thC.)
Faggot master (19thC.)
Fishmonger (19thC.)
Fleece hunter (19thC.)
Forbidden fruit eater (20thC.)

Gap stopper (late 18thC.)
Gay man (19thC.)
Gully raker (19thC.)
Holer (18thC.)
Ladykiller (20thC.)
Lover boy (20thC.)
Make-out artist (mid-20thC.)
Mutton monger (c. 1580)
Passionate Pilgrim (18thC.)
Poopster (19thC.)
Sexpert (1940s)
Skirt chaser (20thC.)
Top diver (late 17thC.-late 18thC.)
Wencher (since 16thC.
Whisker splitter (c. 1785-1840)

† † †

Lothario, Don Juan, and *Casanova* are the big three of *libertinism.*

Lothario was the lech in *The Fair Penitent,* a play by Nicholas Rowe (1703).

Don Juan made his debut in the *Rake of Seville,* and quickly became the dominant *sex symbol* of his age. We also know him from the works of Molière, Corneille, Dumas, Balzac, and Flaubert. He was immortalized by Mozart in the opera *Don Giovanni* (libretto by Lorenzo da Ponte) and came to be most prominently associated with *libertinism* through Lord Byron's *Don Juan.* His figure in fiction proved so popular that it soon overtook reality, helping transform seduction and desertion from malicious sport into an admired and exalted activity. His spirit lives on.

Giovanni Jacopo *Casanova* de Seingalt (1725-1798) was an Italian of Spanish descent who was expelled from the University of Padua at fifteen for gambling and at sixteen for immoral conduct. His first recorded sexual experience was with two young sisters in one bed. An inveterate *f**ker,* he lists 116 *mistresses* by name and claims hundreds of seductions, from noblewomen to chambermaids — done standing, lying down, sitting, in bed, on couches, on boats, floors, and alleyways. His conquests included his own daughter, a nine-year-old child, and a seventy-year-old woman. As he lay on his deathbed — alone — awaiting his maker, his last words were "I regret nothing. I have lived and died a Christian."

† † †

How accessible is a woman? She can be:

The low road (Shakespeare): "trodden by many feet as a hen may be trodden by many cocks." See *to tread* in "The Big F," Chapter 2.

The common shore (Haywood and Massinger, "The Honest Whore"): "Your body is like the common shore that still receives all the town's filth. The sin of many men is within you!"

A hay bag (19th-20thC.): something to lie upon

A hat rack (20thC.): receiving all sizes and shapes

An easy mark (20thC.): frequently punctuated

The town bike, omnibus (c. 1920, Aust., and 20thC., Eng.): ridden by all

The public ledger (19thC.): hundreds of entries

As discriminating as she is democratic, she only

f**ks her friends, and she *doesn't have an enemy in the world* (mid-20thC.).

† † †

The poor had a sexual language of their own derived from the cant and criminal jargon of the English under-class of the seventeenth and eighteenth centuries. Theirs was a world peopled by *morts, dells,* and *culls. Morts* were the more experienced females. *Dells,* according to Bee, were:

> young *buxom* wenches, ripe and prone to *venery* but who have not lost their *virginity* which the upright man [one of the more powerful men in the criminal hierarchy] claims by virtue of his prerogative after which they become free for any of the fraternity.

See the mort and the cull at clicket in the dyke.
Look at the broad and the guy getting it on in the ditch.

The cull wapt the mort's bite.
The fellow enjoyed the wench heartily.

† † †

Women have for a long time been considered *fair game* (late 17th-early 19thC. collective term for *harlots*): *moose* (20thC.), *badgers* (19thC.), and *squirrels* (late 18th-mid-19thC.). The squirrel "covers its back with its tail," Grose).

Students of *horsemanship* (16th-17thC., *copulation*) had their own lexicon. *Pretty filly* was turf talk for a pert young lass. In *Sportsman's Slang,* Captain Bee's classifications were: "*fillies, running fillies* and *entered fillies* which express the condition of town-girls—usually such as attend at races and parts adjacent."

They are not to be confused with *trots* (16th-17thC.), *hobby-horses* (16th-17thC.), and *bob-tails* (17th-18thC.), experienced carriers, ready to be mounted for the right price; or *mares,* a general term for a woman or a wife (16th-17thC.). The *jades* were workhorses, worn out and long past their prime; by the sixteenth century they were treated as contemptible women and *whores.*

Not all *birds* (*harlots* from *c.* 1900) were *high fliers* – fashionable *prostitutes,* women about town who would *job a coach* or *keep a couple of saddle horses* (Bee).

We have had *lady birds* who expressed affection and were often described as life-long companions (as with President Lyndon Johnson's one and only) as well as *coquettes,* literally little cocks, noted for their *flirtatious* manner. Those known best for their inconstancy were the *fly-by-nights* (19th-20thC.); they included *canaries* (18th-early 19thC.), *nightingales* (*c.* 1840), *soiled doves* (late 17th-mid-18thC.), *wrens* (*c.* 1869), *plovers* (early 17thC.), *pheasants* (17thC.), and *partridges* (early 17th-mid-18thC.) – not all "spring chickens," but pigeons all. This is to say nothing of an occasional *bat* (17th-early 19thC.) or *moth* (*c.* 1876).

The Sporting Life

Now that we have agreed on the principle, we must merely be haggling over the price.

— George Bernard Shaw

If you've got the money, honey, I've got the time.

— Popular song, 1940s

Her fee tells you that she means business. It places her clearly *on the batter* (c. 1830), *on the grind* (19thC.), *on the loose, on the business* (c. 1921), or *into the trade.*

What else would she be doing? Maybe *peddling her hips, fluttering her skirt* (c. 1850), *trading on her bottom, selling customhouse goods* (mid-18th-early 19thC.), and *hawking her meat* (19th-20thC.). "Get it while it's hot!"

As a *well-rigged frigate,* she could be found *carrying the broom up* (c. 1820-90), from the time when it was customary to attach a broom to the masthead of a ship that was for sale.

Some missed the boat. When a judge asked the prisoner standing before him, "What are you, young lady?" she replied, "I am *in the vay of life,* your honor" (c. 1823, Grose). Once she was *on the game* (17thC.) or in *a mode of living* (movie newsreel: *News of the World*). Today, she's *in the life* or *into the game.* Don't trivialize it. Just because it's a *game* doesn't mean that it's not a serious matter. As a distinguished *pimp* once put it, "man, the *game* is deep!"

Ho, ho, ho!

Sing *whore*, sing *whore*
Behind and before.
Her price is a shilling
She never gets more.

— Song in Farmer and Henley, *Slang
and Its Analogues*

'Tis pity she's a *whore*, but them's the breaks of the *game*. She's been one since before the twelfth century (Old English *hore).* We once considered her polite, a euphemism for another expression long since forgotten. In fact, she's a relative of the Latin *carus* for "dear." But like all good euphemisms, she too became common, vulgar, and unacceptable.

Back in 1833, Noah Webster sounded an uncertain *strumpet* (*c.* 1327), from the Latin *strupum,* "dishonor"), bowdlerizing the Old Testament and driving all *whores* to cover. *Hoores* had appeared in the first English edition of the Bible in the fourteenth century, but Webster thought it best to replace them with *lewd women* and *harlots.*

More recently, we'd rather not speak of her at all. In 1934, H.L. Mencken noted how New York newspapers reviewing the play *Within the Gates* handled the part of the Young *Whore.* One newspaper referred to her as the Young *Prostitute;* a second, as the Young *Harlot;* the third, as a girl who had *gone astray.* The fourth simply avoided any mention of her at all by ignoring the entire cast.

We've tried to cushion her impact by promoting the British pronunciation *hoor* and the inner-city *ho,* and have disguised her by employing rhyming slang with *Jane Shore, sloop of war* (19thC.), and *two-by-four* (early 20thC., U.S.). But nothing seems to work. In England, you'll still find her blatantly *whoring along the dilly* (Picadilly Circus). In the States we still have the *hard-leg whore,* street-hardened and used up "with millions of miles on her." Tuned up for yet another trip around the square.

Courtesy Pays

And Lais of Corinth ask'd Demosthenes one hundred crownes for one night's business.

—Taylor, *Workes,* 1630

The *courtesan,* like the *whore,* lost her dignity and standing over time. The first *courtesans* were ladies of the court. We later modeled them on the *hetaerae,* and knew them to read and compose poetry and to have fine minds as well as bodies. By the sixteenth century, however, they had a clear-cut reputation, as recorded by traveler Thomas Coryat in his *Crudities:*

As for the number of these Venetian *courtezans,* it is very great . . . at the least 20,000, whereof many are esteemed so loose that they are said to *open their quiver to every arrow.*

The Victorian era elevated the *courtesans'* status slightly, making them somewhat better than your ordinary *streetwalker.* When someone asked Nell Kimball about the *courtesan,* she testily replied, "I knew what a *courtesan* was; it was a high-class, high-kicking *harr!*" Currently we use the term to describe the high-priced *call girl* with a few "select" customers.

An Oft-repeated Tail

A *harlot* with sincerity and a square egg: They both do not exist.

—Japanese proverb

The *harlot's* quite another story. This one takes place in the sixteenth-century French countryside and centers upon the beautiful *Arlette,* or Heleva, daughter of Falbert, a tanner of Falaise. Physically mature beyond her years, but innocence personified, our young maiden made the tragic error of washing her clothes outdoors while naked. Chance had the handsome Robert LeDiable, Duke of Normandy, riding by. Their eyes met, and the rest is history—the birth of William the Conqueror, to be known forever to the world as The Bastard. For her *wanton* behavior, all women so disposed in the future were to carry her name – *Arlette,* or *harlot.*

Would it were true. Unfortunately, the first recorded *harlot* was not a woman but a man. Chaucer even treated him as a good fellow and a somewhat decent chap at that, but between the thirteenth and the fifteenth centuries, his disposition took a turn for the worst, and he became synonymous with a rascal, a knave, and a *fornicator,* a general rogue of sorts. It wasn't until the sixteenth century (about the same time that *Arlette* came into vogue) that we spoke of a woman as a *harlot,* and then only in reference to show-biz types such as jugglers and dancers, a group always deemed suspect by ordinary citizens.

If you're searching for her real roots, you'll probably find them in the medieval Latin *arlotus* for "glutton," though some prefer *hari,* Old German for "war" and *lodere,* Old English for "beggar," making *harlots* into war beggars and *camp followers.* The latter were standard equipment of a medieval army. Charles the Bald of France had more than two thousand such pieces in his entourage, one for every four of his soldiers.

Part and Parcel

I believe the *baggage* loves me.

> – William Congreve, *The Old Bachelor,*
> 1693

Women knew their place in this man's army. The officers' ladies traveled by carriage while those accompanying the common foot soldiers brought up the rear with the supplies and the *baggage* from which they became virtually indistinguishable.

We first used *baggage* (16thC.) to refer to personal belongings that were portable. It later became synonymous with trash, refuse, or dirt, the meaning of which was transferred to *women of a disreputable* or *immoral life*; perhaps related to the French *bagasse,* a *slut.* According to the OED, men employed the term mostly in a "playful" sense (17th-19thC.), often prefacing it with "artful," "cunning," "sly," "pert," and "silly." Though men sought to avoid *heavy baggage* (18thC., women and children), many found themselves holding the *bag* (19thC.) with an old *prostitute.* It was

191

enough to drive a man *satchel-crazy* (20thC., from *satchel,* an old Ozark term for the *genitals*), from all these carryings-on.

By Hook or by Crook

The meanings of most words change frequently, but one has always stood firm over time. The *prostitute* (*c.* 1613) early on took her stance from *pro-statuere* and her willingness to come forward, to stand before her place of business and put herself out for her clients. Her meaning is still intact.

But in today's hurry-up world you have to do more than just stand there and hope they'll come to you. You have to be a *hustler* or a *hooker* to make it. Some believe that our *hooker* was "Fighting Joe" Hooker, the famous Civil War general and one-time commander of the Union Army. In tribute to his reputation as a *ladies' man* and a notorious *quiff hunter,* the *camp followers* of the Union Army quartered on Pennsylvania Avenue were called "Hooker's Division" and "Hooker's Brigade," and the girls themselves were known as *hookers.*

Alas, the first *hooker* appeared on our streets some twenty years before the Civil War, sighted around Corlear's Hook, a notorious section of New York City. Some prefer as her source the Old English *hok,* a long instrument with a hook at the end used for thieving items out of stores and home windows. It's the origin of the word "to hook," as in "to steal," as well as the "hock shop" where pilfered goods were sold. It also gave us the *hooker,* the thief who proved so adept at using the instrument. Given both the *whore's* penchant for petty thievery and her efforts to sink her hooks into a prospective customer, calling her a *hooker* looks to be right. How does it grab you?

Moving Right Along

The *hooker's* also a real *hustler* (same roots, *hokster* or *hochster*) who's always on the move. She has to be, with all that heavy *traffic* (late 16th-early 17thC., from the large amount of business she plies) out there. The *stroll* (20thC., the beat she walks) is crowded with *streetwalkers* (*c.* 1592), *nymphs de pave, pavement pretties, pavement pounders,* and *cruisers* (19th-20thC., also U.S. *homosexual* lingo, 20thC.). It takes all kinds, from all walks of life: not only the *infantry,* your common foot soldier, but also a *princess of the pavement* (20thC., Aust.) and even an occasional *queen* or two.

Ladies of the street have always had to be a few steps ahead of the competition. In ancient Athens, they adopted the practice of placing nails on the soles of their shoes, forming the words "follow me" on the soft streets as they strolled about in search of customers, thereby establishing advertising as the *world's oldest profession.*

Some of the *hetaerae,* the highest class of *prostitutes* in the ancient world, worked the cemeteries, inscribing on the tombstones with eyebrow pencil the names of men in whom they were interested. Prospective patrons would, in turn, write down the names of those *hetaerae* who attracted them. Slave girls would then carry word back and forth, the final negotiations to be consummated in the cemeteries.

In Rome, we had more than a dozen different designations for the *prostitute,* depending on her class, location, and the nature of the services provided. The *lupae* (wolves) proved to be a real howl—frequenting the parks and gardens of the city and attracting customers with a wolf cry.

Girls Will Be Girls

The *girls'* feet carried them everywhere—into the church towers during the fourteenth century and later into the theatres of Restoration England, where they were best known as the *orange girls,* who walked freely about hawking oranges and other fresh fruit together with playbills and odds and ends. They and their friends helped turn playhouses of the time into commodious *brothels* where the play on the stage was only incidental to the other acts taking place.

Through the years, they've been *business girls* (c. 1921), *good-time girls, company girls,* and *sporting girls.*

Party girls (c. 1910) made special appearances at private gatherings, often popping out of cakes and bathing in champagne. They were a must at every *bachelor* or *stag party* (c. 1859), or *stag* (c. 1900), a sure bet to *make* both your party and your party-goers. During the twenties their meaning shifted, and they gained a degree of respectability, becoming flappers, who loved nothing more than partying about. But in the 1950s the meaning changed once more, giving us a young actress or model who was introduced to a client by a third party who set the fee, though she herself retained the prerogative of whether or not to sleep with him, clearly setting her apart from other *working girls.*

Today *working girls* are those on the street, as distinguished from the classier *call girls* (19th-20thC.), who let their fingers do the walking. "A real operator," you say? Not necessarily. We once knew them from the *call house* (18th-19thC.), where the girls were said to be on call. The days of the house call are now but a distant memory. Today, you contact them by calling an *escort service* or by phoning them direct. Thanks to the marvel of modern telecommunications, a touching experience is now within reach of us all.

Tout de Suite

The girls are at their best during periods of great adversity. World War I had its *charity girls* (also *dames* and *molls*) and World War II its *victory* or *V-girls,* who began as amateurs with a particular fondness for boys in khaki and often drifted into *prostitution.* They were generally found around army bases, doing their parts for their country, and giving their all for the war effort. Unstinting in their devotion to duty, they were considered by many to be our first real *patriotutes* (c. 1940s).

Inadvertently, they may also have contributed a colorful new suffix to the language. Examples of its use include:

Astrotutes	First in space
Celebratutes	Catering to the very famous
Flute and tutes	Favoring the woodwind section
Root 'n' tutes	Ride 'em cowboy!
Verisimilitutes	Two for the price of one
No regretatutes	Without guilt·

You too can tute your own:

_____   _____

_____   _____

_____   _____

194

The Lay of the Land

A woman that will be drunk
Will easily play the *punk;*
For when her wits are sunk
All keys will fit her *trunk.*

> —"Cuckold's Haven" in *Roxburghe
> Ballads,* 1871

Once a woman turned professional, she no longer had to travel as an *incognita* (19thC.), an *anoynma* (c. 1860-77), or *just one of them* (19th-20thC.). Instead, she could proudly hang out her shingle, *Ammunition Wife* (c. 1820-1870): "More Bang for the Buck," or select from any of the more than five hundred terms we have to describe her.

Some call her after the hole she has dug for herself and the use to which she has put it. Any of the words which describe her *genitals* may be used for her as well, including *punk* (late 16th-18thC.), from *punctum,* Latin for "a small opening or crack." But let's not forget the *bimbo* (early 20thC.), from *bumbo* (18thC.), a word we once used to describe the female *genitals* via the *bum.* Both the *bimbo* and the *punk* have gone on to become terms of insult; the *punk* is most commonly known on the street today as a nasty urchin and identified with a genre of music noted for its antisocial bent or, in the *gay* lexicon, as a young *catamite.*

Her work has also named her a *put* (18thC.), as in to *do a put, put it in,* and to *play at two-handed put,* perhaps a shortened version of the French *putain.* But if a *put,* why not a *shake* (18th-19thC.), a *flatbacker,* and a *horizontal* (c. 1886), as she was prone to be? For her the nighttime was always the right time as the *nocturnal,* the *nightingale,* the *bat,* and the *lady of the evening.*

Often considered *frail, unfortunate,* and *impure* (as opposed to *pure,* for a proper *mistress*), she still manages to keep her sunny side up as a *joy girl, fille de joie, good-time girl,* and *lady of pleasure.* Always a *lady . . .* of *easy virtue* (c. 1780-20thC.); as the *scarlet lady* and the *painted woman,* she brings color to the scene.

Kissing Cousins

The serving man has his *punk,* the student his *nun . . .*
the puritan his *sister.*

> —Dekker, *Westward Ho,* 1607

Hers is a *family of love* (17th-20thC.), which includes several
*sisters: speedy sister, erring sister, burlap sister, frail (sister), scarlet
sister,* and *street sister . . . sister,* one of my *cousins* (late 17th-early
19thC.) and *my* or *mine aunt* (16th-19thC.).

Summer songs for me and my *aunts*
While we lie tumbling in the hay.

> —Shakespeare, *The Winter's Tale*

Trick or Treat?

"Did you see the score on the blackboard this
morning?"
"Sure I did—87 *tricks* in one week. Let Jenny and the
Nigger match that when there ain't no holidays."

> —Jubilation at Faye's, John Steinbeck,
> *East of Eden*

The *game's* not only deep but *tricky. Trick* as a bout of *love-
making* has been with us for more than four hundred years. During that time folks have both *turned a trick* and *done the trick* (also
a term for a turn of duty aboard ship). And there aren't too many
relationships that haven't been based on some form of trickery.
As one nineteenth-century *wench* put it, "If the little 'un don't do
the trick, me an' him'll fall out (*Derby Day,* 1864).

How's tricks? The ultimate *trick* is the one the *whore* plays on
her customer. She *f**ks* for money and pretends to *come.* As
tricks go, it really isn't much, but even those who know it's a *trick*
love being deceived. As Nell Kimball explained, "It isn't just
nookie—what a girl really sells is an illusion, the idea that the
John is some guy and she's just crackers about his kind of *kip
work.*"

Occasionally, fate plays a cruel trick, leaving her with a
trick-baby, one fathered by a client. There are even those rare in-
stances when a *prostitute* gets personally involved, *getting down*

(doing it for real) while *doing the trick.* But as one Kitty reminded her colleagues in *Gentlemen of Leisure,* "Tricks are *tricks* – that's how they got their name. When they turn around and satisfy you, you're a *trick,* and *tricks* ain't s**t."

The Real Tough Customer

It was a Saturday night around ten. The vice section was overrun with *Johns.* It seemed that every white man in town was over there, scratch in one hand and *rod* in the other ripping and running after the black *whores* with the wildest, blackest *a*ses.*

> —*Iceberg Slim: The Story of My Life,*
> 1967

This is a *trick.* His name is *John. John* was once a *sugar daddy* (early 20thC., *sugar* meaning money) and represented a long-term commitment. Today he's just a customer and strictly a one-shot proposition. *John* is a popular name for the male organ by which he is identified. It also speaks to the anonymity he seeks – "John Doe" – as well as his commonality, his sameness, and his generally undistinguished character.

On first sighting, *John* appears a *deadhead* or a *sightseer;* perhaps he may only have *Georgia* on his mind. *Georgia's* long been a freebie in the trade. To be *georgiaed* meant to be taken advantage of sexually without receiving any money – the ultimate disgrace befalling a pro. If he's a *live one,* he's right on target as a *mark* or a potential *score,* a simple transaction as *trade,* or just so much meat – a *beefburger* (all 20thC.).

John's always been a topic of speculation. In the eighteenth century they asked of him, "Is he foolish or is he *flash?"* (c. 1788, Grose, meaning being into the underworld way of life). Today, we all know that "anyone who spends money on *IT* must be out of his mind."

John couldn't care less what others think. Most *Johns* come from business and industry, with politics and theater a secondary source. As the cream of our country's leadership, they know what our nation needs most and will do everything in their power to see that we get it.

197

The Crack Salesman

Man rules woman. In being a *mack* you acknowledge
this fact. You put yourself in a superior position and
you don't let a woman put you in no position. Most
women are very tricky. They like to have their own
way. But *"women of the night"* don't look up to a
man — they can do anything they want to. He's a *john*
then. Just a *trick*.

> — Susan Hall, *Gentlemen of Leisure*,
> 1972

John often loses his way from the straight and narrow. It's
then he'll turn anywhere for help, even to a known scoundrel. In
this case it's the Old French *pimpreneau,* source of the notorious
pimp (17th-20thC.), one known to never miss a *trick*. In
eighteenth-century London, the *pimp* introduced the wood to
the fire. We still know him best for making introductions. It's a
dirty job, but somebody has to do it.

Currently, he's fancier than ever as a *mack* (or *mac, c.*
1870-90). *Mackarel* was Standard English, from the French
maquereau, "a pimp," a real *player* who's deep into the life with
style. You'll find him decked out in his white mink jacket and
matching cap, his turtleneck, and his red and blue boots, cruising about in his baby-blue hog. Earlier we knew him as *max* and
Hymie; later *Tony* and *Carlo* during the twenties and the thirties;
Louis and *Jacques* in the thirties and the forties; currently he answers to such names as *Red Devil* and *Blue Snapper.*

The *pimp* plays an important role. He's the girl's *sweet man* or
just her *man,* and looking after her is a full-time job. As noted in
Gentlemen of Leisure, "It's almost inevitable that a *prostitute* ends
up with a *player*. It's hand in glove. Birds of a feather. The two
just go together." As one New York *mack* commented: "You
think I take it easy? I have to take care of my *hole,* keep her away
from other guys, get her welfare check on 'Mother's Day' and
take care of myself. It's a tough life." He's also got to replenish his
stock, *cop a new hole or two* (induce new girls to join the *family*),
and let a *hard leg* (one with 50,000 miles on her) out to pasture.

Every major *pimp* has a *stable,* a grouping of *whores* which
belong to him, also referred to as his *family.* Much of his time

goes into maintaining peace between his *wives-in-law*, no easy task and one that might require an occasional *gorilla* (a beating). The "wife" he favors most is his *bottom woman*, his favorite, his *number-one woman*, his *main lady*, who coincidentally happens to be his bread and butter (or his Brie and Chablis). She's something special. Iceberg Slim tells us "ain't more than three or four good *bottom women* promised a *pimp* in his lifetime."

The *pimp* himself is almost unique, one of the few words in *The Erotic Tongue* insulting to man. That is primarily because he lives off the earnings of women. We despise him so much for this that a *mack* was once synonymous with a *bastard*. Yet it is the *pimp* and his trade who have helped make this country what it is today. As one *whore* noted in Susan Hall's *Ladies of the Night*, "Business would crumble without us. We consummate deals. We're like a barter system. In fact we're like money. Our backs are the bridges which link business deals." *Pimping* remains one of the few democratic callings available in our society: from the lowly bellhop with his famous line, "The package you ordered has arrived," to the middle-level junior executive entertaining clients, to lobbyists in Congress who trade *favors* for favors. It's democracy in action.

Food for Thought

He will to his Egyptian *dish* again.

> —Shakespeare, Enobarbus speaking of
> Antony in *Antony and Cleopatra*

John is famished. He's *suffering from the night starvation* (19thC.). The mere thought of a *saucy* or *spicy* female is enough to cause him to *have the flavor*. A little *cooking* (20thC., stirring and teasing) only encourages his appetite further.

If she's *properly tasty* (c. 1890s, sexually alluring), we have but to add a pinch of *salt*. *Salt* dates back to Elizabethan times as an adjective for *lewd*, *amorous*, or obscene:

> . . . As *prime* as goats
> as *hot* as monkeys
> As *salt* as wolves in pride.

> —Shakespeare, *Othello*

Salt (mid-17th-early 18thC.) served as a noun for *sexual intercourse* and as a verb signifying *coition*. As for the other condiments, he could only hope that she was *hot mustard* (19thC.). *Cutting the mustard* was really up to him, and referred to his *virility* and *potency*. *Relish* in Shakespeare only added extra flavor, but by the nineteenth century had come to describe *the act* itself, thus lending whole new meaning to the phrase, "mustard and relish to go."

How Sweet It Is!

A brief snack might hold him – a *crumpet* (woman as an item of sexual pleasure, *c.* 1880) or a *buttered bun*. A *buttered bun* (*c.* 1670-90) was once a *mistress,* later (19thC.) a *harlot* who offered herself to several men in repeated succession. *Pastry* (19th-20thC.) has also traditionally served as a collective term for young and attractive women, the *French* and *Danish* (both 20thC.) varieties being most *accessible*.

Among our more outstanding *pastries* we have the *tart,* though it's gone through some tortuous turns, derived as it was from the Latin *tortus,* meaning twisted. Originally it was a term of endearment, like "honey" or "sweetheart," for a sweet young girl. But by the beginning of the twentieth century we had distorted its meaning into a *fast* or *immoral* woman, and by 1908 made her into a *prostitute,* using the adjective *tarty* (*c.* 1920) to describe her behavior. The *jam tart* (*c.* 1804) has always meant a *mistress* or a *harlot*.

If the *tart's* not to your taste, perhaps you'd like a *cookie;* it's been a *prostitute* and her *genitalia* in both nineteenth-century Scotland and in the Southern Black community as recorded in plantation literature and the lyrics of jazz and blues. *Tarts, cookies,* ane even *pie* (especially *custard pie* among Southern Blacks) have traditionally been *open to the suggestion*. All are variations on a single theme, which some consider a *piece of cake*.

Pleased to Meat You

Which is the best to fit your taste,
Fat pork or scrag of mutton?

The last would suit an invalid,
The first would gorge a glutton.

If fat and plenty is your aim,
Let Phyllis be your treat,
If leaner viands are your choice,
You Pamela may eat.

— Sophia Burrell, *Epigram on Two
Ladies*, late 18thC.

John's particularly *fond of meat*, as befits one who's over-amorous and prone to *wenching*. His taste extends especially to *sweet meat*, a kept *mistress* of tender years, and the *tender part* thereof.

A fine palate, though, is not always adequate to the task: "Is she man's meat?" he asks. Falkland in "Marriage Night," observed, "I have a tender appetite and can scarcely digest one in her teens" (1664). We are also reminded in Bailey's *English Dictionary* that "After sweet meat comes sour sauce, . . . an excellent monitor to temperance and sobriety" (1726).

Throwing caution to the winds, he's off for a wild evening of *meat and drink* (19th-20thC.), making the rounds of the *brothels* and the bars, concluding matters at the *meat house* — often confused with the *meat market* itself (*female pudendum* and *breasts*) — where the *meat merchant* displays his merchandise (all 19thC.).

His tastes generally run to *fresh meat* (one new at plying her trade, or a non-*prostitute*, 19thC.), *meaty* (c. 1820, sexually enjoyable), *white* or *dark* (Caucasian or Negro, 20thC., U.S.), *hot*, and well *done over* (said of a woman with whom one has had *intercourse*, 19thC.). What he more than likely settles for is *dead* or *frozen meat* (an aged *prostitute*) served *raw* (naked in the act, also inexpert and inexperienced); or even just *a bit of fat* (a stout woman as bedmate) — all 19thC. It matters little to *John*. Meat is meat, he's happy whether *in a woman's beef* (18th-mid-19thC.) or in her *mutton* (19th-20thC.).

An angry woman might tell him to simply *beat it* — his *meat*, that is. Any further objectification of women in such a fashion only serves to confirm that she has — ahem — legitimate beefs.

The nearer the bone, the sweeter the meat.

House Calls

It was the seventies. My *house of ill repute* was conveniently located on Melrose between a car wash and nursery school.

— Gail Parent, *David Meyer Is a Mother,*
1976

The street is neat, but there's no place like home. In ancient Greece we had the *porneia* (which, when joined with the graphic descriptions on the walls therein gave us our first glimpse of *pornography*) and in Rome the *lupinari* (home of she-wolves). In 1347, Giovanna I, Queen of Naples, made it official when she took the girls off the streets and legalized the first *houses of sin* in the Christian world. Her intent was to provide a source of taxable income for the State, security for the "girls" by giving them a home, and safe conduct for females everywhere by deflecting overtures aimed at "respectable" women.

French kings used the *bordello* (late 16th-18thC., "a little house") to discourage *homosexuality* and other behavior which they deemed aberrant. We also knew these abodes as *brothels* (c. 1593) from the word for a good-for-nothing man, a wretch of sorts (15thC.), and, later, a *prostitute* whose services he was known to frequent. The *brothel house* (16thC.) soon became the place in which you might find them both; it wasn't long before we dropped the house, leaving us with just the *brothel.*

It took a heap o' lovin' to make a home a *house,* but we soon had one for every taste and mood, more than sixty-five varieties at last count. The best of the bunch include: the *bawdy house* (c. 1552), *call house, can house* (early 1930s), *cathouse* (c. 1925), *fancy house, garden house, gay house* (19th-20thC.), *grinding house, hothouse, house of civil reception* (mid-18th-early 19thC.), house of *ill delight, ill fame,* and *ill repute, naughty house, parlor house* (c. 1867), *slaughterhouse, sporting house* (c. 1890), *vaulting house* (17thC.), and *whorehouse* (16thC.). And that's just for openers.

Learn, Baby, Learn

A vaulting house . . . Where I used to spend my afternoons among superb she-*gamesters* . . . I have cracked a *ring* or two there.

— Massinger, *Unnatural Combat,* 1639

No ordinary houses, these. Many were centers of higher learning known as the *pushing* (17th-19thC.), *vaulting,* or *finishing school* or *academy* (c. 1760-1820). As the *Ladies' College* (18th-early 19thC.) or the *School of Venus* (17th-19thC.) it was your original school of hard knocks where the *rule of three* (18th-20thC. for *penis* and *testes*) was practiced daily. The more serious students of the craft studied under *academicians* (c. 1760-1820) who were known for their strict discipline ("If you don't get it right the first time, we'll do it again and again until you do get it right."). The quest for knowledge continued during Victorian times when the *mottes* placed cards in their tenement windows announcing, "Foreign language school featuring *French* [what else?] lessons."

If you're looking to pursue some form of cultural enrichment today you might try a *library,* often advertised as "well stacked, with *librarians* ready to meet your every need."

For Heaven's Sake

Those three nymphs . . . are three *nuns,* and the plump female is of great notoriety and generally designated the *abbess.*

–Pierce Egan, *Life in London,* 1821

Others sought spiritual uplift through visits to a *nunnery* (late 16th-20thC.). Because nunneries in general never enjoyed a good reputation and all kinds of venal activity was imagined to occur in them, *nunnery* soon became a code word for a *brothel.* *Hamlet*'s injunction to Ophelia, "Get thee to a *nunnery,*" was penned by the bard with that meaning in mind. Several years ago, the New York *Daily News,* in one of its better gaffes, ran a feature story using that as its headline. The story was a somewhat maudlin account of a middle-aged woman's decision to join a religious order. But this was one *nunnery* in which a devout woman in her middle years wouldn't have stood a prayer. For behind the walls of this institution there were only *nuns* (18th-19thC.) *punchable* (18th-19thC., ripe for a man) and *punctured,* who *prayed with their knees upward,* all working diligently at *putting the devil into hell* (18th-20thC.).

The Home Stretch

The eighteenth-century European model introduced elaborate rituals and extravaganzas as well as finely dressed and specially selected girls who were carefully chosen, closely supervised, and under close medical scrutiny. Among the classiest houses were the *seraglios* (late 17th-early 19thC. from *serai*, the Turkish palace where the women were kept). Girls were preselected and sent for in sedan chairs.

The less exotic and less exclusive sites were known as *kips* (*c.* 1766, from the cant word for "sleep") or likened to other business establishments: the *hook shop, flesh* or *meat market, buttonhole factory, bum shop, chamber of commerce, moll shop, bread-and-butter warehouse*, and the *body shop*.

During the late nineteenth and early twentieth centuries we also had *houses of assignation* for couples looking for a secluded rendezvous and as a place where lower-class *prostitutes* and shop girls might supplement their incomes. The better *houses of assignation* catered to a more select clientele, offering food, servants, and posh surroundings, and were generally open only till five o'clock in the afternoon.

Cribs were a twentieth-century invention in the U.S., small cramped areas (roughly four by six feet) not unlike the corncribs from which they got their name. Often they were nothing but mean shacks with a display room in front and a work area in the rear. The earliest *cribs* were on the Barbary Coast and were worked primarily by Chinese slave girls who used to hang out the windows negotiating the fees. A *lookee* was free, a *feelie* or *touchee* went for ten cents, and a *doee*, twenty-five or fifty cents.

We later had the *cowyard*, a three- or four-floor building with long halls and small closetlike rooms off them and two to three hundred *whores* hard at work milking every customer for everything he was worth.

Fighting for Piece

Housing starts have been down in the U.S. since World War II, but there was a brief revival during the Vietnam War with the *boum-boum parlors* of Ankhe, captured so vividly by an American soldier on his visit to the rest and recreation center, also known as *Disneyland East*:

Before I got a pass, I had to pick up a *rubber* and pass an exam on how to use it. I went to a native barber shop where I got a great haircut, manicure, some great pot and a *blow job*. I relaxed for a few hours with the pot and then went out to *Disneyland* and went to one of the houses. I had a drink and the Mama San told me I could get a *boum-boum* for 300 piastres or a *sop-sop* (fellatio) for 500. I got a *boum-boum*. Not bad, though it only took a few minutes. When I left the compound, the MP at the gate told me to wash myself to avoid *clap* or *syphilis*. I went back to the company and got a pro-treatment. The whole deal had cost me about seven bucks, and I had enough pot to last for a couple of weeks.

> – Charles Winick and Paul Kinsie, *The Lively Commerce*, 1971

Signs of the Times

Honi Soit Qui Mal Y Pense
Evil to him who evil thinks.

> – Motto, Order of the Garter, and introduction to *The Blue Book*, the directory of *prostitutes* in New Orleans, 19thC.

It was easy to stray from the beaten path, so to keep a customer from losing his way, houses were marked by large bold numbers, had colored lampshades in the windows, or featured large translucent globes hanging over the sidewalks or doorways – often showing a red light. When we put enough of these together, we had a *red-light district* (late 19thC.).

One version has it that in the early days of the railroad in Kansas City, during the night when freight trains were made up, brakemen would often pass the time with trips to *whorehouses* near the yards, carrying with them their red signal lamps, which they would hang outside the tents or houses to which they were paying a visit. When trains were ready to pull out, the dispatcher would send young boys to retrieve the brakemen, locating them by the red lanterns hanging outside the *bordellos*.

205

It's a story worth sharing, but it doesn't shed much light on the notorious *red-lamp district* which flourished around the Palais Royal in Paris some 150 years before the first railroad.

The French were there first. But for the most impressive *red-light district* in history you'd have to go to New Orleans, the greatest *brothel* city of all time. The area was known as *Storyville* (1897-1917), after Alderman Sidney Story, the creative force who legitimized overt *prostitution* in a thirty-six-square-mile area of the French Quarter. It had no parallel in human history. At its peak, the district housed some 230 *brothels,* 30 *houses of assignation,* and thousands of *prostitutes* — making for what some today might call Super Ball I.

Storyville closed its doors at the beginning of World War I, victim of a concerted drive by authorities looking to protect our boys in uniform from the vagaries of sin. This led critics to protest that our young men might die for their country but not get *laid* for it.

Of the areas less grand in scope than *Storyville,* the *Tenderloin* (*c.* 1887) or *loin* hosted a substantial amount of activity, but never in as concentrated a form as the *red-light district.* The first *Tenderloin* district was located in a section of New York City ridden with *prostitutes* and noted for its meaty payoffs to police (a tenderloin being one of the more expensive cuts of meat). The name *Tenderloin* itself was coined by one of New York's finest.

Call Me Madam

Upon arrival at such an establishment, your first question might be, "Is the madam of the house in?"

Madam(e) (18th-20thC.) has long described the owner and/or manager of the *brothel.* Speculation has it that she originated in the court of Louis XV, a monarch noted for his generous sexual appetite. The royal harem was called *le parc aux cerfs* ("stags"). The *surintendante,* the woman who managed it, kept the girls happy and in line, oversaw the expenses, and maintained order. She was an elderly woman who allegedly came from one of the best families in Burgundy and worked hard to keep her identity a secret. At the *parc* they knew her only as Madame; none ever dared call her by any other name.

I Remember Mama

Mother, how many tails have you in your cab?
How many girls do you have in your bawdy house?

— *Lexicon Balantronicum,* 1811

So an old *abbess,* for the rattling *rakes,*
A tempting dish of human nature makes
And dresses up a luscious maid.

— Peter Pindar, 1819

Madam has long been a term of respect and, in this instance, well deserved. No one would dream of detracting from her stature: "What is a home without *Mother?*" is a common homily you might find over the credenza of a Victorian home or on the wall of the *crib. Mother* (19th-20thC.), also *mother of the maids* or *mammy,* was a designation frequently applied to the central figure of the household. It was she who clothed, fed, and comforted the girls — attending to their every need, *in loco parentis.* As one Victorian *motte* reminisced about the famed *Mother* Willit of London's Gerrard Street:

So help her kindness, she al'us turned her gals out with a clean *arse* and a good tog; and as she turned 'em out, she didn't care who turned 'em up, cause 'em vos as clean as a smelt and as fresh as a daisy.

Mom's status was elevated further as a *mother superior* and an *abbess* (late 18th-19thC.), the ultimate authority in a *nunnery.* When *flagellation brothels* later came into vogue, she became the *governess,* noted for the discipline she maintained and her ability to whip both her charges and her customers into line.

There's the Rub

I do feel rather strongly that an institution [a sauna] associated with fitness, cold water, steam and deep breathing should not suffer the indignity of having to go under the same name as one in which the object is a commercial exercise in sexual stimulation carried out by grim harridans on unhappy men in the shabby back rooms of garishly lit premises in the less pleasant areas of our larger cities.

—*Bernard Levin, London Times, 1980*

Though off the streets, many of the girls still found themselves in hot water. Many were in the *stews,* a throwback to the old Roman baths where folks used to "stew" themselves in hot air or steam, a practice reintroduced to Europe by the Crusaders on their return from the Middle East.

A *stew* had several large tubs which held five or six people at a time as well as smaller ones allowing for greater intimacy. They started off innocently enough, but when gambling, food, drink, and other services were added, together with female camaraderie and associated goings-on, they soon became hotbeds of illicit activity.

Bathing and cleanliness had never been favored by the Christian world, but with the public baths, cleansing of the body took on new popularity. The *stews* flourished until the 1530s and '40s, when authorities closed them down because of an outbreak of *syphilis.* However, we continued to use the word *stews,* both as *brothels* and for those who worked there, through the nineteenth century. Some also knew them as *bagnios* (17th-18thC.), the Turkish baths of Elizabethan times, from the Italian word *bagno* for "bath."

Sound familiar? It's all akin to some of today's *physical culture and health establishments, relaxation clubs* or *parlors, steambaths, saunas* (in England), and, of course, the ever-popular *massage parlors,* which date back to just before World War I. *Massage parlors* have in fact become so closely identified with sexual services that in Las Vegas, city officials tried unsuccessfully to close down two of them that apparently rubbed customers the wrong way—by offering only legitimate massages. City authorities took them to court claiming misrepresentation.

Personal Best

Not everyone fancied such public activity. Those looking for a quieter and more discreet game might try the *personal columns* that have flourished since the late 1970s. The players are most frequently designated as *SWM, DWM, SWF, DWF, GWF, GWM, SBM, DBM, SBF, DBF, GBF, GBM, BI-F, BI-M,* depending on whether you're male, female, Black, White, single, divorced, *gay,* or *bisexual.* Women most often seek a *relationship;* men look to *get laid. Relationships* often prove as abbreviated as the ads themselves.

In the nineteenth century we had the *personal bureau.* One such business was located in New York City in a quiet, modest-looking stationery store on one of the uptown streets near Broadway, convenient to the better class of *demimondaines* who patronized it. Upstairs, atop a counter, sat a large book open to a page on which a lady might write down her name, address, and interests. Men would go through the book, selecting those women consistent with their fantasies. A sample entry was:

> Miss Lavinia — 15 years of age, a beautiful brunette; she likes an old man, blind preferred; must have teeth and money.

The Roman professional was a respectable woman during most of the day – until four or five o'clock in the afternoon, and the afternoon meal. The interlude was know as a *merando,* "a time well earned" (from *mereo,* "I earn"). It also named the women who was most active then, the *meretrix,* (pl.: *meretrices*). Because many people thought the *meretrix* to be cheap and tawdry, she gave us the word "meretricious," which we now use to describe items of little value.

† † †

There are worse things than being called a *whore.* "I may be a *whore,* but I can't be a bitch!" was a cry you might have heard from the mouth of an irate lower-class woman of the late eighteenth or mid-nineteenth century. It's a word which Grose cited as the "most offensive appellation that can be given to an English woman, even more provoking than that of *whore.*"

A *bitch* has been a *lewd* woman since the fifteenth century and in England still has that meaning today. *Bitch* has also served as a verb since Restoration times, meaning to go *whoring.* An interesting trade-off; it left women unhappy but it also gave men something to *bitch* about.

† † †

In England they once distinguished between the *pounce* and the *pimp.* The *pounce* (did he pounce on her, or come from Alphonse?) ran the girl's life while the pimp *solicited* (16thC.) for her. In America he's always been an all-service provider. As her *solicitor* he (or she) has been a *bawd* (*c.* 1362), a *panderer* (*c.* 1450), *procurer* or *procuress* (*c.* 1632), a *gobetween, buttock-broker* (17th-early 19thC.), *flesh-peddler, middleman,* and *wholesaler* (all 20thC.).

As the lady's protecter, he was her *Louis* (*c.* 1935), her *bully,* her *fancy Joseph* (19thC.), or just plain *fancy man* (*c.* 1821). In this category we also have the *souteneur* (*c.* 1906), with his broad-striped jersey, red waistband, apache cap tilted jauntily on his head, and tightly curled lips from which dangled a cigarette.

† † †

It was the *madam* who made the *house* work. She was the one on which everything turned. Experienced, cynical, and intelligent, she ruled with an iron fist but was always sensitive to the needs of her clients. She was adept at recruiting and training, and skilled in providing amusement for her charges and attracting new customers. Her forte was collecting, managing, and spending the money as well as dealing with the law. The more famous American madams include Polly Adler (*A House Is Not a Home*), Nell Kimball, Jew Jenny of Salt Lake City, Silver-Tongue Jean of Detroit, and Mother Lena Hyman of Toledo, noted for her chicken dinners, which she served the police with an accompanying payoff under each plate.

† † †

December 2, 1983

San Francisco (AP) – A judge has ruled that a street preacher has free-speech rights to call working women *whores* and suggested that a woman who had the preacher arrested should just have punched him instead.

The woman, a Mrs. Golden, testified that she was walking across the Civic Center Plaza on May 24 when Rife [the preacher] followed her, pointed a finger in her direction and used her to illustrate his message.

"He said that women who leave their homes and go out to work and carry briefcases and wear suits think they are liberated, and liberated women are *whores*," Golden said.

Rife, who had been ordered by another municipal court judge to stop singling out people during his preaching, denied Golden's allegations after the judge acquitted him. . . .

"The only thing I ever told Mrs. Golden was that Jesus loves her," he said.

ELEVEN

The Wages of Sin

> It is said that President Carter is considering chang-
> ing the Democratic party emblem from a jackass to a
> *condom*, because it stands for inflation, protects a
> bunch of *pr**ks*, halts production, and gives a false
> sense of security while one is being *screwed*.
>
> — Anon., reported by Reinhold Aman,
> *Maledicta*, 1978

The experienced sexual athlete knows enough to shield himself from some of life's contingencies. For short-term protection
he favors the *condom*.

The device is said to draw its name from the mysterious
Dr. Condom or Conton, a physician at the court of Charles II
(*c.* 1660–1685) who allegedly created the item to help put a cap
on His Majesty's growing number of illegitimate children. Students of that period, though, have been unable to locate the good
Doctor, and they're not even sure he really existed.

Alternate theories regarding the origin of the word range from
a Colonel Condum in the Royal Guard to Condom, a town in
Germany recorded as a fortress of considerable strength, to an
oilskin case that held the colors of the regiment (18th–early 19th
C.). Some think the word may even be a unique blend of *cunnus*
(for the female *pudenda*) and "dum" or "dumb" — together rendering the organ incapable of functioning.

Another claim regarding the invention of the *condom*, and its
first published description, was made by Gabriello Fallopio
(1523–1562) — whose name is most closely associated with the

Fallopian tubes— in *De Morbo Gallico,* published two years after his death, in which he encouraged use of linen sheets as *condoms.*

It must have been great between the sheets. From what we know, however, the *condom* actually originated long before, in the slaughterhouses of medieval Europe where lamb intestines and the membranes of other animals were dried and then well lubricated to make them soft and pliant—a time when it apparently took guts to *have sex.*

Letter Perfect

There was a young man of Cape Horn,
Who wished he had never been born.
  And he wouldn't have been
  If his father had seen
That the bloody *French letter* was torn.

     — Anon.

The *condom* achieved its greatest popularity during the seventeenth and eighteenth centuries, often appearing in print as a *c-d-m,* and was most frequently spoken of as a *letter (French, Italian,* or *Spanish*— the letter and envelope being virtually one), a form of correspondence which absolutely, positively, had to be there overnight.

Its ability to deliver the goods was dramatically extolled in a pamphlet coauthored by the Earl of Rochester in 1667, "A Panegyric Upon Cundum," in which he wrote: "Happy the man who in his pocket keeps, whether with green or scarlet riband bound, a well-made *cundum.*" Not everyone agreed. In 1862, Pope Leo XII damned use of the discovery "because it hindered the arrangements of providence"—a statement received in many quarters as so much papal bull.

Steel Yourself

Town blades continued to encourage their cohorts to "take a *letter!*" in spite of the church's attitude. One noted lady of the court, however, found it nothing to write home about, noting that it was "gossamer against infection, steel against love." Other critics described it as *armor,* mocking those who donned the raiment as *pot valiant* (both 18thC.). The *condom* had tried to prove its mettle but was found failing.

New and dramatic developments soon brought the skeptics around. The vulcanization of the rubber sheath in 1876 lent it new-found flexibility and favor. We appropriately named it a *rubber* (20thC.). It wasn't completely foolproof, however. In England an eraser is also called a rubber, which causes untold confusion whenever an Englishman in an American office asks to borrow one.

Wash 'n' Wear

No *glove,* no love.

— John Irving, *The World According to Garp*

You wouldn't go wrong, however, in treating it as an extra garment of sorts, something for the head, perhaps—*la capote anglaise, la capote allemande* (an English or German hood), or a *French cap,* depending upon who you were and which enemy was in vogue at the time. Casanova often came cap in hand and always had a dozen on call. Though he personally favored such headgear, his friend the *nun* seemed less than pleased with their aesthetic effect: "There you are hooded like a mother abbess, but in spite of the fineness of the sheath I like the little fellow better quite naked. I think that this covering degrades us both."

Others saw it as a necessary article with which to brave the elements: a *diving suit* or a *shower cap* (both 20thC.). Though Casanova dubbed it a *redingote d'Angleterre,* an English riding coat, still others thought of it as a *raincoat.* Critics likened it to taking a *bath with a raincoat on.* Yet what better precaution for an evening of stormy *love-making?*

A Tip of the Cap

Grandmother makes cheap *prophylactics,*
She punctures the end with a pin;
Grandfather performs the abortions.
My God, how the money rolls in.

— Sung to the tune of "My Bonnie Lies over the Ocean," 20thC.

A final tribute: No mere *disposable sanitary device* (20thC.), the *condom* has worked hard on man's behalf—some say like a *Trojan* (one of the more popular twentieth-century brand names, after a people noted for laboring energetically and doggedly). It has served him especially well as a *prophylactic* (20th C., from *pro*, "in favor of," and *phylaxis*, "watching or being on one's guard"), forging an effective advance guard whose job is to keep all infections out.

This fear of infection—safety first—rather than concern for the woman *being with child* has always been uppermost in man's thoughts, making the *condom* into an *instrument of safety* (early 20thC.) and also giving us the twentieth-century favorite, a *safety*, which in some people's minds also made *sex* completely *safe* (mid-20thC.).

Catch-As-Catch-Can

He went out a sacrifice and came home a burnt offering.

—A sailor's lament,
mid-18th–early 19thC.

She seemed a stately *pleasure boat*
with tempting good attire;
But little knew that [underdeck]
her Gun-Room was on Fire.

—From a popular Elizabethan broadside

For those who failed to take cautionary measures came the moment of reckoning—the time for the final payment, *the wages of sin*.

Remember the *pleasure boat*, the one with the *finely trimmed sails, high in the bows* and *wide in the beams*? At bottom she was nothing but a *fire ship* (c. 1670–1850). She caught the last guy *napping* (nap: to catch *VD*—"you have *napt* it") and *tipped him the token* (c. 1780; token: a blotch or discoloration, Standard English for the plague). He was really taken in. What he thought was a token of her affection turned out to be nothing but a real *pip* (late 16th–17thC.) and is he *burnt* (16th–20thC.) up!

215

Ay, she quickly poopt him:
She made him roast-meat for worms.

— Shakespeare, *Pericles*

When You Care Enough to Send the Very Best

These London wenches are so stout,
They care not what they do;
They will not let you have a *Bout*,
Without a crown or two.
They double their chops and curl their locks
Their breaths perfume they do;
Their tails are pepper'd with the *Pox*.
And that you're welcome to.

— English ballad, *c.* 1719

Abandon ship! It's *Venus's curse*, the *garden gout*, and the *forget-me-not*. Or it might be the *pox*, with which it was often confused, because the facial disfigurement that resulted bore similarities to that caused by smallpox. Most think it was Columbus and his crew who first discovered this *pox*, having received it from Indian givers and then carried it back to Europe along with other treasures from the New World.

From that point forward, it quickly caught on. Two years later, when Charles VIII of France invaded Italy, he got extra support from Ferdinand and Isabella who sent Spanish troops that brought with them these same glad tidings from the New World. By the time the French had captured Naples, all of Italy had also fallen to the *pox*. The *Neapolitan bone ache* then spread throughout all of Europe, and intrepid sea-going explorers — those folks we learned about in seventh-grade history — soon carried it around the world. Vasco da Gama's crew left it in India, and in 1505 it landed in China. It was truly the *gift that goes on giving* (20thC.).

The French Connection

He suffered by a blow over the snout with a French faggot.
He lost his nose by the pox.

— Grose

No one was quite sure whom to blame. Everyone picked on the French, identified by the whole world as the wellspring of degeneracy (*morbus Gallicus:* the *French disease*, the *French gout*, the *French pox*, the *French measles*). A man was said to wear a *French crown*, a baldness associated with the disease; and an infected *wench* was described as *Frenchified*. Disfigured *testicles* came to be called *French marbles*—though logic, based on an early "cure" which involved submerging the afflicted party in boiling oil, would dictate "Frenchified potatoes." Other nations soon got into the act, including the Spanish, the Italians, and the Germans, giving us the *Spanish gout, German scabies,* and dozens of other permutations. The Spanish even gave the *needle* (c. 1611) to the Americans. There appeared to be no end to it, until the Turks settled such parochial squabbling by treating it collectively as the *Christian disease*.

Love-struck

O, Harvard is run by Princeton,
  And Princeton is run by Yale,
And Yale is run by Vassar,
  And Vassar's run by tail;
But Stanford's run by stud-horse juice,
  They say it's made by hand,
It's the house of *clap* and *syph*,
  It's the *a*shole* of the land.

  —Anon., Univ. of Cal. at Berkeley

It was a poet, however, who had the last word on the subject. The word was *syphilis,* and it first appeared in 1530 in a poem by Girolamo Fracastoro called "Syphilis sive morbus gallicus" (*syphilis*, or the *French disease*), a tract which purported to show both the symptoms and possible treatment of the dreaded malady.

The hero of the piece is a handsome young herdsman named Syphilis, who loses his cattle because of an extended drought. Angry and hurt, he lashes out at the Sun God, blaming him for the misfortune. Apollo, however, does not take kindly to such impiety and afflicts Syphilis with the disease that is soon to bear his name. Miserable and alone, Syphilis is forced to wander the

217

earth's substrata. There he discovers the marvels of the element mercury, with which he treats the disease and cures himself. Humbled by his experience and made wiser by it all, he then dedicates his life to Diana, goddess of chastity.

Many found this such a compelling tale that they adopted its hero's name as an internationally neutral term for the disease. After having known it on more intimate terms, they reduced it to *syph* (mid-20thC.) and *phylis* (early 20thC.). It proved so popular in this form that there still are folks who have not yet received full word of it.

Two for the Money

The Virgin she did prove
a trap, a trap;
The end of all her love
the *clap*, the *clap*.

—Anon., 18thC.

It was evening, I lay dying
Spirit wandering, flame reposing,
But one thought would never leave me
Till poetic form it bore;
Though to you it may appear, Sir,
For a poet rather queer, Sir,
It was about the *gonorrhea*, Sir,
That I'd caught a week before.
And I wrote these warning stanzas,
As I trickled down before,
Trickle, trickle, evermore!

—Victorian parody of Poe's *The Raven*

Syphilis made *sex* a gamble—what some called "the Russian roulette of the *gay* (as in fast-living) set." But as one Victorian wag put it, "The revolver held not one but two bullets." Those fortunate enough to dodge the *big casino* (*syphilis*), had an equally good chance of cashing in their chips on the *little casino* (*gonorrhea*).

218

Gonorrhea comes from *gonos,* "semen" and *rhein,* "flow"—running or flowing semen, named for the discharge identified with the disease, mistakenly thought to be semen. Men so afflicted were said to *p*ss pins and needles* (c. 1780) from the accompanying discomfort and also to *p*ss pure cream* (19th–20thC.), from the results. No mere also-ran, *gonorrhea* is one of our more popular infectious diseases. It is second only to the common cold and nothing to sneeze at.

For the longest time *syphilis* and *gonorrhea* were thought to be different stages of the same disease. It wasn't until 1793 that researchers established *gonorrhea* as separate and distinct. Scientists everywhere applauded the discovery. The rest of the civilized world simply *clapped* approvingly (*clap*—from the French *clapoir*—Standard English late 16th–20thC.).

> *He went out by Had 'em and came around by Clapham home.*
> He went out wenching and got a clap.
> —Grose

Diseased Minds

> Happy *Syphilis*
> and
> Merry *Gonorrhea*
>
> —Graffiti, 1970s

There was no applauding the use of these words. Neither *syphilis* nor *gonorrhea* was deemed verbally proper or permissible in the United States through the 1930s.

The medical fraternity felt especially uncomfortable in their presence. Rather than speak directly of them they made reference to a *certain illness,* a *bad disease,* a *blood disease,* a *preventable disease,* a *secret disease,* and a *vice disease.* If you think that's somewhat vague, you might enjoy Mencken's accounts of doctors treating patients with *specific stomachs* or *specific ulcers.*

Newspapers were equally stiff-necked on the topic, refusing to carry any advertisements or copy which made reference to it until the outbreak of World War II. Mencken recounts how efforts to alert us to the danger (of *VD*, not the war) and to encourage use of *prophylactics* by the U.S. War Advertising Council were protested by the National Commander of Catholic War Veterans, who argued that publication of such information would "weaken the sense of decency in the American people, ... increase immorality by promising to make *promiscuity* safe, and ignore a fundamental fact of human conduct, that shame and embarrassment are among the strongest deterrents to the sins that spread *VD.*"

Venereal disease entered the language in 1658, an innocent enough expression for a discomfort associated with Venus's type of activities, a euphemism for an expression we no longer remember. But people in the States never took kindly to *venereal disease* or its abbreviated successor, *VD*, avoiding both like the plague. They finally agreed upon *social disease,* an all-inclusive term so general and inoffensive as to include everything from bad breath to publicly *breaking wind* and *humping the hostess.*

Germs of Endearment

Times change. Students of the *game* no longer speak of *VD.* Instead they prefer *STD* (c. 1980s, *sexually transmitted disease*). The new Russian roulette of the *gay* (this time as in *homosexual*) is *AIDS, acquired immune deficiency syndrome. Syph* and *clap* have both fallen into disuse—lucky to receive an honorable mention. It's *herpes* (Greek for "to spread or to creep") that's now on everybody's lips—a malaise considered by connoisseurs of the traffic as the "in" disease and the favorite item of discussion at singles bars everywhere. Some can't distinguish *herpes* from true love. The difference, we are told, is that *herpes* is forever.

There are still some for whom the *condom* will always be a conundrum, count Rocky among them. In the third segment of his film epic, his financial advisor asks of our champ, "would you be interested in investing in condominiums?" Rocky turns brusquely away mumbling, "Never use 'em."

† † †

Would you believe three Roman generals all standing guard against *pregnancy: Coitus Obstructus, Coitus Reservatus,* and *Coitus Interruptus.*

† † †

Postal authorities made every effort to halt the contagion of birth control. In 1912–13 Margaret Sanger published her first major document on sex and reproduction, *What Every Girl Should Know,* in serialized form in the socialist newspaper *The Call.*

The article on *gonorrhea* ran without incident. But inspired by Special Agent Anthony Comstock, Secretary of the New Society for the Suppression of Vice, the Postal Service threatened to revoke the newspaper's mailing permit if the section on *syphilis* should appear in the print—citing its authority to bar *lewd* and *lascivious* materials from the mails. The column appeared blank, save the heading, "What Every Girl Should Know," filled only with the word "Nothing."

Ironically, the section was later reprinted and distributed by the U.S. government to its troops during World War II. It would have been a rather nice, if belated, tribute to Miss Sanger if someone had remembered to credit her as the author of the piece.

TWELVE

The Final Act

But don't forget, folks,
That's what you get, folks,
For makin' whoopee!

> — Kahn and Donaldson,
> "Makin' Whoopee," 1928

Sex cannot continue in this wild and abandoned manner. Invariably it settles down into a *relationship*, occasionally stormy, but *hopefully meaningful*. The word *meaningful* lends the requisite legitimacy to all matters sexual. It makes even the *one-night stand* (mid-20thC., a brief *encounter*, 19thC., an *erection*, i.e., one that is very brief) *relevant* as a *meaningful quickie* (c. 1980s).

A *meaningful quickie* may appear to be a contradiction in terms but as the product of fast-food technology and the sexual revolution it must be considered *relevant*. All the best things in life are *relevant*. *Relevant* adds class to *meaningful*. You really can't do much better than a *relationship* that is both *relevant* and *meaningful*.

It was once considered *relevant* to live together *without benefit of clergy* (19thC., a term which originally described denial of the last rites to one who had committed suicide), though it was less so when you were *shacking up* (c. 1940s). We no longer do that kind of thing. Today, we enter into a primary *relationship* with a *significant other* (both c. 1980s).

222

Strangers in the Night

For one so significant, however, the *other* remains some-what vague and nondescript. We know him/her only as *partner, friend, roommate, live-in, lover,* or *cohabitor*. But politics (in this case the U.S. Census Bureau) makes the strangest bedfellow of all—the *posslq*, the person of the opposite sex sharing living quarters. Paeans of praise have already been sung on his/her behalf:

> There's nothing that I wouldn't do
> If you would be my *posslq*.
> You live with me and I with you
> Please, dear, be my *posslq*.
>
> —Charles Osgood, CBS Radio, 1982

You've Got to Be Kidding

> She clung about his neck, gave
> him ten kisses.
> Toyed with his locks, *looked*
> *babies in his eyes.*
>
> —Thomas Heywood, *Love's Maistresse,*
> 1633

Sex with each other leaves nothing—save children—to be desired. The man and woman involved *look babies in one another's eyes* (17thC., seeing cupids therein), but they prefer not to think of it as the *work of increase* (18th–19thC.). The *divine work of fatherhood* (Walt Whitman) is totally inconceivable to them. Rather than *making faces* (mid-18th–early 19thC.) or *making feet for children's shoes* (late 18th-mid-19thC.), he's getting cold feet and making steps.

Lady's Choice

There are steps, however, that he can take—by donning a *contraceptive* or an *anticonceptive* (early 20thC., they're both against *conception*). Most times, however, he'll hop right on, and *ride bareback* (19thC.) without a *saddle* (20thC., U.S. Black for a *condom*).

Fearful that she is the one riding for a fall, the woman traditionally takes such matters upon herself. In ancient Egypt women used pulverized crocodile dung combined with honey and sodium carbonate; since then they've tried a variety of herbs and other nostrums.

Catholics, as everyone knows, have *rhythm* (20thC.) . . . and blues. The results notwithstanding, some still consider it an interesting gamble, a game of *Vatican roulette* (20thC.), but with ten out of every hundred women who play ending up *you-know-how,* it appears that all bets are off.

It was left to Margaret Sanger, founder of *Planned Parenthood* (c. 1920), to take the chance out of it, and she had difficulty finding the right name for her movement. She tried everything from *Malthusianism* (from Reverend Thomas Malthus, who believed that unless restraints were shown, population would soon outstrip subsistence), to *conscious generation, voluntary motherhood,* and *prevenception.* She and her colleagues finally narrowed the choices down to *race control* and *birth-rate control.* After much heated discussion, they agreed on the latter. It was only after a sharp drop in the rate of conversation that we were left with just *birth control.*

Left to Their Devices

When you said *birth control,* to most women of the 1920s and '30s it meant the *diaphragm* (c. 1880, *dia,* through; *phragm,* fence). We once knew such items popularly as *Dutch caps* or *Malthus caps* (both late 19th–early 20thC.). Some more recently have described them as *ladies' saucers,* a metaphor appearing in an old *Realist* cartoon which identified flying saucers as *diaphragms* dropped by nuns on their ascent to heaven.

The *diaphragm* was followed by the *intrauterine device,* invented in the '20s, but not perfected until the '60s. By 1966 it had already been reduced to an *IUD* to help some inarticulate S.O.B. deal with a potential IOU. Its successor, the *birth-control pill,* was introduced in the late '50s and in five years realized such popularity that it came to be simply called the *The Pill,* and everyone – well almost everyone – knew which pill it was. It has caused some confusion; Prince Charles once inquired of a young lady traveling with him on the royal yacht if she had taken her *Pill*. She blushed and stammered, "No,...not really." It was simply an innocent mistake. All the Prince was concerned with was her dramamine, but apparently she had another form of *C* sickness in mind.

Sins of Emission

Disappointed in the options? Hold everything! There's still *coitus reservatus*. The prophet Mohammed never *ejaculated,* believing that reversal of the flow of *semen* (*c.* 1398) back into his bloodstream could invigorate his mental powers and "prepare his sensitive brain and nervous system for self-hypnosis and extrasensory perception."

Another major personage who chose not to share with others was Sylvester Graham (1794–1851), a noted health advocate whose major claim to fame lay in promoting the value of whole wheat and the cracker which was named after him.

Graham's research revealed that loss of an ounce of *semen* was equivalent to a loss of several ounces of blood. Every time a man *came* he reduced his life expectancy. The only solution lay in men adopting restraint and self-discipline, rather than wasting their lives away.

Graham found a large and receptive audience for his ideas. His books (mid-19thC.) were translated into several languages and went through dozens of printings. But today Graham's ideas are mocked, and the entire world knows him simply as crackers.

Gimme a Break!

Beware what a moment of passion can bring
The girl has a baby, the boy has a *fling*.

        —Anon., 20thC.

Even with all the precautions, accidents still happen. Our woman friend fell for him in a big way. In what proved an unfortunate twist of fate, she not only *sprained her ankle* (18thC. for having been *seduced*) but *broke her knees* (19th–20thC.) as well. (The French used to say, "*Elle a mal aux genoux*": "She has sick knees").

225

"Break a leg!" may be good luck in the theater, but no such luck in this instance. In England they once said, *"She hath broken her leg above the knee"* (Beaumont and Fletcher, Cibber, Grose). For a young lady to *break her knees* or a *leg* (c. 1670) meant not only *seduction* and *defloration* but, worse yet, *pregnancy*.

English women still occasionally say, "I *fell*" for "I'm *pregnant*," and there are still parts of the United States where a *broken ankle* announces a blessed event as well as an *abortion*.

Knock, Knock...

No *chupa*, no *shtupa*.
No wedding, no bedding.

– Yiddish proverb

That's what happens when you take a *leap in the dark* (18th–20thC.) – you get *knocked up* (19th–20thC., from 16th–17thC. *knock* for *copulation*, as in *knocking shop* and *knocking house*, all from *nock* for the *c**t*). In England, it's better they knock you up early in the morning rather than you be caught *knapping* (c. 1820–90). It's but another way of saying that *he boomed the census* (20thC.), and she's been *storked* (early 20thC.). No laughing matter this. He had to be *kidding* (19th–20thC.) – but the joke's on her.

In Quite Another Vein

I have no children myself, but
my wife has four, beside
one in *the basket* and two
in the grave.

– Captain Bee, 1823

When it occurs, best you not make *light* (14thC., *lewd* or *wanton*) of it. For some it's sure to hit a sensitive nerve. Witness the seventeenth-century father who cried out, "My faire daughter was *hit on the master vaine* and gotten *with child*" (late 16th–17thC.). Any such remarks were sure to leave both father and daughter with an *inside worry* (17thC.).

Great Expectations

Some maids will get a lip-clip
but let them beware of a *lap-clap*.

—"Poor Robin," 1707

Say what you like but don't say *pregnant* (c. 1545). We've been uncomfortable with the word for several hundred years. As Johnny Carson reminded us, as late as 1964 you still couldn't say it on TV.

Now that she's *with child,* everyone speaks of her *delicate state of health* (Dickens, c. 1850) or being in a *way* or *condition* described as *certain, delicate, interesting,* or *family* (19thC.). When they say in a *familiar way* (c. 1891), someone knows she's done *naughty things,* done a *lap-clap* (mid-17th–18thC.: to get *pregnant*), and been *playing tricks* (20thC.). After all, it's rather *obvious* (c. 1897–1914), also described as *awkward* (19th– 20thC.), *bumpy, lumpy* (c. 1810–1910), *high-bellied* (c. 1850), and *apron up* (19th–20thC.). Everyone knows that as a *lady in waiting,* she's *expecting* (c. 1870), *infanticipating* and *heir-conditioned* (c. 1940s).

Rounding Out the Picture

Big as a barn? Consider her *clucky* (c. 1942, Aust.), *in pup* (c. 1860), or *in pig* (c. 1870). Many women, however, didn't particularly like being described this way. Neither did they want to be considered *up the stick* (c. 1920) or suffering from an *ITA,* an *Irish toothache* (c. 1909).

Hoping to lend their state a touch of class, they borrowed *"Je suis enceinte"* from the French. The phrase became extremely popular in the States during the early part of the century and recently enjoyed a revival among the suburban set. However, there's really no escaping the bestial nature of the act. According to Mencken, *enceinte* was also used during the 1920s by Iowa pig farmers, often as *insented,* to describe the condition of their sows.

Enceinte itself derives from the Latin "to gird," and was once used to describe the works which surrounded a fortified palace. *Pregnant* ladies also once surrounded themselves with a special

227

scent making them *fragrant* (early 20thC.). But for that air of finality, most preferred being *gone* (mid-19th–20thC.) as in "She's six months *gone*," though everyone could figure out where she was headed.

Her departure was seen by many as a matter of sweet justice, a woman's just desserts, often described as a *bellyful of marrow pudding,* qualifying her for *membership in the pudden* or *pudding club* (19th–20thC.). Since Restoration days, *pudding* has played a triple role: as *semen virile,* as a *penis* (from the *pudden,* a shortened version of the *pudendum*), and as *the act* itself. *Hasty pudding* is an eighteenth-century English term for an *illegitimate child* (c. 1673), settling once and for all the speculation as to the origin of the famous Harvard University club of the same name, or as one *Lampoon* member put it, "We've always known what *bastards* they were."

Babes 'n' Arms

After having been joined in *union,* does this mean that nine months later, a woman goes into organized labor?

—Alan Sherman, *The Rape of the Ape,*
1973

"Son-of-a-gun!" Truly an appropriate comment made by a man discovering he is about to become a father. It fits especially well when speaking of a *bastard* sired by a soldier, though folk etymology provides us with an even more colorful origin.

In nineteenth-century England, it was customary for women to accompany ships' crews on long voyages, providing sorely needed female companionship to help wile away those lonely hours at sea. But, unfortunately, with the inevitable *slip-ups* also came children *born out of wedlock.* Naval vessels were ill prepared for the event, and ships' surgeons often had to improvise when delivering a baby. To insure the requisite privacy, they frequently selected the closed section of the gun deck to perform the operation. As a result, the child literally came into this world "under the gun." Being of uncertain paternity, such a child, when later asked as to his father, would simply point to the nearest stationary object, thus making himself into a son-of-a-gun. It's a neat and perfectly logical explanation, though some felt the language misfired by failing to take into account the birth of a daughter.

Taking Issue

Remember the woman who was so many months *gone?* Well, apparently she *made a trip* (*c.* 1823) – for no legitimate reason.

It was really no big deal – only an *incident* (*c.* 1909), a *by-blow* (late 16th–20thC.), but *voilà!* a *love child* (19thC.) or *chance child* (*c.* 1838), *the product of their union,* thus *merry-begotten* (Grose).

We're not positive about his origins. Most believe he was *born on the wrong side of the blanket* (18th–19thC.) or *came through the side door* (*c.* 1860). Closer examination, however, shows them both to be popular misconceptions. The *bantling* (17thC.) began life on the German *bank,* for "bench," while the poor *bastard* (*c.* 1327) originated with the *bast,* the pack saddle used by mule drivers as a bed on which many an *illegitimate child* (*c.* 1673) was spawned.

Pledging Allegiance

Ere the scythe cut
the grass, I met a
pretty lass
And I gave her a
dainty *green gown.*

– "When Flora had on her new gown,"
Bristol Drollery, 1674

Of one thing you can be sure: the *son-of-a-gun* could easily have been a *misfortune* (19th–20thC.). The father, having given her a *green gown* (18thC., *a turn in the grass,* referring to the stains), could have left her a *grass widow* (16th–early 19thC.), burdened with a *bachelor's baby* (mid-19th–20thC.). Fortunately, according to Tobias Smollet, he considered it a *pledge* ("In a few hours, a living *pledge* of my love and indiscretion saw the light " – *The Adventures of Peregrine Pickle,* 1751).

There'll be no need to talk of force and *shotgun weddings* (19th–20thC.) – not by a long shot. He chooses instead to *make*

229

an honest woman of her (c. 1506), to which she will enthusiastically respond, "This is so sudden!" (c. 1920).

The End

He that get a wench with child and marry her afterwards is as if a man should s**t in his hat and then clap it on his head.

—Samuel Pepys, *Diary,* 1663

Marriage often spells the end of *sex* as we know it. It's a time when relationships cease being *meaningful.* But folks do adapt and do manage to *carry on* (20thC.). These arrangements are now called *extramarital* or *comarital.* Many make light of them, reducing them to a mere *fling* (a penile thrust, early 16thC; a brief *relationship,* 19th–20th C.), ignoring their complex nature. Such arrangements, however, are anything but simple. An *entanglement* (20thC.) often foreshadows dire consequences—an *intrigue,* or a *liaison* (two CIA agents *getting it on* in a telephone booth?)—but can be highly instructive (*extracurricular activities,* mid-20thC.).

A Place in the Sun

"What has she got that I haven't?"
"Nothing at all, my dear, but it was available."

—Anon., *c.* 1930s

Much work has gone into making *amours* delicate and discreet, but with only limited success. They were considered innocent and open dalliances during medieval times, but once they added a sexual dimension, around the seventeenth century, they became secret and illicit. They soon lost their innocence and fell from grace, ending up somewhere outside the bounds of propriety and on the other side of good taste. The *amourette* (19thC.) was of so trivial a nature as to pass quickly in the night. But the *tryst* (14thC.), though it started life as a simple appointment, ended up with its people *getting involved* (mid-20thC.). It's now a heavy word conveying images of clandestine meetings on lonely street corners and in dark alleyways. Two people having a *tryst* sounds like something requiring immediate medical attention.

230

Mind Your Affairs

I love my wife,
but oh you kid!

—Anon, *c.* 1916–40

With *sex* on its way out it's definitely time we got our *affairs* in order. It's important, though, to distinguish between *affaires d'amour* (those primarily sexual), *affaires de coeur* (those primarily of the heart), and ordinary *affairs* (late 16thC.), the female *genitals*. *Current affairs* fall somewhere between the *one-night stand* and the *relationship*. We also have foreign affairs, in which nations give it to one another, and social affairs such as weddings, bar mitzvahs, and showers. Thinking of throwing an affair? For an affair to remember, it should be catered. Anything less would be considered gauche.... "Excuse me, Miss, would you please pass the *peccadillos?*"

That Was No Lady

But where's your lady, captain,
and the *blowing* that is to be
my *natural,* my *convenient,* my *pure?*

—Charles Shadwell, "Squire of Alsatia"
in *Works,* 1720

The first *affair* occurred when man discovered the wifely function was to raise a family and administer the household, and that for pure pleasure and excitement he had to look elsewhere.

The Old Testament sanctioned such activity with the *concubine* (from the Latin *concubitus,* "lying together"), who was to serve as his *consort* on a regular and exclusive basis. Man later referred to her as his *mistress, inamorata,* or *paramour* (14thC., originally two words, *par* and *amour,* hence being in love through or by sexual love), though there was a time when it described spiritual love, as in the medieval poem where Mary spoke of Jesus as "myne own dere sonne and paramour." On a less lofty plane, she became his *sparerib, side dish, tackle* (17thC.), and *flame.*

Verbally, she always did far better than the wife. The wife

was relegated to a *conveniency* (17th–19thC.), an *ordinary* (17th–20thC.), a *comfortable* (17th–20thC.), and, at times, an *impudence* (17th–20thC.). It was conceded on occasion that she was a *necessary* but that term, along with a *convenience,* also referred to a *water closet,* putting her in somewhat less than distinguished company. The *mistress,* though at times deemed *peculiar* (17th–19thC.), has always been his *natural* and his *pure* (both 17th–19thC.) and—when counted among the very best—his *purest pure* (17thC.).

But it's been downhill ever since. When man started playing for keeps, she became a *kept woman* (18th–20thC.) and he, her *keeper,* leaving us with images of a caged female held at bay with chair and whip. Her glory faded further with the appellation, a *wife in watercolors* (c. 1780–1840), "like their enjoyments, easily effaced or dissolved." Her slide continued with the *brazen hussy,* finally hitting rock bottom as *the other woman* and *a little on the side.*

Faithfully Yours

When we were boys the world was good
But that is long ago:
Now all the wisest folks are *lewd,*
for *adultery's* the go
    The go, the go,
    Adultery's the go.

                —Victorian ditty

Conjugal infidelity is not a subject you casually *fool around with* (mid-20thC.). To be caught *cheating* (20thC.) is unspeakable and a topic of *criminal conversation* (19thC.). Some dare call it *treason* (17thC.), *fleshly treason,* or *smock treason.*

Most adults prefer practicing *adultery,* but even with practice, it's still hardly adult behaviour—in fact, it's not even adolescent. "Adult" and "adolescent" both derive from the Latin *ad* and *alere,* "to nourish or raise toward maturity." *Adultery,* on the other hand, comes from *ad* and *alterare,* "to change into something else," as to corrupt another, or from *ad* and *alterum,* "to turn to another."

Currently, *adultery* itself has been badly corrupted. It began when Mencken dubbed it "democracy applied to love," and culminated in today's *swingers* and what some call *open marriage* (c. 1970s).

So too with the word "adult." We label more and more of our contemporary activities adult as they become increasing puerile. It's enough to drive one to an *adult-entertainment* zone for some *adult reading matter*.

The Horse of Another Color

"Thou play'st the *stallion* every
where thou comest.... No man's bed's
secure, no woman's unattempted by thee.
—George Chapman, *Al Fooles,* 1605

The impulse for such activity often occurs around middle age, a time for prancing about and nostalgic talk of playing the *stud,* once known as a *stallion*.

Middle-aged males have most closely identified with the colt (a horse four years old or under known to be frisky). They were once described (late 14th–19thC.) as *showing their colt's tooth,* "imagining they have a notion to taste a fancy bit which as often turns out mere vanity and vexation of spirit." *A colt's tooth in her head* "is said of a woman in years who retains the lechery of youth" (Bee). Some think it best we put them both out to pasture.

Sugar 'n' Spice

The *colt's tooth* also favored such sweets as *sugar* and *sweet brown sugar* (c. 1930, U.S. Black) for any attractive young Black woman. But there was also a *bit of jam* (c. 1850) for any pretty and *accessible* female, or a *jelly,* for a *buxom,* good-looking girl—perhaps from the manner in which she shook.

To have a bit of jam (c. 1897) was to partake of the sweets of sexual pleasure. *Jam* by itself served both as the female *pudenda* and as a sweetheart or a *mistress;* a broadside ballad proclaimed, "He made this young girl feel queer when he called me his *jam,* his *pet,* and his *lamb*" (c. 1880). *Real raspberry jam* (c. 1883–1915) was that of exceptional quality and *elderly jam* (c. 1880–1915), stuff long past its prime.

A Slice of Life

Easy it is of a cut loaf
to steal a shive, we know.

— Shakespeare, *Titus Andronicus*

However, two can play at that game. And women play it
equally well. It's easy enough to *take a slice* (mid-18th–mid-
19thC.), it being unlikely that anyone would ever miss a piece
from an already cut loaf. Just make sure you don't get caught *in
flagrante delicto* (Latin, "while the crime is blazing") with your
rem in her re (c. 1860, "a thing in a thing"); that could prove nasty,
no matter how you cut it.

For the Birds

The mere thought of it was enough to drive a husband
cuckoo. The cuckoo is a bird which lays its eggs in the nests of
other birds. Dr. Johnson tells us that townspeople used to alert
an unsuspecting husband to the presence of an *adulterer* by calling "cuckoo" after him. Over time, the cry became identified
with the husband instead. He was now said to be *cuckolded* or to
have been *made a cuckold of* (13th–20thC.). To *cuckold the parson*
(late 18th–late 19thC.) was to put one over on the local minister,
i.e., to "sleep with your wife before she is" (Grose). *Sharing a
mistress* was an activity considered somewhat less cuckoo, the
partners being known as *brothers starling* (17th–19thC.) for having built in the same nest.

The Horns of the Dilemma

And fear of *horne* more
grief of heart hath bred
Than *wearing horns* hath
caused an aching head.

— Song, "Good Susan be as Secret as
You Can," 17thC.

Once she flew the nest, the wife was free to express her
previously suppressed *horniness.* She was now *selling horns*
(17th-mid-19thC.); the husband was *wearing* them, and was said

to be *horned* or *hornified* (17th–18thC.)—expressions which originated with stags in the *rutting* season who, when they lost a female in contest to another, also lost the respect and association of their colleagues. People further certified this condition by making a *V*, the sign of the horn, at him, with the first and second fingers forked out.

As you can imagine, it was hardly the proudest moment in a man's life. *Giving* or *getting a bull's feather* (17th–19thC.—Fr., *planter des plumes de boeuf*) was anything but a feather in one's cap.

It's somewhat curious, though, that given such a surfeit of old terms to describe the injured husband, we have no contemporary expressions to draw upon.

Barking Up the Wrong Tree

Men have always vacillated on the subject of the *unfaithful* wife. The definitive stand on the subject was taken by King Boleslaw II of Poland during his war with Russia. Concerned about the rapidly increasing incidence of *infidelity* on the home front and its impact upon troop morale, he introduced some rather unusual measures. Boleslaw legislated that children born of such *trysts* be taken to the woods and allowed to die and the offending women be obligated to nurse puppies in their stead. The women were further required to take these dogs wherever they went, often appearing publicly with them on their laps. Boleslaw, however, would have been surprised at the results of his edict. The practice proved so commonplace and ultimately so popular that it also become quite fashionable—giving birth to the notion of the lap dog.

Try and Try Again

His rod and its butting head
Limp as a worm.
His spirit that has fled
Blind as a worm.

—William Butler Yeats, *The Chambermaid's Second Song,* early 20th C.

With *adultery's* work completed, there's little left to do. The torrent of sexual activity is reduced to a dribble. Man now *sleeps like a cow,* i.e., "with a *c**t* at one's *a*se.*"

Coming Up Short

Twenty to thirty, night and morning
Thirty to forty, night or morning
Forty to fifty, now and then
Fifty to sixty, God knows when.

— Anon.

'Tis only reality — not sex — which now rears its ugly head. How can we put it? *Dominie-do-little* (mid-18th–early 19thC.)? There's *no money in his purse* (19th–20thC.) and *the flute has fallen silent* (18th–19thC.). He looks to be *impotent* (literally "powerless"), what one seventeenth-century punster called *impudent* — and he's that too. Some thought him a *nincompoop* of sorts, breaking the word down as *no income pooping,* "poop" being an old term for *copulation,* as in the seventeenth-century expression, "I saw them close together at *poop-noddy.*" With luck it'll prove only a simple *genital dysfunction* (*c.* 1980s) set right by a visit to your friendly neighborhood *sex-surrogate* (*c.* 1980s). Hope springs eternal, perhaps another day to rise.

Here lies John Penis
Buried in the Mount of Venus;
He died in tranquil faith
That having vanquished death
He shall rise up again
And in Joy's Kingdom reign.

— Count Geoffry Potocki de Montalk,
"Here Lies John Penis," 1932

Mistress has been a title of respect since the four-teenth century and also an honorable term for a sweet-heart or lover. She's the source of both "Miss" and "Mrs." "Miss" is her first syllable, and "Mrs." a contraction of the word ("mis'ess"). According to Pope, it was common during the reign of George II to refer to a single lady as Mrs. So and so. "Mrs." as a married label came only much later, and "Ms.," of course, our most recent invention, was a product of the women's liberation movement of the seventies.

The *Miss* became most closely identified with a *paramour* during the seventeenth century, as when speaking of Charles II's *Misses*. Since that time, when-ever we speak of a *mistress* we also think of her in those terms.

† † †

Looking for a new angle? It's a matter of plane geometry. We once had a *love triangle* (early–mid-20th C.). Now that's been replaced by an ever-widening *circle of love* (Helen Gurley Brown)—transforming all its critics into squares.

"I love my wife, but oh Euclid!"

THIRTEEN

The Last Word

Take your course, use your force
Kill me, Kill me, if you please;
Nay. I'll *die* willingly
In this sweet *death,* I find such ease.

— Anon., *Roxburghe Ballads,* 1871

Is this the end? Is *sex* dead? *Necrophiliacs* argue that it is. The rest of us are hardly prepared to agree. "Not over my dead body!" we say.

There is a consensus that *sex* is a deadly serious business. Most favor the *mort douce* ("sweet death"), also known as *dying in the saddle* or *with one's boots on.* It has claimed many a prominent figure who found it quite a way to go. When the producers of TV's "Hill Street Blues" had to explain the circumstances surrounding the death of Sergeant Esterhaus (coinciding with the real death of actor Michael Conrad) they had him die in the arms of his *paramour.* Others allegedly exiting in this fashion included a former Vice President of the United States, and a French Archbishop locked in a *conjugal embrace* in a *house of ill repute.*

However, it also happens under more traditional circumstances. Death has frequently been used as a metaphor to describe the *sexual spasm.* As Benedick promised Beatrice (in *Much Ado*), "I will live in thy heart, *die* in thy lap and be buried in thy eyes." But no need to mourn. Samuel Butler reminded us, "O 'tis a happy and heav'nly death when a man *dy's* above and a woman beneath" ("From Love," mid-17thC.).

I will *die* bravely
like a smug bridegroom.

— Shakespeare, *King Lear*

Never Say Die

Others also consider *sex* a dying activity. The scientific news magazine, *Discover*, in a 1984 article entitled, "Why *Sex*?" discovered that *sex* is an inefficient, risky way for an organism to reproduce itself. For the first time in recent memory, *sex* faces tough competition from an alternate lifestyle. The word is out about "the new *celibacy*" (from the Latin *caelebs,* "unmarried," which originally referred to a state of living alone and only later to *sexual abstinence* and renunciation of marriage), a practice which has recently generated a small but loyal following. Germaine Greer, who campaigned for female equality and sexual freedom in the 1970s, has now come out in favor of *chastity,* and recent surveys show jogging to be a more popular form of recreation than *sex.*

Though *sex* appears to be in decline, let us not be too hasty in writing it off. Reports of its demise may well be premature. Agreed, it's no longer in the full flush of youth, but neither is it ready for interment. Perhaps it's best we think of it as being in the intensive-care unit. And desperately in need of your support.

But *if you can't say it, you can't do it* (mid-20thC. teen-age aphorism). And that could be the death of us all. Now is the time for all good men (and women) to come to the aid of the life force. Isn't it time you also did your part and finally agreed to give a...

......FUCK.

The Erotic Tongue is a living thing, working tirelessly to help keep the English-speaking world clean. You can join in its work by sending in any additional phrases, terms, expressions, anecdotal material, or bilious commentary that might help comprise a sequel. Do *IT* now! Lick dirty talk with *The Erotic Tongue.*
Write to:

The Erotic Tongue Revisited
11230 75th Avenue, NE
Kirkland, WA 98034